The Fellowship

Of the Mystery

The Book of Ephesians

The Fellowship of The Mystery

The Book of Ephesians

by

Dr. Steve Combs

ISBN: 978-1-7336063-2-5

Printed in the USA
By The Old Paths Publications
http://theoldpathspublications.com/

Copyright © 2019 by *Steve Combs*

All rights reserved. No part of this publication may be reproduced or transmitted in any form or by any means, electronic or mechanical, including photocopy, recording, or any information storage and retrieval system, without permission from the copyright owner, Steve Combs, in writing, except for fair use.

You may contact the author through the web site:
www.bpsglobal.org

ISBN: 978-1-7336063-2-5

Cover Photo by Jordan Klein
A photo of the old Roman Theater in Ephesus
originally posted on Flickr, licensed under cc-by-2.0
obtained from Wikipedia 13 Dec. 2017
en.wikipedia.org/wiki/Ephesus

All Bible quotations are from the Word of God
the Authorized Version (the King James Bible)

By The Old Paths Publications
http://theoldpathspublications.com/

Table of Contents

	Introduction to Ephesians (Eph. 1:1-3)	7
1	Blessings in Heavenly Places In Christ (Eph. 1:3-23)	18
2	Election and Predestination (Eph. 1:4-5)	43
3	The Dispensation of the Fullness of Times (Eph. 1:7-12)	72
4	Reconciliation of Jews and Gentiles in the Church (Eph. 2:1-22)	89
5	The Mystery of the Church (Eph. 3:1-13)	122
6	Paul's Second Prayer for the Church (Eph. 3:14-21)	146
7	The Doctrinal Unity of the Church (Eph. 4:1-6)	160
8	Unity of Love in the Church (Eph. 4:7-32)	188
9	The Moral Unity of the Church (Eph. 5:1-17)	219
10	The Filling of the Spirit for the Church (Eph. 5:18)	247
11	The Music of the Church (Eph. 5:18-21)	270
12	Marriage: A Picture of the Church (Eph. 5:21-33)	282
13	More Relationships of the Church (Eph. 6:1-9)	301
14	The Warfare of the Church (Eph. 6:10-24)	314
	About the Author	332
	End Notes	333

Other Books by Steve Combs

The Power of the Gospel: A Survey of Romans

Every Word for Every People: Seven Reasons Why We Must Translate God's Word

INTRODUCTION TO EPHESIANS

PAUL'S LETTERS COVER A VAST FIELD of doctrine, life, and ministry. The Book of Romans gives the fullest explanation of our salvation and Galatians contrasts the grace of God with the Law. 1 Corinthians deals with some of the most difficult practical challenges faced by the church. In 2 Corinthians, we find the heart of the pastor who has a struggling church. First Thessalonians is probably the best book for a new Christian, because it was written to recent converts, reminding them of the initial teaching they received. The Book of 2 Thessalonians concentrates on the second coming. 1 and 2 Timothy and Titus are books written to advise young pastors and missionaries. Paul wrote Philippians and Colossians at the same time as Ephesians, when he was in prison in Rome in Acts 28. Philippians speaks of dedication to Christ, firm faithfulness in any circumstance, and interpersonal relationships. Colossians expounds on the deity of Christ, relationships, cults, and the Christian life. [1] The Book of Philemon, also written from prison in Rome, was a personal letter to Philemon.

The Book of Ephesians is the greatest book in the New Testament on the doctrine of the church. All the other books have some truth about the church and the life of a Christian, but the Book of Ephesians specifically explains the origin, nature and unity of the church. Nowhere else will you find such a rich depth of truth about the church. The theme of the book is that the church is one body in Christ. The Church is not two bodies, Jewish and Gentile, but one body in Christ. It is not multiple bodies, but *one* body *in Christ*.

Chapter one talks about the blessings of every believer in Christ. In this dispensation, the Jews no longer have a privileged place in the blessings of God. Gentile believers stand on an even footing with them, being equally blessed in Christ. Chapter two and three explain the spiritual nature and unity of the church. Chapter four describes the walk of the church; its doctrinal unity, gifts, ministries, and relationships. Chapter five outlines the necessity of holiness in the church, including being filled with the Spirit and its results. Finally, chapter six continues the results of Spirit filling and finishes the epistle by describing the warfare of the church and how to gain victory over Satan.

The Book of Ephesians is a very challenging book. It is also a book that reveals a lot of truths that can enable us to live successful and godly Christian lives. I have found it to be challenging and helpful personally. While I submit to all its truths, I do not profess to have perfectly implemented all its truths, but, as Paul said, "I follow after, if that I may apprehend that for which also I am apprehended of Christ Jesus" (Phil. 3:12). It is my desire to apply these truths to my life along with you.

In Paul's Day, the city of Ephesus was the fourth largest city of the Roman world, after Rome, Alexandria in Egypt, and Antioch in Syria. It boasted about 300,000 inhabitants. Ephesus was the capital of the Province of Asia. It was situated on the western coast of what is now Turkey. The city had a harbor and was a busy commercial center. Entertainment was important to the people of Ephesus with ceremonies and parades on the beautiful main street of the city (pictured on the cover), which led from the Temple of Diana to the harbor. There were plays, musical performances, and reading of poetry. The great theater of Ephesus (also pictured on the cover) measured 495 feet in diameter and held an estimated 25,000 people. The uproar surrounding Paul's ministry mentioned in Acts 19:23-41 took place in the theater. Ephesus was a center for the worship of the female deity known as Diana to the Romans and Artemas to the Greeks. The temple of Diana was one of the seven wonders of the ancient world. The sale of statues of Diana was an important part of the economy of Ephesus. The silversmiths, who made the idols, caused the uproar of Acts 19, because the preaching of the gospel was hurting their business. [2]

Paul visited the city of Ephesus several times. The first time was after his ministry to Corinth in Acts 18. Arriving in Ephesus, he took just enough time to preach to the Jews, then he left Aquila and Priscilla there, and sailed into Syria (Acts 18:18-22). After his visit to Antioch, he returned to Ephesus where he had a fruitful three-year ministry (Acts 19). Toward the end of his three-year ministry, the silversmiths raised the famous uproar to stop Paul's preaching. They were unsuccessful. Afterward, Paul departed on a preaching tour of Macedonia and Greece. Finally, he returned to the vicinity of Ephesus on his way back to Syria at the end of his third missionary journey. However, he did not go all the way to Ephesus, but to the nearby city of Miletus. From there, he called the elders of Ephesus and they came to him in Miletus. He gave them his farewell address, being convinced that he would not see them again (Acts 20:17-38).

Three final considerations remain before launching into the body of Ephesians. First, I have chosen to base this exposition on the King James Version of the Holy Bible. It is necessary to mention this, because there can be only one final authority when seeking the truth. Since there are textual issues that cause other versions to conflict with the KJV at various places and many of those conflicts are based on conflicting Greek texts (the UBS Text or the Received Text or the Majority Text), a decision must be made as to which English Version and which Greek text will be relied on as the truth and as the Word of God. An example of these differences is in Romans 8:1. The last half of the verse as it is in the KJV is missing in nearly all modern versions.

After many years of study in manuscript evidence, Greek, English, and history, I am convinced that the KJV is the most correct and exact English Version available and the Received text is the right Greek New Testament. I have never found an error in the KJV and I never expect to find one. Therefore, I accept the King James Version as the Word of God without error in the English language. For this reason, this exposition will be based on the wording of the KJV.

Second, at times, I may draw illustrations and definitions from the Greek Received Text, from which the KJV was translated. Some may object to this. I think, however, that their objection is because many have made references to the Greek and Hebrew texts to prove that the KJV is translated incorrectly. That is not what I do. I use this text to confirm, defend, and explain the King James as it is translated.

Finally, there is the matter of repetition. The reader will find that I have repeated some truths, principles, and verses in various places. The reason for this is two-fold. First, the same verses and principles apply in more than one place in Ephesians. Rather than make the reader refer to other parts of the commentary, I have repeated some things mentioned before. Second, repetition is one of the keys of learning. The more you hear or read something the easier it is to remember.

Paul's Introduction to Ephesians

Ephesians begins:

1 Paul, an apostle of Jesus Christ by the will of God, to the saints which are at Ephesus, and to the faithful in Christ Jesus:
2 Grace be to you, and peace, from God our Father, and from the Lord Jesus Christ. (Eph. 1:1, 2)

Paul identified himself as an apostle, one who is called and sent forth with the gospel. Paul often said that

God called him to be an apostle and his apostleship was according to the will of God and the commandment of God (1 Cor. 1:1; Gal. 1:1; Col. 1:1; 1 Tim. 1:1).

The English word *apostle* is a word brought into the English language from Greek. Its use in English has come to be limited to "a disciple of Christ commissioned to preach the gospel" and applied only to a few specifically mentioned individuals in the New Testament, particularly, Paul and the twelve who followed Jesus. However, the use of the term in the Greek world of New Testament times was not limited to this strict application. The term means "a delegate, messenger, one sent forth with orders." [3] It is applied to messengers sent by others, such as Epaphroditus in Philippians 2:25, where the word "messenger" is translated from the Greek "apostolos." In the case of those specifically God called apostles, the word means the same. It is *one sent forth by Christ to declare the Word of God.* However, in the church *Apostle* is a specific office and ministry.

There are more apostles in the New Testament than the twelve and Paul. The qualifications listed in Acts 1:21-22 for an apostle to replace Judas did not hold true for Paul, so they are not the universal qualifications of an apostle. The other apostles include James, the Lord's brother (Gal. 1:18-19) and Barnabas (Acts 14:14). The "we ... as the apostles of Christ" in 1 Thess. 2:6 certainly includes Timothy and Silas. Apollos was an apostle (1Cor. 4:6-9) and, possibly, also Andronicus and Junias (Romans 16:7). Some have equated an apostle with a missionary. There is a similarity in that an apostle went out to places other than his home town to preach the gospel. However, there is also a difference. Apostles in New Testament times were able to exercise sign gifts, such as healing and miracles (2 Cor. 12:12) to confirm the preached Word. These signs faded out after the New Testament was written.

As an apostle, God separated Paul to the gospel (Rom. 1:1) and specifically sent him to the Gentiles (Rom.

11:13; 1 Tim. 2:7), although he had a ministry to the Jews also (Rom. 1:16). Paul felt that he was not fit to be called an apostle and he was the least of the apostles, because he had persecuted the church (1 Cor. 15:9). Yet, when defending his ministry, he was willing to acknowledge that he was not less than any of the other apostles (2 Cor. 11:15). However, at the same time, he acknowledged that all he was and all he had accomplished was by the grace of God (1 Cor. 15:10). Paul's entire life was centered on one object and one alone. He expressed it this way: "For to me to live is Christ, and to die is gain" (Phil. 1:21).

The Christians in Ephesus were called "saints" and "faithful." These are both designations for the same group of people, but these designations are not limited to the Christians in Ephesus. God calls *them* saints and faithful so that all the rest of us will know that this is our identity too (Rom. 1:7; 1 Cor. 1:2; 2 Cor. 1:1). It applies to all Christians. We are all *saints*.

The words *sanctified* and *saints* come from the same Greek word, *agiazo*, which means *holy*. A *saint* is a *holy one* and to be *sanctified* is to be *made holy*. 1 Cor. 1:2 uses the verb form of the Greek word and it is translated *sanctified*. Even though a saint is a person who is holy in God's eyes, it certainly doesn't mean that we are sinless and perfect. When a person believes the gospel, God sanctifies him in the sense that he is separated as a special possession of God. This is initial sanctification. After this, we progressively become increasingly separated from sin in our practical living. Some day, when Christ returns, we will be sinless (1 John 3:1-3; Romans 8:28-30), but in this life we struggle to live an obedient life separated from sin.

In the beginning of the Christian life, salvation is by grace through faith (Eph. 2:8-9), justification is by grace through faith (Rom. 4), and our initial *sanctification* is by grace. This is evident from the example of the Corinthian church. The Corinthian Christians were carnal (1 Cor. 3:1-4), there were contentions and divisions among them (1 Cor. 1:10-13), there was fornication and pride among them (1 Cor. 5:1-6), there was selfishness and lack of love among them (1 Cor. 11:17-22). Despite all this and more, the Lord inspired Paul to address 1 Corinthians to "the church of God which is at Corinth, to them that are *sanctified* in Christ Jesus, called to be *saints*."

Upon trusting Christ, we are holy, sanctified because of two things. First, we are set apart from the world to God as His possession. To sanctify is "to separate from profane things and dedicate to God ... consecrate things to God ... dedicate people to God ... free from the guilt of." [4] God has set us apart as His special people (Titus 2:14). We belong to Him. We no longer belong to ourselves; He has purchased us with the blood of Christ (1 Cor. 6:19-20).

Second, we are *justified*. When we put faith in the Lord Jesus Christ, God counts us to be righteous. Romans four explains this and cites Abraham as the prime example. *"Abraham believed God, and it was counted unto him for righteousness"* (Rom. 4:3). Paul explains Abraham's faith:

> 20 He staggered not at the promise of God through unbelief; but was strong in faith, giving glory to God;
> 21 And being fully persuaded that, what he had promised, he was able also to perform.
> 22 And therefore it was imputed to him for righteousness.
> 23 Now it was not written for his sake alone, that it was imputed to him;
> 24 But for us also, to whom it shall be imputed, if we believe on him that raised up Jesus our Lord from the dead;
> 25 Who was delivered for our offences, and was raised again for our justification (Rom. 4:20-25).

Salvation and sanctification that come to us when we trust in Christ never changes or goes away. We always hold the position of "sanctified in Christ Jesus." However, as we grow in Christ, our practice, actions, attitudes, thoughts, and activities must progressively become more sanctified, that is, separated from sin. As Peter wrote:

> **13 Wherefore gird up the loins of your mind, be sober, and hope to the end for the grace that is to be brought unto you at the revelation of Jesus Christ;**
> **14 As obedient children, not fashioning yourselves according to the former lusts in your ignorance:**
> **15 But as he which hath called you is holy, so be ye holy in all manner of conversation;**
> **16 Because it is written, Be ye holy; for I am holy. (1 Peter 1:13-16)**

The Ephesian Christians are also called "faithful in Christ Jesus." The word "faithful" (Greek *pistos*) is used in the New Testament in two ways: "to be trusted, reliable" and "believing, trusting, relying." [5] It is the latter sense that is meant in Ephesians 1:1. The Christians in Ephesus were *holy* because Christ had bought them by His blood and *justified* them by faith and they were *faithful* in that they continued in their trust and faith in Christ.

One of the most important things to notice about these initial verses is that the Book of Ephesians is not meant to be restricted to the Ephesian church only. Ephesians is the only book that fully explains what Paul calls the "mystery," the fact that all saved Jews and Gentiles have been gathered together into one body in Christ. The mystery is mentioned in Colossians, but little detail is given there. The truth explained in this current study applies to everyone who is in Christ. Those "in Christ" are not classed into various groups. We are all *one* in Christ (Jn. 17:21). As we will see, the key phrase in the Book of Ephesians is *in Christ*.

Paul wishes them grace and peace. The grace of God, the undeserved free mercy and loving kindness of God, comes to us, who are saved, for two purposes. Grace is that which saves us when we trust in Christ (Eph. 2:8; 5:2). We are saved by grace and we are justified by His grace (Rom. 3:24). However, the grace meant in this verse is grace that helps in daily living and in facing the challenges of life (2 Cor. 12:4-10). "Let us therefore come boldly unto the throne of grace, that we may obtain mercy, and find grace to help in time of need" (Heb. 4:16). The Bible says God is a very present help in time of trouble (Ps. 46:1). Our entire lives as Christians are lived by grace (2 Cor. 1:12), so we must always rely on God, not ourselves: "Not that we are sufficient of ourselves to think anything as of ourselves; but our sufficiency is of God" (2 Cor. 3:5). "For the LORD God is a sun and shield: the LORD will give grace and glory: no good thing will he withhold from them that walk uprightly. O LORD of hosts, blessed is the man that trusteth in thee" (Ps. 84:11-12).

Two types of peace are relevant to a Christian. The first is *peace with God.* This requires faith in the Lord Jesus, His death and resurrection (Rom. 5:1-2). The result is forgiveness of sin, justification, reconciliation with God, and peace with Him. We were once rebels at war with God, but now we are forgiven and accepted with Him.

The second type of peace (and the one in view here) is *inner peace of heart and mind.* This is a treasure of great value. Everyone seeks it. God's peace gives us relief from guilt, worry, and stress. It gives us strength to face pressure, problems, and trouble. It is a supernatural peace that defies understanding. Peace of heart is obtained through trust in God. "Thou wilt keep him in perfect peace, whose mind is stayed on thee: because he trusteth in thee" (Is. 26:3). We can express faith in prayer by looking to God for the fulfillment of our needs and, with thanksgiving, making request to Him for everything that concerns us. Philippians 4:6-10 gives us the Biblical formula for peace of heart and mind.

**6 Be careful for nothing; but in every thing by prayer and supplication with thanksgiving let your requests be made known unto God.
7 And the peace of God, which passeth all understanding, shall keep your hearts and minds through Christ Jesus.
8 Finally, brethren, whatsoever things are true, whatsoever things are honest, whatsoever things are just, whatsoever things are pure, whatsoever things are lovely, whatsoever things are of good report; if there be any virtue, and if there be any praise, think on these things.
9 Those things, which ye have both learned, and received, and heard, and seen in me, do: and the God of peace shall be with you.
10 But I rejoiced in the Lord greatly, that now at the last your care of me hath flourished again; wherein ye were also careful, but ye lacked opportunity.**

We can make a list of the steps we need to take from these verses:

1. "Be careful for nothing." To be *careful* means to be full of care or to worry. We are not to worry. Therefore, don't focus on the problems. Focus on the God who has the solutions and the strength needed. *"Looking unto Jesus the author and finisher of our faith; who for the joy that was set before him endured the cross, despising the shame, and is set down at the right hand of the throne of God"* (Heb. 12:2).

2. Go to God boldly and talk to Him about your problems and needs. Make your requests known to Him. "Ask, and it shall be given you; seek, and ye shall find; knock, and it shall be opened unto you" (Mt. 7:7); "ye have not, because ye ask not" (James 4:2).

3. At the same time, be thankful. This requires that you focus on your blessings. The Bible says that we are to be thankful during every occurrence, good or bad, *"In everything give thanks: for this is the will of God in Christ Jesus concerning you"* (1 Thess. 5:18). The Bible doesn't stop there. It says to give *"thanks always for all things unto God"* (see Ephesians 5:20 and comments). Not only are we to give thanks no matter what kind of problem is going on, but we are to *thank God for the problem*. Remember, *"all things work together for good to them that love God"* (Rom. 8:28).

4. Continual peace can come from following up prayer with fixing our minds on God, heaven, positive, and helpful things (Col. 3:1-3; Phil 4:8-9).

5. Follow God. Paul was an example of this (v.9).

The greeting in verses one and two is typical of Paul's letters. The greeting itself is gracious. We generally have lost sight of this kind of gracious approach to correspondence. But, some still use it. Recently, a dearly beloved brother and pastor in Togo, West Africa began his email by saying, "Warm greetings from my family and the brethren in the name of our glorious Lord and Saviour Jesus Christ." [6] Perhaps, we should consider doing more of this.

CHAPTER ONE
BLESSINGS IN HEAVENLY PLACES IN CHRIST
Ephesians 1:3-23

Blessed be the God and Father of our Lord Jesus Christ, who hath blessed us with all spiritual blessings in heavenly places in Christ: (Eph. 3:3)

THE WORD "BLESSED" IS AN OFTEN MISUNDERSTOOD word. Perhaps this is because the word "happy" is often used in connection with it, especially in Webster's dictionary. "Blessed" does not always mean "happy." Easton's Bible Dictionary gives four definitions:

> (1.) God blesses his people when he bestows on them some gift temporal or spiritual (Gen. 1:22; Gen. 24:35; Job 42:12; Ps. 45:2; Ps. 104:24, Ps. 104:35).
> (2.) We bless God when we praise Him or thank Him for a benefit He has bestowed or a work He has done (Ps. 103:1, Ps. 103:2; Ps. 145:1, Ps. 145:2).
> (3.) A man blesses himself when he invokes God's blessing (Is. 65:16) or rejoices in God's goodness to him (Deut. 29:19; Ps.49:18).
> (4.) One blesses another when he expresses good wishes (or gives good gifts-author) or offers prayer to God for his welfare (Gen. 24:60; Gen. 31:55; 1Sam. 2:20). [7]

The Book of Ephesians   19

The second definition applies to "Blessed be God" and the first definition applies to "blessed us."

The blessings, spoken of in Ephesians chapter one, are *spiritual* blessings, not material. Someday, after Jesus comes again we will have material blessings, such as, a new body (Phil. 3:20-21) and heavenly homes (John 14:1-2). The blessings of Ephesians 1 are spoken of as past tense, "God ... hath blessed us." That is, they are already given and secure. We already have them. They are also said to be "in Christ" and "in heavenly places." Therefore, we must get *in Christ* to get them; that is, we must get saved.

Heavenly places are just that, places in Heaven. It has often been pointed out that the KJV translators supplied the word "places," therefore the translation should be "in the heavenlies," as if the Bible is pointing to some indistinct, undefined spiritual sphere that we cannot quite understand.

At best, this criticism is amateurish interpretation and translating. The Greek word for "heavenly" is *epouranios*. It is a neuter plural adjective. As elementary Greek students know, a Greek adjective modifies a noun or a pronoun, as adjectives do in English. The Greek sentence has *no expressed* noun or pronoun for this adjective to modify. Therefore, a noun is implied by the gender and number of the word, neuter plural. As a result, a noun can *accurately* be supplied in the English translation. Since the Greek word is neuter one cannot supply the word "women" or the word "men." The Greek word is neuter and plural, therefore, the correct word to supply can only be *places or things*. Only the word "places" fits the context.

So how is it that our spiritual blessings have come to us in heavenly places in Christ? What does this mean? And, how is it that we have received the blessing already, even though we are on earth, rather than in heaven? Believe it or not, these are simple questions to answer. However, the answer is not easy to believe, or to understand. The answer to all these questions is in chapter two verses five and six: It is because God "hath raised us up together, and **made us sit together in heavenly places in Christ Jesus**." Though alive on earth, God has made believers to sit together with other believers in heaven in Christ. Some people find this hard to swallow. Here is the Biblical logic. When you trust in Christ and are saved, God puts you spiritually *into* Jesus Christ (John 17:21; Rom. 12:5; 1 Cor. 1:30; 2 Cor. 5:17; Gal. 3:28). We are completely united with Him. Every believer, whether alive or dead, is *in Christ* and Christ is now in heaven, seated at the right hand of the Father (Eph. 1:20). So, it follows that all believers are also seated in heavenly places *in Christ*. You are saved, you are in Christ, Christ is seated in heaven, therefore, you are seated in heaven and you are partakers of the spiritual blessings in Christ in heavenly places.

It is evident, by the nature of the blessings, that they have an effect and application to our lives on earth.

What are the blessings? They are in verses four through fourteen and can be listed as follows.

1) Chosen before the foundation of the World to be holy (1:4)
2) Predestinated to the adoption of children (1:5)
3) Accepted in the beloved (1:6)
4) Redemption (1:7)
5) The forgiveness of sins (1:7)
6) Abundant grace (1:8)
7) The revelation of the mystery (1:9)
8) Gathered in Christ (1:10)
9) Predestinated to an inheritance (1:11)
10) The privilege of being destined to bring God glory (1:12)
11) The privilege of having heard the gospel of our salvation (1:13)
12) Sealed by the Holy Spirit (1:13)
13) Given the earnest of the Spirit (1:14)

14) The promise of the redemption of the purchased possession (1:14).

Some say these blessings are given according to God's will with no influence from man. God's will is spoken of as if it is some arbitrary thing on God's part. Verse five says, "Having predestinated us ... according to the good pleasure of his will." John Gill explains verse five this way:

> The will of God is the rule of all his actions, and of all his acts of grace and goodness; and the good pleasure of it appears in the predestination of men to grace and glory: and from hence it is manifest, that foreseen faith, holiness, and good works, are excluded from being the moving cases of predestinating grace; and that it is wholly to be resolved into the good will and pleasure of God. [8]

This is a statement like many that teachers make about God's will. The Lord's will is spoken of as if it is based on nothing more than God's whims. God certainly does all things according to the good pleasure of His will (v. 5) and according to His good pleasure (v. 9) and according to His purpose (v. 11) and after the counsel of His own will (v. 11). God certainly did not consult man when he laid out His purposes and plans for the universe. However, His will is based on a great deal more than just His "pleasure" and He has revealed what that is. His will is based on His wisdom and prudence (v. 8) and His grace (v. 7) and His purpose that is obviously wise and well thought-out (v. 9, 11). His will agrees with all that He is in His nature and person.

The wonderful thing is that God has revealed His wisdom, will, and purpose. If we believe God's will is based on His own wise counsel, then we should accept that wise counsel wherever we find it in the Scriptures and whatever the Scriptures say it is. This is true *even if we find that God has decided to do or not do certain things depending on the response of man to His commands.* He has clearly done so in some cases, since God tells man *if you do this, I will do that* (e.g. Deut. 28).

All the blessings in our list are connected. In fact, they each flow out of the previous one. This is clear from the connecting words used. For example, the blessings of verse three are "according as" God has chosen us in verse four. Then God chose us to holiness (v. 4) "having" predestinated us (v. 5). The predestination of verse five flows out of the choice of verse four. These connections continue all through the section. Let us take each one.

Chosen in Him and Predestinated to Adoption

**4 According as he hath chosen us in him before the foundation of the world, that we should be holy and without blame before him in love:
5 Having predestinated us unto the adoption of children by Jesus Christ to himself, according to the good pleasure of his will (Eph. 1:4-5)**

At this point I will say very little about "election," God's choice of us in Christ. I will take up the subject in detail in chapter two. For now, let it stand that God chose us in Christ and predestinated us before the foundation of the world for certain purposes. Those purposes are that we will be holy and without blame before Him in love and that we will obtain the adoption of children.

Accepted in the Beloved

To the praise of the glory of his grace, wherein he hath made us accepted in the beloved. (Eph. 1:6)

The "beloved" here is the Lord Jesus Christ. This is the One of whom the Father said, "This is my beloved Son, in whom I am well pleased" (Mt. 3:17). Jesus Christ is the creator and sustainer of the universe (Col. 1:16-17), the image of God (Col. 1:15), and the One in whom all fullness dwells (Col. 1:19). He died for us (Rom. 5:8) and redeemed us by His blood (Col. 1:14) and rose from the dead (Rom. 4:25; 1 Cor. 15:1-4). He took sinners like us (Rom. 5:8), who were dead spiritually in trespasses and sins (Eph. 2:1), alienated and enemies separated from God (Col. 1:21), having no hope (Eph. 2:12), and reconciled us to God by His grace through faith (Rom. 5:10; 2 Cor. 5:18; Col. 1:21). We are now fully and completely without conditions *accepted* by the Lord Jesus Christ, who is not only beloved of the Father, but also the One who is beloved by the church.

Grace is the cause of God's acceptance. Grace is God's loving-favor which He bestows on people, who in no way deserve it. We are completely undeserving and unworthy, yet God loved us so much, that He gave His only begotten Son to pay for the sins of a world of wretched hopeless sinners (John 3:16). The election and predestination of verses four and five are also results of God's grace. All God does for us is a matter of grace, because we do not deserve any of it. The blessings of God's grace cause praise to God for that grace.

Redemption and the Forgiveness of Sins

In whom we have redemption through his blood, the forgiveness of sins, according to the riches of his grace (Eph. 1:7).

In Christ we have redemption and the forgiveness of sins. The word redemption here is from the Greek word *apolutrosis*. It means freedom, deliverance, or forgiveness gained from the payment of a ransom. [9] All our lives, we have been in bondage to sin, the flesh and Satan, the god of this world (Eph. 2:1-3). Now the Lord Jesus Himself has paid the price of our forgiveness. That price was the blood of Christ.

Redemption not only means the price paid, but also the deliverance it purchased. Forgiveness is that deliverance.

So, redemption comes inseparably with forgiveness. Redemption goes beyond forgiveness and extends to the deliverance of the body from corruption, as mentioned in 1 John 3 and Philippians 3:20-21. We will look at the redemption of the body further under Ephesians 1:14.

The Abundance of His Grace

7 In whom we have redemption through his blood, the forgiveness of sins, according to the riches of his grace;
8 Wherein he hath abounded toward us in all wisdom and prudence; (Eph. 1:7-8).

The grace of God is a blessing all by itself. It is the substance from which all other blessings flow. The grace of God is tied inseparably with His love. The Bible says, God is love (1 John 4:8). It is by grace and love that Christ died for us, that He obtained redemption for us, that we are justified, and that we are eternally saved. Grace gave us the Word of God, which can build us up and give us an inheritance among the saints (Acts 20:32). It is by grace that God calls us to service (Rom. 1:5). Grace is the source of our spiritual gifts (Rom. 12:6). Boldness and wisdom come through grace (Rom. 15:15; 1 Cor. 3:10). Whatever we are and whatever we do that pleases God is by grace (1 Cor. 15:10). Godly conduct is by the grace of God (2 Cor. 1:12). Grace enables us to unselfishly give to meet the needs of others (2 Cor. 8:1-2, 7). God's grace is enough to meet the needs of all our weaknesses (2 Cor. 12:1-9). Since God meets all our needs by grace (Heb. 4:16), grace is with us all day every day, abundant and free.

The Revelation of the Mystery and the Gathering in Christ

9 Having made known unto us the mystery of his will, according to his good pleasure which he hath purposed in himself:

10 That in the dispensation of the fulness of times he might gather together in one all things in Christ, both which are in heaven, and which are on earth; even in him: (Eph. 1:9-10).

The blessings here are two-fold. First, the mystery, which has been hidden all through Old Testament times (Eph. 3:5), has been revealed to us and, second, there is a blessed gathering of all things in Christ. The consensus of many commentators seems to be that the dispensation of the fullness of times is the millennial reign of Christ. I disagree. The dispensation is an inseparable part of the mystery and the mystery is what the Book of Ephesians is all about. I believe the dispensation of the fullness of times is our current dispensation of the church. It is a time when all things (believing people) are gathered together in one body in Christ, whether they are Jew or Gentile. The Bible only speaks of one group as being "in Christ" and that is the church. The Old Testament saints are never said to be "in Christ." Neither are the millennial saints said to be "in Christ" at any time. God has given this privilege to the church alone. The mystery is explained in Ephesians chapters two and three. The mention of this mystery here is an introduction to the topic that lies at the heart of the Book of Ephesians, the church, the body of Christ. We will look at the dispensation of the fullness of times in more detail in chapter three of this commentary.

Predestined to an inheritance

11 In whom also we have obtained an inheritance, being predestinated according to the purpose of him who worketh all things after the counsel of his own will:
12 That we should be to the praise of his glory, who first trusted in Christ. (Eph. 1:11-12).

We have already mentioned predestination, so the additional blessing here is that we are *heirs of God.* "The Spirit itself beareth witness with our spirit, that we are the children of God: And if children, then heirs; heirs of God, and joint-heirs with Christ; if so be that we suffer with him, that we may be also glorified together" (Rom. 8:16-17). It's no wonder the Lord also says, "For I reckon that the sufferings of this present time are not worthy to be compared with the glory which shall be revealed in us" (Rom. 8:18).

We will be "to the praise of His glory." God will be glorified in us. All the blessings of chapter one will abound to the glory of God. In verse twelve, it is the fact that God has graciously bestowed on us a heavenly inheritance and predestinated us to it that brings Him glory. In verse six, election and predestination give glory to God. The gift of the earnest of the Spirit (verse 14) results in the praise of God's glory. Paul's prayer in chapter three closes with the request that the church will give Him glory through all ages. It is a privilege to give God glory. Our ultimate purpose as Christians is to glorify God in all we do. "Whether therefore ye eat, or drink, or whatsoever ye do, do all to the glory of God" (1 Cor. 10:31).

As His children, we are heirs of God (v. 17). The Lord Jesus, the only begotten Son of God, has an inheritance from God the Father. We will share in that inheritance and, so, are joint-heirs with Christ. The inheritance relates to the end of the church age and the beginning of the Millennium, when Christ will reign for one thousand years (Rev. 20:1-6). Christ illustrated His inheritance in His parable of the nobleman in Luke 19:12-27. A nobleman went into a far country to receive a kingdom, as Christ has now ascended into heaven and is awaiting His second coming. The nobleman returned and received the Kingdom. The Bible tells us that when Christ returns after the Great Tribulation, he will rule the earth (Mt. 24:21; Luke 1:33; Mt. 25:31; 19:15). After the nobleman had become the king, he called his ten servants, to whom he had given ten pounds, when he went into the far country. He judged them as to how well they had traded and gained profit on the money. In our case, we will be judged as to how well we have served Him with the abilities and opportunities He has given us (Rom. 14:10; 1 Cor. 3:11-15; 2 Cor. 5:10). The servant who had gained ten pounds received authority over ten cities. The servant who had gained five pounds received authority over five cities. However, the servant who had received one pound and had gained none, because he was too timid to try, received no authority and the pound he had was taken and given to him who had gained ten pounds. The servants were all granted the privilege of sharing in the inherited kingdom of the nobleman. They became joint-heirs with him. If we please Him in our service, we will also receive the blessing of ruling with Christ in His Millennial Kingdom (Rev. 1:6; 2:27; Rev. 5:10; Rev. 20:1-6).

Romans 8:17 adds "if so be that we suffer with him, that we may be also glorified together." The verse seems to be telling us that our inheritance depends on whether we suffer with Christ or not. What seems clear from cross references is that ruling with Christ depends on suffering. "If we suffer, we shall also reign with him: if we deny him, he also will deny us" (2 Tim. 2:12).

This verse says that if we deny Christ in our lives here, he will deny us. It is not that He will disown us or deny knowing us. That would leave us out of His kingdom altogether. Verse thirteen says that even if we do not believe Him, He will abide faithful. He cannot deny Himself (2 Tim. 2:13) and we are part of Him (Eph. 5:30). So, it must be that He will deny us the privilege of reigning with Him. I suspect that those of us who do not reign with Him will be priests for Him, since Rev. 5:10 says, "And hast made us unto our God *kings and priests*: and we shall reign on the earth."

Nevertheless, you can be encouraged about this. It is not hard to come by opportunities to suffer with Christ. We do not have to suffer with the same severity Paul did. He was whipped, stoned, starved, imprisoned, shipwrecked, in peril, and in need (2 Cor. 11:23-28). No, the truth is "all that will live godly in Christ Jesus shall suffer persecution" (2 Tim.

3:12). It may only be a sneer here or a snicker there or a snide remark, but it is suffering with Christ. Others may think it strange you do not do what they do and say ugly things about you behind your back (1 Pet. 4:4). In fact, the process of seeking to live godly has its own variety of suffering. Jesus said, "If any man will come after me, let him deny himself, and take up his cross daily, and follow me" (Luke 9:23). Deny yourself; die to yourself. To deny yourself your own pleasure and to discipline your own behavior doesn't necessarily *feel* good. In fact, it hurts sometimes. All you must do is commit yourself to obey God with all your heart and tell others about Him and you will experience some measure of suffering.

There are things that await us that are unconditional. First, we will have a new body that is like the Lord's body. Philippians 3:20-21 describes this new body, "For our conversation is in heaven; from whence also we look for the Saviour, the Lord Jesus Christ: Who shall change our vile body, that it may be fashioned like unto his glorious body, according to the working whereby he is able even to subdue all things unto himself." His body could eat but did not need to (John 21:9-12), was heavenly flesh (1 Cor. 15:39-49), would never die, was forever perfectly healthy, youthful, energetic (1 Cor. 15:42-43), could pass through walls (John 20:19, 26), and could appear or disappear at will (Luke 24:31), yet it was a physical body, a body of flesh and bone (1 Cor. 15:39-41). We all will have this type of body. When we get this body, it is referred to as the "redemption of the body" (Rom. 8:23) and the "redemption of the purchased possession" (Eph. 1:14).

Jesus also promised us, "In my Father's house are many mansions: if it were not so, I would have told you. I go to prepare a place for you" (John 14:2). The Lord has prepared a home in heaven for us. Our homes are in God's city, New Jerusalem, near the throne of God. New Jerusalem is described in Revelation twenty-one. Its size has been estimated at fifteen hundred miles in length and breadth and height. It will have a wall with foundations made of precious jewels, twelve gates of pearl, and a street of pure gold (Rev. 21:12-21). It is a glorious bright happy place of no death, sorrow, tears, weakness, pain, crime, conflict, or disease (Rev. 21:4). We will have a new body, a new home, and riches built up by our years of serving the Lord (Mt. 6:19-21). We have much to look forward to, much awaiting us beyond this life. Remember:

> **1 If ye then be risen with Christ, seek those things which are above, where Christ sitteth on the right hand of God.**
> **2 Set your affection on things above, not on things on the earth.**
> **3 For ye are dead, and your life is hid with Christ in God.**
> **4 When Christ, who is our life, shall appear, then shall ye also appear with him in glory. (Col. 3:1-4).**

"For I reckon that the sufferings of this present time are not worthy to be compared with the glory which shall be revealed in us" (Rom. 8:17). Suffering takes on a whole new perspective when viewed in comparison to what God has for us in the future. The future will be glorious for all of us, without exception. God has great beauty, happiness, and wonder in store for us. There will also be great glory revealed through us. We will be the display of the glory of God's grace (Eph. 1:6, 12, 14). The wonder and beauty of what God has done for us will be seen and glory will be given to God. We, new creatures in Christ created for God's glory (2 Cor. 5:17; 1 Cor. 10:31), will be able to glorify Him throughout eternity. In 2011, I lost a friend to complications of cancer. The day he died he told a mutual friend, "This is what I've lived my whole life for!"

The Gospel of Our Salvation

> **12 That we should be to the praise of his glory, who first trusted in Christ.**

> **In whom ye also trusted, after that ye heard the word of truth, the gospel of your salvation: in whom also after that ye believed, ye were sealed with that holy Spirit of promise (Eph. 1:12-13).**

These verses mention two groups, those "who first trusted in Christ" (v. 12) and those who "also trusted." Those "who first trusted in Christ" is a group who trusted Christ before the Ephesian Christians. Paul himself was part of that group (notice the "we" in the early part of verse 12). Since Paul was a Jew and spent a lot of effort in Chapters two and three to show that saved Jews and Gentiles are now equal in Christ and are both part of the body of Christ, the first group certainly refers to saved Jews. He says that those Jews who first trusted in Christ are to the praise of God's glory. Now the Ephesians, who were mostly gentiles, have trusted Christ and they also are to the praise of God's glory.

The Ephesians trusted Christ "after that ye heard the word of truth, the gospel of your salvation." God has commanded the Church to preach the gospel to every man, woman, and child on the planet in every generation (Mark 16:15). 1 Corinthians 15:1-4 defines the gospel in this way: 1) Christ died for our sins, 2) He was buried, 3) He rose physically from the dead, and 4) we must believe it to be saved. The message of the gospel is the total foundation on which our salvation rests. The gospel is considered the word of truth because it comes from "the God of truth, who cannot lie; and because of the concern which Christ has in it, who is truth itself, and was the author, subject, and preacher of it, and who confirmed it by his miracles, and his death; and on account of the Spirit of God, the dictator of it, and who leads into all truths ..." [10]

Sealed by the Holy Spirit (Eph. 1:13)

> **... in whom also after that ye believed, ye were sealed with that holy Spirit of promise** (Eph. 1:13).

Three specific things stand out in this verse: 1) The Holy Spirit is the *means* of the seal, 2) we receive the blessing listed here *after* we believe, and 3) we are *all* sealed. First, we need to answer the question, "What is a seal?"

The Definition of the Seal: The Webster Dictionary, 1828 edition, says a seal is "That which confirms, ratifies or makes stable; assurance" and "That which effectually shuts, confines or secures; that which makes fast." [11] The term comes from the historical practice of sealing documents with an instrument that makes a mark of a distinctive design, usually in wax or ink. The seal thus made conveys security and authority to the document. Smith's Bible Dictionary says, "The importance attached to seals in the East, is so great that, without one, no document is regarded as authentic. Among the methods of sealing used in Egypt, at a very early period, were engraved stones, graved stones, pierced through their length, and hung by a string or chain, from the arm or neck, or set in rings for the finger." [12]

The Bible often mentions seals and acts of sealing. In 1 Kings 21:8, Jezebel wrote letters and sealed them with the King of Israel's seal, thus giving them authenticity and the authority of the king. Isaiah 8:16 speaks of sealing the law. Evidence of a purchase was sealed in Jer. 32:11-14, 44. This makes the purchase sure and certain; it makes the purchase *final.* Perhaps the most definitive example in the Old Testament is Esther 8:8, "Write ye also for the Jews, as it liketh you, in the king's name, and seal it with the king's ring: for the writing which is written in the king's name, and sealed with the king's ring, may no man reverse."

The Lord God is obviously a much greater King than the king of Persia. If no one can reverse a document sealed by a king of Persia, then certainly no one can change something the great King of heaven has sealed. So then, a seal is placed on a thing to show it is authentic and secured. God alone can place a permanent seal on a person.

The Holy Spirit is God's seal on us. The Spirit's seal means we are absolutely secure in Christ. Just as no one can reverse the king of Persia's seal, Jesus said, "My Father, which gave them me, is greater than all; and no man is able to pluck them out of my Father's hand" (John 10:29). Just as we are saved by the grace of God, through faith (Eph. 2:8-9), we are "kept by the power of God through faith unto salvation" (1 Pet. 1:5), rather than through any effort of our own. Being born into the family of God and now called the children of God, we are in His family forever (John 1:12; 3:3). Nothing can change that.

The timing of the seal: Eph. 1:14 says, "... in whom also after that ye believed, ye were sealed with that holy Spirit of promise." The preposition *after* is used, stating that belief came prior in sequence to sealing. It is not that the sealing of the Spirit is some later second blessing. Rather, it is merely stating that there is a sequence of events in salvation. As far as our experience is concerned, the things that happen when we are saved seem simultaneous. However, they are all conditioned on belief. Therefore, belief is first.

Some say that the word *after* is a mistranslation. [13] The Greek word for "after that ye believed" is an "aorist participle," one past tense Greek word translated into four English words. Another possible way to translate the word is "having believed." That would make the verse read, "In whom, having believed, ye were sealed with that Holy Spirit of promise." The fact is, there is no difference in meaning. Those theologically trained individuals who have studied Greek and prefer "having believed" know that "after that ye believed" is a perfectly correct way to translate the Greek participle. Nevertheless, they prefer the other way, thinking it more supports their way of looking at the verse. Notwithstanding, the verse means the same either way. "Having believed" is past tense, presenting a sequence of events where faith comes first, just as "after that ye believed" means the same. Everything depends on belief. Faith comes before forgiveness and regeneration and sealing and the Baptism of the Spirit and every other aspect of salvation. We must first believe and then we are immediately sealed and given the earnest of the Spirit. The verse, "Believe on the Lord Jesus Christ and thou shalt be saved" (Acts 16:31), expresses a sequence of events. Thank God He has made it so simple.

The sealing applies to all Christians. The language of Eph. 1:13-14 makes it clear that every Christian is sealed. All Christians are sealed and are given the earnest of the Spirit. This is what makes it important that sealing takes place after belief. Sealing is conditioned on belief, so *all who believe* have been sealed. This blessing is no more dependent on man's efforts than salvation itself is. It is a free gift to all who believe.

The Holy Spirit's ministry is to implement all aspects of salvation in those who believe, as well as to convince the world of sin, righteousness, and judgment (John 16:7-11). Dr. H. D. Williams, of Old Paths Publications, suggested RIBS as an acronym that can help people remember some of the works of the Holy Spirit.

> R = Regeneration
> I = Indwelling
> B = Baptism
> S = Sealing [14]

The Earnest and the Redemption

Which is the earnest of our inheritance until the redemption of the purchased possession, unto the praise of his glory. (Eph. 1:14)

The Holy Spirit "is the earnest of our inheritance..." (Eph. 1:14). The earnest is also mentioned in 2 Cor. 1:22 and 5:5. An "earnest" is from the Greek word *arrabon* which means "money which in purchases is given as a pledge or down payment that the full amount will subsequently be paid." [15] This is also the meaning of the English term. So, an earnest is a down payment in a purchase transaction and it carries with it a promise that the full payment will be made later. For us, the initial payment is the Holy Spirit. He Himself is a down payment that carries God's promise of the full payment later.

The Earnest is the guarantee of the inheritance. The redemption spoken of here is the redemption of our bodies (Rom. 8:23). Our human spirit, which was dead in sin, has been born again (John 3:3, 6). Our souls are saved (James 5:20; 1Peter 1:9). But what can we say about the salvation of our bodies? The body, along with the rest of the person, has been purchased by the blood of Christ. "What? know ye not that your body is the temple of the Holy Ghost which is in you, which ye have of God, and ye are not your own? For ye are bought with a price: therefore glorify God in your body, and in your spirit, which are God's" (1 Cor. 6:19-20). Our bodies are bought by the blood and we are to glorify God in our bodies, but there is a problem. Sin is still present. "For I know that in me (that is, in my flesh,) dwelleth no good thing" (Romans 7:18). This morally corrupt human nature is still present in the Christian, in the flesh, and will not be gone until the body dies. What is God's plan? His plan is the redemption of the body (Rom. 8:23) which is described in the great resurrection chapter, "So also is the resurrection of the dead. It is sown in corruption; it is raised in incorruption: It is sown in dishonour; it is raised in glory: it is sown in weakness; it is raised in power: It is sown a natural body; it is raised a spiritual body. There is a natural body, and there is a spiritual body" (1 Cor. 15:42-45). Our future blessings include a new body that is pure and sinless and will never experience weakness, sickness, or death. The Holy Spirit is given to mark us as God's possessions, to make us utterly secure until we receive our inheritance; and the Holy Spirit is God's promise and guarantee that we will receive the inheritance.

The guarantee is until the redemption. The sealing and earnest will carry us through until the "redemption of the purchased possession." Since that refers to the time when we get a new body, the seal and the earnest of the Holy Spirit carries us on through this life all the way to the resurrection mentioned in 1 Thess. 4:13-18 and the end of the Church Age. This also means that once we are sealed and given the earnest of the Spirit, it never has to be repeated.

Paul's First Prayer for the Church (Eph. 1:15-23)

15 Wherefore I also, after I heard of your faith in the Lord Jesus, and love unto all the saints,
16 Cease not to give thanks for you, making mention of you in my prayers;
17 That the God of our Lord Jesus Christ, the Father of glory, may give unto you the spirit of wisdom and revelation in the knowledge of him:
18 The eyes of your understanding being enlightened; that ye may know what is the hope of his calling, and what the riches of the glory of his inheritance in the saints,
19 And what is the exceeding greatness of his power to us-ward who believe, according to the working of his mighty power,
20 Which he wrought in Christ, when he raised him from the dead, and set him at his own right hand in the heavenly places,
21 Far above all principality, and power, and might, and dominion, and every name that is named, not only in this world, but also in that which is to come:
22 And hath put all things under his feet, and gave him to be the head over all things to the church,
23 Which is his body, the fulness of him that filleth all in all. (Eph. 1:15-23).

Paul was motivated to pray for the Ephesian Christians by two things: their faith and their love to all the saints (v. 15). This prayer is the first of two detailed prayers given in the Book. The second is in Ephesians three. There are other prayers of Paul in other books, where the detailed requests are listed. One of these is in Colossians 1:9-12 and another is in Philippians 1:9-11. These prayers are important for two reasons. First, they tell us God's desires and goals for us. Second, they reveal prayer requests that are according to the will of God and that we ought to pray for one another. God tells us to pray for all saints (Eph. 6:18).

It is significant that Paul says, "I ... cease not to give thanks for you, making mention of you in my prayers (Eph. 1:16). The statement is reminiscent of Samuel's answer to Saul when the king asked for prayer, "God forbid that I should sin against the LORD in ceasing to pray for you" (1 Sam. 12:23). In all his letters, Paul assured the recipients that he prayed for them, except the church in Corinth and the churches of Galatia. These churches are the churches with which Paul had the most trouble. In Philippians 1:6, Paul expressed confidence that God would continue a good work in the lives of the Christians in Philippi. His confidence was because they were participants in the grace God had given Paul (Phil. 1:7). Why did grace given to Paul make a difference to the Philippians? The grace of God given to Paul motivated and enabled him to pray for the Philippians (Phil. 1:3-5). His prayers had a powerful effect on those for whom he prayed. I suspect he failed in his prayer responsibilities for the Corinthians and the Galatians, leaving them vulnerable to the attack of the enemy.

"That the God of our Lord Jesus Christ, the Father of glory, may give unto you ..." (Eph. 1:17) is a phrase indicating the source of answered prayer. God is the source of all good things; "Every good gift and every perfect gift is from above, and cometh down from the Father of lights, with whom is no variableness, neither shadow of turning" (James 1:17). Prayer moves God to work in our lives. He works in us with the same power he used when He raised up Jesus from the dead (Eph. 1:19-20). In chapter three Paul includes this evaluation of God's resources, "Now unto him that is able to do exceeding abundantly above all that we ask or think, according to the power that worketh in us …" (Eph. 3:20). We have the assurance that "God shall supply all your need according to his riches in glory by Christ Jesus" (Phil. 4:19). The God who said, "Ask, and it shall be given you" (Mt. 7:7), added, "Ye have not, because ye ask not" (James 4:2).

"God … may give unto you the spirit of wisdom and revelation in the knowledge of him; the eyes of your understanding being enlightened" (Eph. 1:17-18). The entire prayer is for "revelation" from God so the Ephesians would have knowledge, understanding, and wisdom. It is correct to seek these things from God because "Great is our Lord, and of great power: his understanding is infinite." (Ps. 147:5). These three are the consistent refrain of the Book of Proverbs and are frequently mentioned throughout the Old Testament. In fact, the entire book of Proverbs was written to reveal knowledge, understanding, and wisdom (Prov. 1:2-4).

The gospel itself is an example of knowledge, understanding, and wisdom. When a person hears that the Lord Jesus died for his sins and rose from the dead, he gains a new and wonderful *knowledge*, but does he understand it? *Understanding* comes when he realizes that he, himself, is a sinner condemned before God and Jesus' death and resurrection is his only hope of salvation. However, he is not yet wise. *Wisdom* is realizing that he must come to Christ in faith. He must believe. Only when he takes the step to put his faith in Christ is he wise.

The source of wisdom, understanding, and knowledge is in Prov. 2:6, which says, "For the LORD giveth wisdom: out of his mouth cometh knowledge and understanding" (Prov. 2:6). This being the case, it is clear where we may find the words that come out of God's mouth (Mt. 4:4). They are in the Scriptures, the Bible. So, the prayers of Proverbs 2 and of Ephesians 1:15-23 are prayers for revelation from God's Word, the Bible. Remember also the advice of James 1:5-7: "If any of you lack wisdom, let him ask of God, that giveth to all men liberally, and upbraideth not; and it shall be given him. But let him ask in faith, nothing wavering. For he that wavereth is like a wave of the sea driven with the wind and tossed. For let not that man think that he shall receive any thing of the Lord." So, let us cry out for knowledge, understanding. and wisdom: "Yea, if thou criest after knowledge, and liftest up thy voice for understanding ..." (Prov. 2:3).

The Bible is God's source of knowledge, understanding, and wisdom. The Bible admonishes us to get these three in Proverbs 2:4-5, "If thou seekest her as silver, and searchest for her as for hid treasures; Then shalt thou understand the fear of the LORD, and find the knowledge of God." This is the attitude we are to have when we approach Bible reading and study. Yet, too much Bible study begins and ends in the wrong place. When many read a passage of Scripture, they say, what does that mean? This is the wrong question. It is an understanding question. The first question we should ask is what does this say? This is a knowledge question. You must know before you can understand. You must first look closely at the passage and obtain any definitions and necessary cross references. When you are confident you know what it says, you can ask what it means. Finally, once you know what it says and what it means, you can apply it to your life, so you can obey it. This is wisdom.

Specifically, Ephesians 1:17 says, we should look for "the knowledge of him." The focus of our hearts and minds should be on Him, the Lord Jesus Christ. One of Paul's major goals was, "That I may know him, and the power of his resurrection" (Phil. 3:10) exactly as these final verses in Ephesians 1 say. Peter admonishes us to, "grow in grace, and in the knowledge of our Lord and Saviour Jesus Christ (2 Peter 3:18). When we get to know the Lord Jesus, we will find wisdom, because He "is made unto us wisdom, and righteousness, and sanctification, and redemption" (1 Cor. 1:30). In Him "are hid all the treasures of wisdom and knowledge" (Col. 3:2). To repeat, we get to know Him through the Scriptures. He said, "Search the scriptures; for in them ye think ye have eternal life: and they are they which testify of me" (John 5:39).

The prayer for knowledge, understanding, and wisdom is so that we might "know what is the hope of his calling, and what the riches of the glory of his inheritance in the saints, and what is the exceeding greatness of his power to us-ward who believe, according to the working of his mighty power" (Eph. 1:18-19). God wants every Christian to know the hope of His calling, His inheritance, and His power. There is a call to repentance and faith that all believers have answered (Luke 5:32). That calling gives us a special *hope*. We are "looking for that blessed hope, and the glorious appearing of the great God and our Saviour Jesus Christ" (Titus 2:13). Our hope is in the second coming of the Lord Jesus Christ; "we know that, when he shall appear, we shall be like him; for we shall see him as he is" (1 Jn. 3:2).

The Lord also has an *inheritance*. In the Old Testament, Israel was His inheritance. In the New Testament, it is "the saints," that is, His church.

This passage describes God's *power*. Paul's personal goal, according to Philippians 3:10, was to know His power. To *know* His power means more than to simply read about it. It means to learn it by experience, to see God at work in your own life and heart.

God demonstrated His power by raising Jesus from the dead and "set him at his own right hand in the heavenly places" (Eph. 1:20). God works in us with the power necessary to raise the dead. God's power is not limited. He can create all the universe down to the smallest particle. God's power is not limited as to what He can do in or through us. If there is any limit, it is not due to His inability. It is due to our lack of faith and our disobedience.

Verse twenty should settle forever the identity of the "heavenly places." God's throne, according to Revelation 5, is in New Jerusalem in the Third heaven. The Lord Jesus is seated there at God's right hand. The phrase "heavenly places" refers to New Jerusalem (Rev. 21).

Seated in the heavenly places, He is "far above all principality, and power, and might, and dominion, and every name that is named, not only in this world, but also in that which is to come" (Eph. 1:21). Principalities and powers refer to satanic forces (See Ephesians 6:12) and to governments (Titus 3:1). However, whether they are satanic or governments or both or any other power, the Lord Jesus has been exalted above them all. He is above every name in this age (world) and the next age, the millennium. God has put "all things under his feet." After His resurrection, He Himself said, "All power is given unto me in heaven and in earth" (Mt. 28:18).

Setting the Stage

Finally, we come to the definition of the church; "and gave him to be the head over all things to the church, which is his body, the fullness of him that filleth all in all" (Eph. 1:22-23). The church is defined, by God Himself, as *Christ's body* and as the "fullness of him that filleth all in all," with Jesus Christ as the *only* head of the church. At this point, that is all that is said about it, but it sets the stage for what is to come. The details of this definition are in chapters two and three. Later, a cardinal doctrine is that this body is *one* body (Eph. 4:4).

There are many who say that Paul was speaking of the Ephesian church only; He was not speaking of all believers being in one body. Instead, he was speaking of the believers in each local church being in one body in that local church. That would mean there was, at that time, one body of Christ in Jerusalem and a separate body in Thessalonica and a different body of Christ in Corinth and another body in Ephesus, etc., but there was not one body that incorporates them all. Is this really what God is saying in the Book of Ephesians? The questions we must ask are this: How many bodies does Christ have? Does He have one body, unified in Him and including every believer (as the text *says*)? Or, does He have many bodies in various places - split, splintered, and separated from one another? Is Christ divided? We are not speaking of denominations here or multi-church fellowships or any kind of earthly organization. We are seeking to understand the spiritual reality that is "the church." By God's grace, that is what we shall do.

One incontestable fact about this book is that all its truths apply to all believers and they are individual in nature. Every blessing applies to every individual Christian, in or out of a local church, regardless of his affiliation. Every Christian is saved because of the gospel. Every Christian is sealed and has the earnest of the Spirit. Every Christian has the same hope and the same redemption. Every Christian seeks the same wisdom, understanding, and knowledge from the same book, the Word of God. God has chosen and predestinated every individual Christian. All Christians experience the same power from the same God. None of this is limited to the Ephesian church or to any local church. Every Christian is in Christ and every Christian is seated in heavenly places in Christ. These truths apply to every individual Christian, even if some of those Christians happen to currently not belong to any local church or if they belong to a church you don't like.

Are we now to believe that of all these truths *only the body of Christ does not apply to every Christian*? Some tell us that the body of Christ only refers to the local church. There is no single body of Christ that includes all Christians. Yet, every truth in Ephesians applies to all Christians without exception. Why not the body of Christ also? We are led to believe that a Christian is in the body if he is a member of a local church, but if he leaves that church and does not join another right away, he is not in the body of Christ any longer. Then when he gets into another local church, he is now in the body again. This cannot possibly be true in light of the teaching of the Book of Ephesians.

Paul said in 1 Corinthians 12:13, "For by one Spirit are we all baptized into one body, whether we be Jews or Gentiles, whether we be bond or free; and have been all made to drink into one Spirit." Paul included both himself and the Corinthians in the one body he mentions. He said "we." So, he said they were both baptized by the Spirit into *the same* body. However, Paul was never baptized into the Corinthian local church, either by the Spirit or by water. Yet, he said he was a member of the same body they were and they all got there by an action of the Spirit, baptism. This body must be a spiritual body, because we enter it through being baptized by the Spirit of God. This body is not a visible body. It has no earthly organization. Its head is in heaven and some of its members are on earth and others are in heaven.

If the term "body of Christ" refers only to the local church, then Christ has many separate bodies, rather than "one body." Is there one body or many? This is a question that is at the heart of the Book of Ephesians. May the reader discover the answer by the time he has finished this study. The Book of Ephesians will reveal the nature of the church and the practical outworking of its principles in daily life.

CHAPTER TWO

ELECTION AND PREDESTINATION
Ephesians 1:4-6

4 According as he hath chosen us in him before the foundation of the world, that we should be holy and without blame before him in love:
5 Having predestinated us unto the adoption of children by Jesus Christ to himself, according to the good pleasure of his will,
6 To the praise of the glory of his grace, wherein he hath made us accepted in the beloved. (Eph. 1:4-6)

MANY COMMENTATORS SEEM to equate these verses with the teaching of John Calvin (1509-1564) on *unconditional election*. A simple statement of the doctrine of unconditional election is this: In eternity past, before the foundation of the world, God knew everyone who would ever live and out of these He arbitrarily chose some to be saved, whom He predestinated to salvation. This choice is called election and it was not based on foreknowledge or on any good deed or any choice the chosen one would ever make. It was not based on foreseen faith on the part of the chosen one. Other related doctrines of Calvinism are Total Inability (people are completely depraved and unable to choose God or salvation-see Chapter Four in this commentary), Limited Atonement (Christ died only for the unconditionally elected), Irresistible Grace (some call it the "effectual call" - when God calls you to Himself you cannot resist), and Perseverance of the Saints (this is not eternal Security, because the saints do not persevere. God keeps them).   Together these are called *Calvinism* or *Sovereign Grace* or *the doctrines of grace*. Unconditional election is the teaching that before the foundation of the earth, in eternity past, God chose certain people to be saved and left the rest to remain unsaved. The motive for this choice was entirely in the good pleasure of God's will and not because of some merit, choice, or faith He foresaw in those chosen.

Calvinists usually assume that God's choice (or "election" as it is translated elsewhere) in Ephesians 1:4 is a choice to salvation.

> Election, according to Calvinism, is God's choice of certain persons for his special [16] favor. ... The sense that primarily concerns us here, however, is the choice of certain persons to be God's spiritual children and thus recipients of eternal life. [17]

They sometimes refer to this as to as *predestination*. God, they would say, chose some to be saved and predestinated them to salvation.   The 1689 Baptist Confession puts it this way in chapter three paragraph three:

> By the decree of God, for the manifestation of His glory, some men and angels are predestinated, or foreordained to eternal life through Jesus Christ ... to the praise of His glorious grace ... others being left to act in their sin to their just condemnation, to the praise of His glorious justice. [18]

Since the teaching of unconditional election is that before the foundation of the world and according to the good pleasure of His will, God chose only a few (not all) to be saved, it automatically leaves the rest (the majority) to

The Book of Ephesians   45

remain unsaved and go to hell. They call this "grace." John Calvin said it plainly:

> By predestination we mean the eternal decree of God, by which he determined with himself whatever he wished to happen with regard to every man. All are not created on equal terms, but some are preordained to eternal life, others to eternal damnation; and, accordingly, as each has been created for one or other of these ends, we say that he has been predestinated to life or to death. [19]

Many have departed from Calvin, saying that the Bible never says the non-elect are predestined to go to Hell, although they agree with him on unconditional election of the saved. I wholeheartedly agree that the Scriptures never declare that God has predestined anyone to Hell. However, if God has arbitrarily, before the foundation of the world, chosen some (and *only* some) to be saved and go to Heaven, then He has automatically left others to go to the only place they can, Hell. This, too, is clearly by His choice. All must go either to Heaven or Hell. There is no other alternative. If the door is shut to Heaven, the non-elect have only one other destiny left, to go to hell. According to predestination theologians, God alone made that decision. This is the simple reality of the doctrine of unconditional election.

The Sovereignty of God

Another related matter is the doctrine of *the sovereignty of God.* This is a key doctrine (perhaps *the* key doctrine) in Calvinistic teaching. Erikson, in *Christian Theology*, explains this:

> Calvinism's second major concept is the sovereignty of God. He is the creator and Lord of all things, and consequently he is free to do whatever he wills. He is

not subject to or answerable to anyone. Humans are in no position to judge God for what he does ... This concept of the divine sovereignty, together with human inability, is basic to the Calvinistic doctrine of election. Without these two concepts the remainder of the doctrine makes little sense. [20]

The 1689 Baptist Confession, Chapter three, *God's Decree*, states the Reformed Doctrine relating to God's sovereignty.

> God has decreed all things that occur, and this he has done in himself, from all eternity, by the perfectly wise and holy counsel of his own will, freely and unchangeably.
> Yet he has done this in such a way that God is neither the author of sin, nor does he share with anyone in sinning, nor does this violate the will of the creature, nor is the free working or contingency of second causes taken away but rather established.
> In all this, God's wisdom is displayed in directing all things, as is his power and faithfulness in accomplishing his decree ...
> Although God knows everything which may or can come to pass under all imaginable conditions, yet he has not decreed anything because he foresaw it in the future, or because it would come to pass [anyway] under certain conditions. [21]

It is readily admitted that God is sovereign and that all He does is according to the good pleasure of His own will (Eph. 1:5). However, the above statements contain both truth and error. God is the Creator and Lord of all things. He does have a program and plan that neither mankind nor Satan nor angels can change or prevent (Is. 46:10-11). God does as He pleases (Ps. 115:6). God is not answerable to mankind. Mankind certainly is not able to judge God (Rom. 9:20). God can do all that He pleases and all He wills.

But, does God plan every little incident in every life? The 1689 confession sounds like He does when it says, "God has decreed all things that occur." There is not a single word of Scripture that makes this statement. It cannot be found.

Let's be logical about this a moment. The Confession tells us that God is not the author of sin, does not participate in sinning, and does not violate the will of the creature (you and me). Yet, they are saying that God has determined (decreed) that mankind should fall and that people should sin, sometimes terribly, every day. They say it happens because God wills it, regardless of what the creature wills. Sin occurs because it is God's plan and God's decree. Yet, at the same time God is not the author of sin. On one hand they say God is the author of all things and He decreed all actions that take place, including sin, and yet He is not the author of sin. I say this is poppycock. They imply that God has planned each person's thinking and all occurrences in their lives and God hasn't violated their free will, even though it happens by his will, with no regard to what they will. The sinner certainly wills to sin. However, the sinner wills to sin because God planned that he would choose to sin. God decreed it from eternity past. Remember, all things are done by the good pleasure of God's will, without regard to man's will. Man's will has nothing to do with God's decrees.

There isn't one word of Scripture that makes these statements.

Furthermore, these Reformed mental contortionists, take away from God one of His Sovereign tools: His omniscience. They say, "he has not decreed anything because he foresaw it in the future." God foreknows all things as these theologians say. However, to arbitrarily forbid God to use His omniscience when He made His plans for the universe is ridiculous. Romans 8:28-30 and 1 Peter 1:2 connect God's foreknowledge with both Election and

Predestination. They further state that foreknowledge came first. The Scriptures do not make the statement these teachers make.

God has permitted many things. He permitted sin to enter the world. However, the Scriptures nowhere tell us that God decreed sin in eternity past. The contradiction in this is enormous. For example, regarding marriage, God declares, "What therefore God hath joined together, let not man put asunder" (Mk. 10:9). Yet, they have God decreeing that some people will divorce, sometimes two and three times. God foreknew sin's entrance into the world, but the Bible does *not* say He decreed it.

Those who say God has not decreed anything based on His foreknowledge have no Scriptural basis for their belief. But that's not all. They may also have limited faith in God. God does not have to *fix* all things for His plan to work out. God has the wisdom and power to accomplish all His plan and program in spite of some actions being done by the free will of man and contrary to the will of God.

God can and will do all His will. But, what has He willed? God has the power to do anything, but He has not willed to *do everything*. No one can keep God from doing His will, but there are some things God *cannot do*. With God all things are possible (Mt. 19:26; Mk. 10:27; 14:36), that is God has the power to accomplish anything. At the same time, when God made a promise, "it was impossible for God to lie" (Heb. 6:18). God is the "LORD God of truth" (Ps. 31:5) and "all his works are done in truth" (Ps. 33:4). Therefore, God cannot lie when He confirms His promises. *He is limited by His own nature.*

God's sovereignty is only one of His many attributes and all His attributes work together in perfect harmony. God is not only sovereign and almighty, He is all-knowing, just, holy, gracious, kind, merciful, longsuffering, and wise (Is. 40:28; Job 37:16; 1 John 3:20; Ps. 145:17; Jer. 12;1; Ps. 99:9; 1 Pet. 1:15-16; Ps. 103:8; 2 Pet. 3:9; Rom. 11:33). God is also *love* (1 John 4:8-16). The will of God is not arbitrary. God will do what he chooses to do (Is. 46:9-10), but when His will operates it is not separated from the influence and constraint of all that He is. His will is controlled by who and what He is. For example, His will is based on all His wisdom and counsel (Eph. 1:7-9, 11). His will is never arbitrary or based merely on a whim bent to accomplish His pleasure. His will operates in accord with His wisdom, justice, love, and all His other attributes.

The fact that God's attributes include love, mercy, and grace is very pertinent and important to this discussion. I think that a discussion of election often forgets or are willfully ignorant that God's love, mercy, and grace are directed toward all mankind, not just a select few, and they help guide His sovereignty. It is not enough to say that God will do all His pleasure. We must find out *what* His pleasure and what His will *is* regarding the salvation of mankind. God's attributes of love, mercy, and grace are key elements in finding that knowledge.

Total Inability

Dr. Erikson said that the sovereignty of God and the doctrine of the inability of man are the two foundational doctrines of Calvinism. He further said that the rest of the so-called doctrines of grace make little sense without them. We have briefly looked at the sovereignty of God. We will look at the subject of inability in chapter 4 of this commentary.

"We Take These Truths to be Self-Evident."

These words from the Declaration of Independence remind us that there are certain *unchangeable and inviolate truths* that should be understood and should never be forgotten. Certain truths of Scripture about God and His plan of salvation fall into this category. Whatever the truth is about election and predestination, it will not contradict certain inviolate truths. These are truths that are absolutely foundational. All truth is rooted in the person and character of God Himself, whether it is election and predestination or love and mercy. God *never* contradicts Himself.

The first thing any doctrine of election cannot contradict is that "God is love." These words from 1 John 4:8 and 16 bring up a subject that God says is "the greatest of these" (1 Cor. 13:13). Love is not simply a characteristic of God. Love is what God *is*. It isn't that love is what God *does* (John 3:16), love is an essential part of God's nature; not just a characteristic of His nature, but it is an essential part of *what* God is.

What is love? When John says that God is love (1 John 4:8, 16) he connects the love of God with our Christian love for one another. "Beloved, let us love one another: for love is of God; and every one that loveth is born of God, and knoweth God. He that loveth not knoweth not God; for God is love" (1 John 4:7-8). We receive the love we have for the brethren from God. 1 Corinthians 13 (the love chapter) describes in detail this love that we are to have for one another. To summarize that chapter, love consists of both attitude and action. The basic truth is that love seeks the good, welfare, and happiness of the objects of love. Since love of one Christian for another is from God, *because* God *is* love, then when God loves, He is doing the same; *He seeks the good, welfare, and happiness of those He loves.*

The love chapter says, "And now abideth faith, hope, charity (love), these three; but the greatest of these is charity." This not only shows what our attitude is to be, but it reveals the attitude of God. He considers love to be greater than faith and hope. Earlier, the chapter compares love to speaking in tongues and prophesying. A person speaks in tongues by the power of God and one can prophecy only according to what God has revealed. God said that anyone doing these things is *nothing* unless they do them *in love*.

Seeing that this is the attitude of God, it is clear that the good pleasure of His sovereign will is guided by His love.

Who does God love? Certainly, God loves His Son (Mt. 3:17) and His children (John 16:27). God's love for all sinners is revealed in the well-known verse, "For God so loved the world, that he gave his only begotten Son, that whosoever believeth in him should not perish, but have everlasting life" (John 3:16). This speaks of God's provision of salvation for all of mankind. John, the Baptist declared of Jesus, "Behold the Lamb of God, which taketh away the sin of the world" (John 1:29*). It cannot be denied that God loved the world.*

However, some have said that "the world" here means *the elect*. From this, they have concluded that Jesus only died for the elect. They call this "limited atonement." God loved the *world* and Jesus came to take away the sin of the *world*. What is meant by "the world?" It is true that there are times when the term has a limited or qualified definition that is clear from the context, but does it here?

John 3:16 is talking about God's provision of salvation for people. John the Baptist spoke of Jesus taking away the sin of people when he said, "Behold the Lamb of God, which taketh away the sin of the world" (John 1:29). So, the focus is on people. In Mark 16:15 Jesus commanded, "Go ye into all the world, and preach the gospel to every creature." The goal of gospel preaching is "all the world" and "every creature." Jesus then is telling them to preach the gospel throughout the world that exists under heaven and to all who live there. If the gospel is to be preached to all of them, then it was "every creature" for whom Christ died.

Indeed, we find that the Scripture confirms this. "And he is the propitiation for our sins: and not for ours only, *but also for the sins of the whole world*" (1 John 2:2). "Propitiation" means that Christ's death satisfied the penalty for sin. "Ours" in this verse refers to believers, the elect. So, let us paraphrase this statement and say, "He is the propitiation for the elect's sins: and not for the elect's sins only, *but also for the sins of the whole world."* Therefore, God loved the entire world so much that He gave His only begotten Son to die for both the elect and the non-elect, or rather, for those who would accept Him by faith and for those who would reject Him. Therefore, the term "world" in John 3:16 should be understood in its normal meaning to include every person in the world past, present, and future; not just the elect. *God loved the world and Jesus died for everyone in the world, not just those called "the elect."*

The second truth that any doctrine of election cannot contradict is the fact that God desires and wills that everyone be saved. According to unconditional election, it is the good pleasure of God's will to save only some people, a remnant out of all mankind, and leave the rest to die in their sins to spend eternity in Hell. Condemnation must have been His will if they are right. How many people have lived in all of history? It is unknown, but it must have been many billions. We can tell that because about seven billion are living now. One thing history appears to show is that a minority of people have been saved in every generation. Let's get some idea of the magnitude of what we are saying. How many are saved today? Ten percent? Twenty percent? Let's say that a full fifty percent of all people living on earth today are elect and will be saved. It is probably not near that number in reality. That still leaves fifty percent of them, or 3 billion 500 million who, according to unconditional election, are not elect and will go to hell by the good pleasure of God's will! That's only among those living today. It doesn't count the 6,000 years of human history before today! *Is it truly God's will that all these people go to Hell?*

How do we know God wishes everyone to be saved? Simple Scripture, that's how.

1) John 3:16, sets the stage revealing two things: God loved all unsaved human beings, elect or not, and He gave His son to provide for their salvation.

2) "And he said unto them, Go ye into all the world, and preach the gospel to every creature. He that believeth and is baptized shall be saved; but he that believeth not shall be damned" (Mark 16:15-16). Jesus' last command was to preach the gospel to every human being, *sincerely* inviting all of them to come to the Savior.

3) "No man can come to me, except the Father which hath sent me draw him: and I will raise him up at the last day" (John 6:44). "And I, if I be lifted up from the earth, *will draw all men unto me*" (John 12:32). People cannot come to Christ on their own power. The way the Father enables people to come is to "draw" them. Jesus promised that if He would be lifted up from the earth (crucified, see verse 33), *He would draw everyone.* Therefore, he enables everyone.

4) "... the Comforter ...will reprove the world of sin, and of righteousness, and of judgment: Of sin, because they believe not on me; of righteousness, because I go to my Father, and ye see me no more; of judgment, because the prince of this world is judged" (John 16:7-11). Jesus promised that the Holy Spirit, the Comforter, will convict every person in the entire world of sin, righteousness, and judgment to come. The world the Spirit reproves is the same world in the context that the devil is prince over. Therefore, the Spirit's reproving work is on unsaved people, some of whom will never get saved, because that is who are under the prince of this world.

5) "The same (John the Baptist) came for a witness, to bear witness of the Light, that all men through him might believe. He was not that Light, but was sent to bear witness of that Light. That was the true Light, which lighteth every man that cometh into the world" (John 1:7-9). Jesus Christ enlightens *every human* who comes into the world. According to Thayer the Greek word for light, *photizei*, in this context means, "To enlighten, spiritually, imbue with saving knowledge." [22] So, spiritual enlightenment is given to every single person ever to be born.

These verses teach us how God is dealing with every sinner. God commands us to preach the gospel to every individual and God promises that He will enlighten each of them, thereby helping them understand the gospel. He will convict each of them of their sin, the necessity of righteousness, and their judgment to come. Finally, He will draw every one of them, thereby enabling them to come to Christ and believe. These benefits come to everyone. We may not understand how He does all this, but He does, nonetheless. This is consistent with the fact that He loves all people and wishes them to be saved. Nevertheless, He still has more to say.

6) "For this is good and acceptable in the sight of God our Saviour; who will have all men to be saved, and to come unto the knowledge of the truth (1 Tim. 2:3-4). This is a clear statement that it is God's will that "all men" be saved. The Greek word for "will," the verb *thelo*, means "to will, have in mind, intend." [23] The same word in noun form is used in Eph. 1:5, 11, "the good pleasure of his will" and "the counsel of his own will." Do you want to know what the good pleasure of God's will is? God's will, His mind, His intention, and the counsel of His own will is *that all men be saved and come to the knowledge of the truth!* This is truth that no correct doctrine of election can violate or contradict, as the doctrine of unconditional election does. According to God's own statement, if the total inability of man is true (See comments on Ephesians 2 in chapter four) and God must so manipulate an elect person that he will be saved regardless of any other factors, then God would elect everyone, because He wills, has in mind, and intends that they all be saved.

7) "The Lord is not slack concerning his promise, as some men count slackness; but is longsuffering to us-ward, not willing that any should perish, but that all should come to repentance" (2 Pet. 3:9). This does not teach that God is delaying the second coming and the end. What it does say is that God has worked out the timing so that the maximum

number will get saved before the end. Why? Because He is *not willing* that *any* should perish. The Greek word for "willing" here is *boulomai* and means "to will deliberately, have a purpose, be minded." [24] According to this definition and 2 Pet. 3:9, God has never had an eternal purpose or deliberate intent that anyone should perish. Yet, the only conclusion we can come to from the Calvinistic, Sovereign Grace teaching of unconditional election and the sovereignty of God is that God has done just that. He has made a deliberate plan that some individuals would be born already predestinated for Hell from birth. If two people knock on your door in a cold snowy night and you open the door and choose only one to let in to the warm house, you have automatically, deliberately chosen to allow the other to remain out in the cold. Unconditional election says that God not only does this (some go to Heaven and the rest go to Hell), but that He planned and purposed and decreed to do it before the foundation of the world. 2 Peter 3:9 says that God doesn't do that. *It says that God does not make a deliberate purpose or plan that leaves some to go to hell unconditionally.* The doctrine of unconditional election teaches that He did exactly that and, thereby, contradicts Scripture.

8) A very good reason for believing that God wants everyone to be saved is *the purpose for which He sent the Lord Jesus Christ.* Following the very powerful words of John 3:16, we read these words: "For God sent not his Son into the world to condemn the world; but that the world through him might be saved" (John 3:17). For you scholars out there, the Greek words for "that ... might be saved" are *ina sothe*. *Sothe* (might be saved) is in the subjunctive mood. For those of you who do not know what that means, it means the word expresses a *wish* and a *hope*. It expresses a *distinct possibility.* John Pappas, Th. D., explains it this way in his Greek grammar: "The Greek subjunctive is the mood of possibility ... In grammar it is the mood of uncertainty, a wish,

or an uncertain condition ... The subjunctive mood expresses an action which is not really taking place but which is objectively possible." [25] Both the Greek and the English of John 3:17 expresses the objective possibility that all the world can get saved. They are not *all* getting saved, but they all *can* get saved. It is an *objective possibility*. The presence of *ina* in the Greek text makes the subjunctive a purpose statement. It was God's *purpose* to save everyone in the world through Christ. That is the *reason* He came. There is no possible way that God limited the number of individuals who *could* get saved or that He determined to leave anyone out.

9) Finally, when Paul preached in Athens, he stood on Mars Hill and drew the audience's attention to their rampant idolatry, declaring, "And the times of this ignorance God winked at; but now commandeth *all men every where* to repent" (Acts 17:30). According to Calvinism, people are unable to make any good spiritual decisions. Therefore, only the elect can obey this command, because God enables them. Still, God commands all men everywhere to repent, even those who cannot repent, because God will not enable them to do so. Still, God holds them responsible and punishes them for disobedience. This is a truly twisted theology. The natural and normal view would be that if God commanded them to repent, they *can* or He *will enable* them to repent. This command goes out to every individual on earth and that implies that all can repent and be saved.

The third truth that no doctrine of election can contradict is that there is no respect of persons with God. The phrase that God does not have "respect of persons" is found in the Bible six times (2 Chron. 19:7; Acts 10:34; Rom. 2:11; Eph. 6:9; Col. 3:25; 1 Pet. 1:17) and others are warned against having respect of persons three times (Prov. 14:23; 28:21; Jas. 2:1). "And if ye call on the Father, who without respect of persons judgeth according to every man's work, pass the time of your sojourning here in fear" (1 Pet. 1:17). God clearly is without respect of persons in judgment. The phrase, "respect of persons," means to show favoritism to some, while taking it away from others. God doesn't play favorites. Yet, that's exactly what the doctrine of unconditional election has Him doing, showing favoritism in judgment.

The doctrine of unconditional election, or as some call it "sovereign grace," contradicts each of these truths. God's sovereignty is not the greatest thing about Him, because His sovereign activity is guided by His wisdom, His grace, His loving-kindness, His justice, His mercy, and all His other attributes, especially His love. His love makes Him desire the welfare, good, and happiness of all His created creatures. The doctrine of unconditional election has Him deliberately consigning more than a majority of His human creatures to eternity in Hell with no genuine opportunity to escape it. Some say He is just to do so. But, this is true only if people have free will. Calvinism teaches that God determines the choices people make.

It is because of His love and mercy that God sent His only begotten Son into the world to die for sinners and provide a way to escape for everyone. God wills that all people everywhere be saved. Unconditional election, on the other hand, says that it is His will that only a few be saved and that the rest go to Hell. God does not make a purpose to consign people deliberately unconditionally to Hell. He is not willing that any perish. Yet, unconditional election says He certainly is willing and that it is a purposeful part of His plan. God does not show respect of persons, play favorites, in judgment. He is equally fair in His judgment to all. Yet, unconditional election has him picking favorites, who will be saved, while His rejects will be left to go to Hell. It makes God look like a capricious arbitrary hateful despot. Unconditional election is contrary to the nature and the *revealed* will of God.

The Real Story

What is Scriptural election all about, then? The first thing to understand is that the choice spoken of in Ephesians 1:4 *is not a choice to salvation.* The verse clearly says that the goal of the choice is to make us "holy and without blame before Him in love;" that those who are in Christ will finally and forever be confirmed in holiness. That condition is the goal of the entire Christian life and will ultimately be realized at the second coming. God wants us to strive to be holy and blameless in behavior now (1 Thess. 5:23). But, the Bible also points to a perfection of holiness as an ultimate end goal of the Christian life. "Who shall also confirm you unto the end, that ye may be blameless in the day of our Lord Jesus Christ" (1 Cor. 1:8). The choice of Ephesians 1:4 is that in eternity past God chose those who would be in Christ to reach a certain destiny of holiness.

This view of Eph. 1:4 is confirmed by the connection of election with predestination in verse five, which says, "Having predestinated us unto the adoption of children by Jesus Christ to himself." The key that points to the end of the Christian life is the "adoption of children." Scripture clearly defines adoption: "… ourselves also, which have the firstfruits of the Spirit, even we ourselves groan within ourselves, *waiting* for *the adoption, to wit, the redemption of our body.*" The adoption is the redemption of our body, which will take place at the second coming. This is the Bible's own definition of the term. "Beloved, now are we the sons of God, and it doth not yet appear what we shall be: but we know that, *when he shall appear*, we shall be like him; for we shall see him as he is" (1 John 3:2). "For our conversation is in heaven; *from whence also we look for the Saviour, the Lord Jesus Christ*: who shall change our vile body, that it may be fashioned like unto his glorious body, according to the working whereby he is able even to subdue all things unto himself" (Phil. 3:20-21).

For those who say we are adopted when we get saved, I have a news flash. We were *not* adopted into God's family; we were *born* into it (John 3:3-7; 1:12-13). It is our spirits that receive the new birth, because they were dead (John 3:6; Eph 2:1). The new birth does nothing for our bodies. They are not saved yet. The body cannot be born again, so, it must be adopted. We do not yet have the adoption; if we do, *why must we wait for it*? We have the *Spirit* of adoption now (Rom. 8:15), but the adoption itself, or redemption, of our bodies will take place at the Rapture (1 Thess. 4:13-18). This view of adoption also explains the mention of predestination in Rom. 8:28-30. The goal of predestination in those verses is to be "conformed to the image of his Son." This will be perfected at the Rapture and includes the redemption of the body and holiness, in accordance with the verses in 1 John 3:1-3 and Philippians 3:20-21. Therefore, election and predestination in Eph. 1:4-5 focus on the *end* of the Christian life, *not the beginning*.

Election to Salvation

There is an election to salvation. Some of the key verses to explain this aspect of election are found in 2 Thessalonians 2:13-14 and 1 Peter 1:2:

> **13 But we are bound to give thanks alway to God for you, brethren beloved of the Lord, because God hath from the beginning chosen you to salvation through sanctification of the Spirit and belief of the truth:**
> **14 Whereunto he called you by our gospel, to the obtaining of the glory of our Lord Jesus Christ. (2 Thess. 2:13-14)**

> **Elect according to the foreknowledge of God the Father, through sanctification of the Spirit (1 Pet. 1:2)**

2 Thessalonians 2:13-14 uses a different Greek word for "choice" than the word in Ephesians 1:4, which uses the Greek word *eklegomai* or (in noun form) *eklektos*. That word means *to choose, chosen*. [26] The word in 2 Thessalonians is *aireomai* and it means *to choose*. [27] Some criticize the use of 2 Thessalonians 2:13 to explain election, because it does not use the word *eklektos*. However, this is a failure to understand language. The two words are synonyms; they both mean *to choose*. A normal characteristic of languages is words that mean the same and are interchangeable. In English it would be proper to say, "He was elected" or to say, "He was chosen." Both are proper and both mean the same. Also, 1 Peter 1:1-2, the companion verse to 2 Thessalonians 2:13, uses the word *eklektos*.

Some will no doubt object to using 2 Thessalonians 2:13-14 to explain election to salvation based on context. The context talks about the future tribulation period that will precede the second coming of Christ. It says the antichrist will come "with all deceivableness of unrighteousness in them that perish; because they received not the love of the truth, that they might be saved. And for this cause God shall send them strong delusion, that they should believe a lie: that they all might be damned who believed not the truth but had pleasure in unrighteousness" (2 Thess. 2:11-12).

These are people who will perish in the Great Tribulation. Why do they perish? Was it because they were not among the elect? Will God send strong delusion to them that they might believe a lie because they are not elect? Their election status was not the reason at all. They will perish, because they had a chance to get saved and refused it. They could have been saved, but they "believed not the truth." They could have "received the love of the truth," but they refused.

Paul is contrasting the situation of those who perish with the salvation of the Thessalonian Christians. Those who perish could have believed the truth and gotten saved, but they refused the truth. On the other hand, the Thessalonian Christians were chosen to salvation *because they believed the truth*. The salvation of the Thessalonians included a salvation from the wrath of God in the Tribulation. However, it was more than that. The salvation was received when they were "sanctified by the Spirit." That is, they were saved when they believed the gospel. When we trust Christ, we get a lot of salvation in one big package. Our spirits are born again, our souls are saved, and we have guaranteed salvation of our bodies and salvation from wrath in the coming tribulation. We get it all at once. So, the salvation Paul is talking about in 2 Thessalonians 2:13-14 is that whole package we get the day we receive Christ and are sanctified by the Spirit.

The verses in 2 Thessalonians clarify the truth about God choosing us to salvation. He clearly states, "God hath from the beginning chosen you to salvation." The verses define the timing of the choice, the means by which the choice is made, and the vehicle used to call the sinner. This may sound strange to some, because no one who believes in unconditional election to salvation will express these things in this way. Commentators sometimes mention 2 Thessalonians 2:13-14 regarding this topic, but very briefly. It is often mentioned to show that the choice took place in eternity past before creation. In reality, the verses say exactly the opposite.

The timing of the choice is "from the beginning." The timing in Ephesians 1:4 is "before the foundation of the world." The two statements are not the same. Another timing statement is found in John 1:1, "In the beginning." So here are three statements about the beginning. "Before the foundation" equals "before creation." "In the beginning" equals "at the time of creation." "From the beginning" equals "sometime after the creation" or "starting at creation." It's that simple. So, the timing of 2 Thessalonians 2:13-14 is *beginning at creation* or *sometime after creation*. The election to salvation took place in *time*, not eternity past!

In addition, the phrase "the beginning" doesn't always refer to creation. In 1 John 1:1, it refers to the life of Christ: "That which was *from the beginning*, which we have heard, which we have seen with our eyes, which we have looked upon, and our hands have handled, of the Word of life." In Acts 26:4-5, Paul uses the phrase to refer to the beginning of his productive life in the Jews religion. John 6:64 applies the phrase to the beginning of Christ's ministry. The same is true of John 15:27. "From the beginning" is a general phrase that could refer to the beginning of any ongoing activity. So, the meaning *sometime after creation* is appropriate.

To what does the phrase apply in 2 Thessalonians 2:13-14? There is an application of the phrase "the beginning" that is like the examples above and sheds some light on the question. Philippians 4:15 expresses it as "in the beginning *of the gospel.*" This phrase means "when the gospel first came to you." After that it would be expressed as "from the beginning of the gospel." The phrase, "the beginning," clearly carries the same meaning in the context of 2 Thessalonians 2:13-14. This is verified by the reference to the gospel in verse 14 and the other references to sanctification and belief. The phrase "from the beginning" in 2 Thessalonians 2 means "from the beginning" of gospel preaching among them. For these reasons, it is clear that God *chose us to salvation in time*, not eternity past.

Another example of the phrase "from the beginning" is found in Revelation 17:8.

> The beast that thou sawest was, and is not; and shall ascend out of the bottomless pit, and go into perdition: and they that dwell on the earth shall wonder, **whose names were not written in the book of life from the foundation of the world**, when they behold the beast that was, and is not, and yet is.

This verse has been used by Calvinists to prove that election to salvation occurred before the foundation of the earth in eternity past. However, the verse says just the opposite. They argue that the verse says names were written in the Lamb's Book of Life *before* creation. That would require the Greek word to be pro, before. It is not. The Greek word is apo, which in regard to time means from or since, anmd it is translated "from" in Revelation 17:8. So our definition above applies to this verse. "From the foundation" means starting at or since the creation. Therefore, the Book of Life was not written before creation, but rather after creation. As people have gotten saved, their names have been added to the Book of Life. The Book was not completed in eternity past and does not prove unconditional election.

God made the choice through means. That is, there was a method to how God made the choice. The verses say God chose us *"through* sanctification...and belief..." Webster defines the term *through*: "By means of; by the agency of; noting instrumentality." [28] So, 1 Thessalonians 2:13 means, "God hath ... chosen you ... through (*by means of)* sanctification ... and belief." An example of this use of the term is found in John 17:17, "Sanctify them through thy truth: thy word is truth." How are we sanctified? It is "through" or "by means of" His truth. Regarding salvation, 1 Peter 1:2 says the same thing: "Elect according to the foreknowledge of God the Father, through (by means of) sanctification of the Spirit." So, God *chose us to salvation* by *sanctifying us* with the Spirit. This is the plain statement of God almighty, who works all things according to the good pleasure of His will. It was the good pleasure of His will to choose us to salvation *in time,* not eternity past, *by means of* sanctification and belief of the truth.

When were we sanctified by the Spirit? The first use of "sanctify" in the Bible is Exodus 13:2, where the Lord told Israel to sanctify the firstborn to Him. Every Biblical use of the word in all its forms refers to something that is done in time, not eternity. It never refers to eternity. You were sanctified by the Spirit when you got saved. This did not happen in eternity past. It happened during your life time. So, you became one of the elect, regarding salvation, in time, not eternity past, although God *foreknew* (1 Pet. 1:2) your election in eternity past.

To confirm this, God also chose us "through ... belief of the truth." So, our faith itself became a vehicle by which God chose us. Belief also took place in time, the same time that we were sanctified, not in eternity past.

God calls the sinner to salvation by the gospel. "Whereunto he called you by our gospel, to the obtaining of the glory of our Lord Jesus Christ" (I Thess. 2:14). "Whereunto" refers to the salvation of verse 13. The "call" of a sinner to salvation does not come through some inner compulsion or conviction. It comes through the gospel. The Holy Spirit convinces sinners through the Word of God. We can add that the drawing of the sinner to come to Christ (John 6:44) is done through the Word of God, also. John 6:45 says, "It is written in the prophets, And they shall be all taught of God. Every man therefore that hath heard, and hath learned of the Father, cometh unto me." What do they hear? Do they hear some voice from heaven or a voice whispering in their ear? Or, do they hear the Word of God? Jesus said, "He that *heareth my word*, and believeth on him that sent me, hath everlasting life" (John 5:24). Those who hear the Word and believe are those who have heard and learned of the Father. Specifically, it is the gospel they hear (1 Cor. 15:1-4). The call of God and the drawing of the Spirit come through hearing the Word of God. This is especially important because "faith cometh by hearing, and hearing by the word of God" (Rom. 10:17). Faith (Rom. 10:9-10) comes through hearing the gospel. Faith is part of the means by which God chooses us to salvation. This also proves that election to salvation takes place in time, because our faith occurs in time.

One important ingredient regarding predestination and election is foreknowledge. Rom. 8:28 says, "For whom he did foreknow, he also did predestinate ..." and 1 Peter 1:2 says, "Elect according to the foreknowledge of God the Father." Clearly foreknowledge is part of the process. However, a Calvinistic view would deny that foreknowledge has anything to do with it. The 1689 Baptist Confession, Chapter Three, *Of God's Decree*, paragraphs one through three, says:

> God hath decreed in himself, from all eternity, by the most wise and holy counsel of His own will, freely and unchangeably, all things, whatsoever comes to pass ... yet hath He not decreed anything, *because He foresaw it as future* ... By the decree of God, for the manifestation of His glory, some men and angels are predestinated, or foreordained to eternal life through Jesus Christ, to the praise of His glorious grace; others being left to act in their sin to their just condemnation, to the praise of His glorious justice. (Emphasis added.) [29]

This is "theology," but it is not truth. Regardless of the opinions of men, God's Word says otherwise. The Greek word translated foreknowledge, *prognosis*, is the word from which we get the English word *prognosis*, which is an *educated prediction of the future condition* of a medical patient. It has to do with prior knowledge. Acts 2:23 ("Him, being delivered by the determinate counsel and foreknowledge of God") uses this word and contrasts it with the "determinate counsel" of God. In the death of Christ, both determination and foreknowledge were involved, and both specifically and separately mentioned, indicating they are not the same.

These verses do not explicitly state what God foreknew. He certainly knew everything about each of us and our lives. He definitely knew that we would put our faith in the gospel. However, the word foreknowledge is specifically mentioned about salvation. Regarding, predestination, Romans 8:28-30 places foreknowledge first in the list of God's actions: foreknowledge, predestination, calling, justification, glorification.

Closely akin to *prognosis* is the Greek word *proginōsko*, which literally means "to know beforehand. The word *proginōsko* is translated with this meaning every time it's used in the New Testament except once. It is translated as "foreordained" in 1 Peter 1:20, "Forasmuch as ye know that ye were not redeemed with corruptible things, ... But with the precious blood of Christ ... Who verily was *foreordained* before the foundation of the world, but was manifest in these last times for you..." (1 Peter 1:18-20). *Foreordain* means to "appoint before." The word is used referring to Christ's death. In His case, His death was part of God's "determinate counsel." It means that before creation Christ was appointed to die. The Bible does not say individual salvation is appointed or, even, determined beforehand. This word is never used in the sense of foreordained any other time. Acts 4:23 makes it clear that God not only foreknew Christ's death, but it was also determined beforehand and foreordained. The KJV translators correctly rendered it "foreordained" for this reason. The Bible never states that the salvation of specific individuals was foreordained or determined before the foundation of the earth.

Conclusion

No doubt, it is very apparent that I am not a Calvinist. I believe very strongly in the grace of God, but not like those who believe in the Calvinistic version of "the doctrines of Grace." However, I am certainly not an Armenian either! Armenians have a much weaker view of God's grace, believing that Christians can lose the salvation God so graciously gave them. They believe we are saved by grace through faith, but we must be obedient to God if we are to keep our salvation. As important as obedience is, it is not required to keep your salvation any more than it is required to obtain your salvation. The grace of God is as necessary and effective after we get saved as before.

For centuries there has been a false dichotomy drawn between Calvinism and Armenianism. The idea is that, If you are not a Calvinist, you must be an Armenian. This is a false dichotomy. I try to be a Bible believer, no matter whose doctrine the Scriptures contradict. In this case, my view of the grace of God is much stronger than those who say they believe in the "doctrines of grace." In their view God only has enough grace to give salvation to a select *few*, while deliberately leaving the great majority of people to go to Hell. Grace that leads to salvation is not genuinely offered to them. On the other hand, I believe God's grace genuinely offers salvation to everyone and that anyone can come to God through Christ by the grace of God. Our God sincerely wishes every person to come to the knowledge of the truth and be saved. This is the true doctrine of grace.

What shall we say then? Many theologians and thinkers and students of the Bible see in the Scriptures what they call Sovereign Grace or the doctrines of grace or Calvinism, that, before creation, God unconditionally chose certain individuals throughout history to be saved and chose to allow all others to die in their sins and go to hell. On the other hand, many of them also clearly see that the Bible depicts and treats people as if they have free will and can choose salvation when they hear the gospel. They all know that the gospel call goes to all, whether elect or not, and it is preached that "whosoever will" may come. This clearly gives the impression that a free and equal opportunity for salvation is offered to everyone. They say, "It is a mystery." They cannot see how free will and their view of election could both be true, but many of them say they believe both. Charles Spurgeon, a famous preacher and a Calvinist, addressed that conflict this way.

That God predestines, and that man is responsible, are two things that few can see. They are believed to be inconsistent and contradictory; but they are not. It is just the fault of our weak judgment. Two truths cannot be contradictory to each other. If, then, I find taught in one place that everything is fore-ordained, that is true; and if I find in another place that man is responsible for all his actions, that is true; and it is my folly that leads me to imagine that two truths can ever contradict each other. These two truths, I do not believe, can ever be welded into one upon any human anvil, but one they shall be in eternity: they are two lines that are so nearly parallel, that the mind that shall pursue them farthest, will never discover that they converge; but they do converge, and they will meet somewhere in eternity, close to the throne of God, whence all truth doth spring. [30]

    I have heard it explained in college something like this: Free will and unconditional election are like the two rails of railroad tracks. They run parallel and seem to come together in the far distance. Election and free will are parallel truths and we do not see how they reconcile, but they do reconcile and someday we will understand it. Until then it is a mystery. Spurgeon would agree. However, we are dealing with the doctrines of salvation here. There is no way God would leave such matters as a mystery that we cannot understand. He said, "The secret things belong unto the LORD our God: but those things which are revealed belong unto us and to our children for ever, that we may do all the words of this law" (Deut. 29:29). Spurgeon and those who use this excuse are wrong.

    The problem is that those who teach unconditional election start off with unscriptural definitions which they impose on Bible verses and they refuse to believe the plain statements of Scripture as it is written. The truths of election and free will are easily understood when you believe the plain words of God in their ordinary meanings and when you define words according to their use in Scripture.

In reality, the railroad tracks of Calvinistic election verses free will *never* come together, regardless what they "appear" to do and unconditional election *cannot* be reconciled with free will. However, there are others who openly reject free will. I believe we can understand the truth about this so-called "mystery" right now, if we accept and believe the plain, clear statements of Scripture.

Ephesians 1:4 is a profound and deep statement of truth. However, election is not a mystery. It can be understood by believing precisely what we read in the word of God. In Ephesians 1:4, before the foundation of the world, God chose all who would be in Christ to ultimately be made permanently and fully morally holy. To that end He predestinated them to the adoption of children. In the past, He saved our souls and gave a new birth to our spirits. In the future, we are predestined to have new bodies and we will be completely holy. He will save us from the very presence of sin in our lives. In this way, we will finally be confirmed in complete holiness and love before God. This is the plan and the assurance for the final destiny of all believers. The same truths are taught in Romans 8:23-30.

The doctrine of unconditional election flatly and forthrightly contradicts some cardinal truths of Scripture. God loved every individual in the world to the point that He sent His only begotten Son to die for them and pay the penalty of their sins. He died for everyone. Calvinism teaches that Christ only died for the elect. This is a genuine problem in understanding of the gospel. It is God's desire that everyone be saved and come to the knowledge of the truth. Unconditional election teaches that God only wants a few to be saved. In fact, the Scriptures teach that God is not willing that any perish (2 Pet. 3:9). Yet unconditional election teaches that God's plan determines that only a part of mankind will be permitted to be saved and the rest will perish. Finally, unconditional election makes God a respecter of persons in judgment. God shows favoritism in judgment toward a few unconditionally chosen ones. The Scriptures teach that God's judgment is consistent for all. He has offered a way out of eternal punishment to all through the death and resurrection of Christ. He has declared that whosoever will, may believe and be saved. Those who won't shall perish. This judgment is applied without partiality or favoritism.

God does choose us to salvation (2 Thess. 2:13 -14; 1 Peter 1:2). He makes this choice in time, "from the beginning," which means sometime after the beginning of gospel preaching among you. Therefore, He did not make the choice to salvation *before* the foundation of the world. The timing is further defined as being when we were sanctified by the Spirit and when we believed the gospel. This definition places the time God chose us to salvation at the same time we got saved. Sanctification of the Spirit became the means by which God chose us. The choice was also according to God's foreknowledge.

The Bible tells us, "Hold fast the *form* of sound words, which thou hast heard of me, in faith and love which is in Christ Jesus" (2 Tim. 1:13). There are many words that have been written and spoken on the topic of unconditional election. Some of these words make sense and some do not. Many of them have a strong flavor of human logic and philosophy applied to the subject. When I was in college, during one class, a philosophy professor started with a Calvinistic view of the Sovereignty of God (he did not prove this view by Scripture) and built a complete Calvinistic structure based entirely on philosophical logic, without one word of Scripture. So, words are piled upon words and volumes are written to the point where God's truth is complicated beyond any recognition. However, the words that count are not the words of John Calvin or the Reformers or the 1689 Baptist Confession or any professor or any pastor or any other commentator, including me. The only words that count are the words of Scripture. These are the form of sound words, to which Paul referred.

There is simplicity in Christ (2 Cor. 11:1-3). When we listen to His words in the Bible and judge the words of men by His words, many things become clear. This is what I have tried to do here. In Acts 17:11, God commended the Bereans because, when Paul taught them, they "received the word with all readiness of mind, and searched the scriptures daily, whether those things were so." Steve Jones, a former Calvinist, wrote a paper challenging the major points of Calvinism. In his concluding remarks he agrees:

> The average Calvinist may be amazed at just how weak his system is when scrutinized in the light of revealed truth. May our brethren see fit to adopt a Berean spirit (Acts 17:11) and honestly rethink their Calvinism. We would urge them to, for a time, lay aside the commentaries of Calvin and Gill, the theology of Warfield and Hodge. With an open Bible and mind, may they take a second look at the so-called "doctrines of grace" to see if they truly are the doctrines of Christ. [31]

As you proceed through this commentary, you will find other places where I explain aspects of Calvinism as contrasted with Scripture. For example, in Ephesians 2 (Chapter 4 of this commentary), we will look at what the Bible says about Total Inability.

CHAPTER THREE
THE DISPENSATION OF THE FULLNESS OF TIMES
Ephesians 1:7-12

7 In whom we have redemption through his blood, the forgiveness of sins, according to the riches of his grace;
8 Wherein he hath abounded toward us in all wisdom and prudence;
9 Having made known unto us the mystery of his will, according to his good pleasure which he hath purposed in himself:
10 That in the dispensation of the fulness of times he might gather together in one all things in Christ, both which are in heaven, and which are on earth; even in him:
11 In whom also we have obtained an inheritance, being predestinated according to the purpose of him who worketh all things after the counsel of his own will:
12 That we should be to the praise of his glory, who first trusted in Christ. (Eph. 1:7-12).

I **HAVE INCLUDED ALL THESE VERSES** because they are one complete sentence and they are all inter-related. The truth contained in the sentence is based on the grace of God (v. 7), in which He has abounded toward us in all wisdom and prudence. It is that grace that has made the mystery of His will known to us. What is that mystery? It is "that in the dispensation of the fullness of times he might gather together in one all things in Christ." What is this dispensation? How are we to identify it?

To begin, we need to take note of the clues God has given us in these verses. First, the dispensation is connected with a "mystery." This mystery is called the mystery of "His will," which is based on His good pleasure and His purpose. Second, the dispensation involves *something* (described as "all things") being gathered together. All these things (whatever they are) are to be gathered together "in Christ." Third, the "dispensation" is a part of the "mystery." Fourth, the "all things" that are gathered together in Christ are in heaven and on earth. Fifth, the dispensation includes "fullness" and it includes "times." Sixth, the dispensation relates to an inheritance, which is obtained through predestination. All these things, and all the other blessings listed in Ephesians 1 are done in God's will and according to his purpose (verses 9 and 11). His will is based on motives "in Himself" and nowhere else. It is based on His good pleasure, but also in His wisdom and prudence (v. 8). However, God's will is not arbitrary. It is not based on whims. God's will springs forth from His wise well-thought-out purpose and plan and His character.

Definitions

The first word we need to define is *dispensation*. The Greek word for dispensation is *oikonomia*. According to *Thayer's Greek Definitions*, the word means "the management of a household or of household affairs." [32] The word is translated "dispensation" (1Cor. 9:17; Eph.1:10; Eph. 3:2; Col. 1:25) and "steward" (Luke 16:3, 8; Tit. 1:7) and "stewardship" (Luke 16:2-4). Webster gives this definition of the English word *dispensation*: "The dealing of God to his creatures; the distribution of good and evil, natural or moral, in the divine government." [33] A steward is someone "employed in great families to manage the domestic concerns." [34] Therefore, the word refers to how God manages His governing of the world and the affairs of men.

Another definition is "The method or scheme according to which God carries out his purposes towards men." [35] It first involves a revelation and "dispensing" of God's divine truth and of His will to mankind; second, it involves testing mankind according to the responsibilities God reveals. An examination of the Biblical history of revelation makes it clear that God gives that revelation progressively; some now and more later. Abraham knew more of God than did Noah. Moses knew more about God and His law than did Abraham, and so on.

Traditional dispensationalists generally recognize seven dispensations in Biblical history. Theologians give these dispensations various names, but the period of history designated for each has remained very consistent. *The Dispensation of Innocence* covers Genesis 1-3, the creation, Garden of Eden, and the fall. The *Dispensation of Conscience* goes from Genesis 4 until the Flood. *The Dispensation of Human Government* follows the Flood until Abraham's promises of Genesis 12. The *Dispensation of Promise* goes from Genesis 12 until the giving of the Law on Mount Sinai in Exodus 20. In Exodus, the *Dispensation of the Mosaic Law* began and continued until John the Baptist (Luke 16:16). The *Dispensation of the Church* is next, from Pentecost until God takes the church of the world at the event which we call the Rapture (1 Thess. 4:13-18). Finally, the *Dispensation of the Millennial Kingdom* will start at the second coming and continue for one thousand years. Each of these dispensations begin with new revelation from God, but some of the old revelation and responsibilities may remain in effect. For example, the beginning of the Dispensation of Human Government did not erase human conscience and the inauguration of the Dispensation of Promise did not stop human government or abolish the promises and covenant given to Noah. On the other hand, with the creation of the church, the Law was abolished for the believer (2 Cor. 3:13 with context).

The "fullness of the times" needs some definition. The terms "fullness" and "times" are ordinary terms that may be understood in their everyday meaning. We know what is meant by filling something until it is full, but Biblical writers apply the term in scripture in special ways. *Vine's Complete Expository Dictionary of New Testament Words* defines the word *fullness* this way:

> Pleroma ... denotes "fullness, that of which a thing is "full"; it is thus used of the grace and truth manifested in Christ, Joh 1:16; of all His virtues and excellencies, Eph 4:13; "the blessing of Christ," ... the conversion and restoration of Israel, Rom 11:12; the completion of the number of Gentiles who receive blessing through the gospel, Rom 11:25; the complete products of the earth, 1Co 10:26; the end of an appointed period, Gal 4:4; Eph 1:10; God, in the completeness of His Being, Eph 3:19; Col 1:19; Col 2:9; the church as the complement of Christ, Eph 1:23. [36]

"Fullness," then, means something that is filled, or it can mean something that is complete. It can also mean the arrival of an appointed time, as Galatians 4:4 seems to be saying.

Likewise, "times" is used in specialized applications in the Scriptures. It comes from the Greek word *kairos* which *Strong's Hebrew and Greek Dictionaries* defines as "an *occasion*, that is, *set* or *proper* time." [37] The KJV variously translates it *time(s), season(s), always, opportunity, convenient,* and *while.* So, the dispensation in question involves set and proper times or occasions. Also, notice Gal. 4:4, "...when the fulness of the time was come, God sent forth his Son..." There the phrase "fullness of the time" means "when the set and proper time was fully come." So, the phrase "the fullness of times" in Eph.1:10 can be understood in one of three ways: first, the times that are characterized by fullness or, second, the completion of the times or, third, the times that are right and proper for a certain purpose have fully come. This will all make more sense as we gather the facts together.

The phrase "gathered together in one" also needs some examination. This comes from one Greek word, *anakephalaiomai,* which only occurs in the New Testament here and Rom. 13:9, where it is translated "briefly comprehended." The word basically means "to sum up (again), to repeat summarily, to condense into a summary." [38] This is like an orator whose speech covers several points and at the end he repeats them by drawing them together into one brief summary. G. Abbott-Smith reinforces this definition and supports the translation in the KJV in *A Manual Greek Lexicon of the New Testament*: "to sum up, gather up, present as a whole." [39] "To sum up" is *not* strictly how the word is translated, however. The underlying idea of summing up or gathering up is to be translated *according to the context in which it is found.* It carries the idea of condensing several ideas into one basic summary (as in Rom. 13:9) or gathering many individual things together into one whole or group (as in Eph. 1:10).

Albert Barnes, in his commentary, tells us "the word means to collect under one head, or to comprehend several things under one; Rom 13:9. 'It is briefly comprehended,' i. e., summed up under this one precept, sc., 'love.'" [40] However, the inclusion of "head" is not part of the word's definition, according to the lexicons. By "head," Barnes likely means under one subject or category. Moreover, the meaning of the word in Eph. 1:10 does not include gathering everything together under Christ as the Head, but, rather, it specifically says that all things are gathered together into one group and placed *into* Christ. The Lord Jesus Christ is still the central figure in the gathering, but while it may be implied that the "things" of Eph. 1:10 are submitted to Him as Head, the focus is on the fact that they are gathered together *in Him.* "In

Christ" is very technical terminology in the Pauline epistles. Keep this in mind. It will be very significant later.

Finally, what is meant by *all things*? This "all things" includes things located in heaven and on earth. First, you must realize that it could not possibly mean *all things without exclusion*. If it did, that would then include angels, demons, Satan, animals, nature, and saved mankind, and unsaved mankind. There *never was* and *will never be* a time when all these things will be *in Christ*. Even in the "times of restitution of all things" (Acts 3:19-21) nothing is said about anything being placed in Christ at that time. Therefore, this "all things" must be *limited to whoever or whatever is or will be in Christ*. If one would search "all things" in a concordance, he would find the phrase to be usually limited by something in the context. For example, Romans 14:2, "For one believeth that he may *eat all things*: another, who is weak, eateth herbs." Obviously, the "all things" in that verse refers to food. He certainly was not speaking of eating the wood from a boat on the Sea of Galilee! In at least one place, the phrase refers to people: "For as the woman is of the man, even so is the man also by the woman; but *all things* of God" (1 Cor. 11:12).

Therefore, at the very least, "all things" in Eph. 1:10 refers to all *people* who are gathered together *in Christ*. The only people *ever* referred to in the Bible as being *in Christ* are Christians, living on earth or in heaven. The first time the phrase "in Christ" is found in the Bible is Acts 24:24 and the last time is 1 Peter 5:14. There was no one *in Christ* in the Old Testament or anytime before the church and no one is *in Christ* in the Book of Revelation. However, it seems that there are others who see it differently.

What Do the Commentators Say?

One thing most commentators seem to have in common on this subject is consistency. Harry Ironside, the former pastor of Moody Memorial Church, said, "By-and-by there will be another glorious economy, 'The dispensation of the fullness of times.' That will be in the last glorious age, which has been called ever since the dawn of the Christian era, 'The Millennium'..." [41] Albert Barnes put it this way, "The period referred to here is that when all things shall be gathered together in the Redeemer at the winding up of human affairs, or the consummation of all things." [42] Jamieson, Fausset, and Brown identify it as both the church and the millennium. [43] John Wesley even points to the end and consummation of all things: "That in the dispensation of the fullness of the times - In this last administration of God's fullest grace, which took place when the time appointed was fully come. He might gather together into one in Christ - Might recapitulate, re - unite, and place in order again under Christ, their common Head. All things which are in heaven, and on earth - All angels and men, whether living or dead, in the Lord." [44] Scofield agrees with the general consensus: "The Dispensation of the Fulness of Times. This, the seventh and last of the ordered ages which condition human life on the earth, is identical with the kingdom covenanted to David." [45] The same is true for Hindson and Woodrow in the *KJV Bible Commentary* [46] and MacDonald and Farstad in the *Believers Bible Commentary.* [47]

Many commentators simply assert that the dispensation of the fullness of times is the millennium without giving the reasons for thinking so. However, two papers presented on the internet take the time to list reasons for believing this. One is by Joyce Pollard and her conclusion seems to be that the dispensation of the fullness of times occurs at the end of the millennium:

> I believe that we may conclude that the fulness of times refers to *a time when all God's plans have been completed* and there is nothing else that needs to be done. I think we may conclude from how it is used that the term 'dispensation of the fulness of times' tells us that *when everything is ready, God will*

> *manage His household according to the fact that all His plans have been completed* (Emphasis added). [48]

The second article is by Dr. Paul M. Elliott who believes this dispensation to be the millennium:

> God is going to re-gather all things under the headship of the Lord Jesus Christ ... *'All things'* in Ephesians 1:10 encompasses not only the redemption of believers, but of the entire creation. It will be consummated when Christ comes again (Emphasis added). [49]

These two articles make some specific arguments to support their conclusion. It seems they can be summed up (*anakephalaiomai!*) into four main points:

    1) *Fullness* means *completed*. That is, this dispensation is the arrangement that occurs when God has completed His plans for all His times.
    2) Gathered together (anakephalaiomai) should be re-gathered.
    3) Gathered together (anakephalaiomai) means to gather under Christ's *headship*.
    4) "All things" means the entire creation.

These are points that should be considered. There are weaknesses in each of them. Some have been considered under the section on definitions above. Therefore, *anakephalaisometha* (we will gather together) our facts.

Fullness does not always mean completion, neither by Greek definition nor by English definition. Even if it did, "fullness of times" would not necessarily mean "a time when all God's plans have been completed" (Pollard). *Times,* as mention above, does not mean *plans*. Similar terms are used in Galatians 4:4, "But when the fulness of the time was come, God sent forth his Son." This is a reference to the virgin birth, long before the final consummation of history. The phrase "fullness of the time" certainly does not mean all God's plans have been completed; it means "when the time was fully or finally come." Gal. 4:4 refers to only one time and Ephesians 1:10 to more than one, but, there is nothing in Ephesians 1:10 to indicate that *all* God's times or plans are in view.

Points two and three above are related, so we will look at both here. We have previously looked at the definition of *anakephalaiomai*. To reiterate, the meaning of the word is to sum up or to gather up. It is not to "head up." Ephesians 1:10 does not *mean* putting everything under Christ as head. What it *says* is that all things will be gathered together *in one in Christ.* This is what it says in English and in Greek. To give it a different meaning is to *change what the Scriptures say*, a tactic used by the serpent in Genesis 3. The belief some have that *anakephalaiomai* means to *head up* apparently is based on the mistaken idea that the word comes from *kephalē*, the head. It does not. It comes from *kephalaion*, the sum, the chief thing, the main point. [50]

Regarding the statement that this is a re-gathering, Dr. Elliott points out that in Genesis 1 all things were in harmony under Christ as head. This harmony was broken by sin and someday God will re-gather all things under Christ as head once more. The only dispensation in which this will happen is the millennium. The idea of re-gathering or gathering *again* is taken from one part of the word *anakephalaiomai*. The first three letters, *ana*, are a prepositional prefix. The idea is that *ana* means "again." However, that is not the only meaning of *ana*. The usual meaning is "upwards, up ... among, between." [51] However, when it is used as a prefix, there are times it can mean again, but, to repeat, this is not always true. For example, *anayennan* means born again, *anabaino* means to go up, and *anablepo* means to look up or to recover sight. [52] In the definitions I gave above, Vine's gives the definition of *anakephalaiomai* in part as "to sum up (again)..." This is the only inclusion of "again" in any lexicon examined. Barnes explains this the use of again, "The word used here -

anakephalaioō - means literally, to sum up, to recapitulate, as an orator does at the close of his discourse." [53] Often a public speaker will repeat his main points at the end of his speech as part of his summary and conclusion. The meaning is not that he said it once today and in five years he will say it again. No, it means a repetition *in the same speech.* So, the idea that all things once were under Christ's headship and someday they will be again is true, but that is not what is meant in Ephesians 1:10.

I will not argue the point about *all things* meaning *all creation.* By the time we finish, it will be quite clear to what this phrase refers. Remember that Ephesians 1:10 does not say that all things will be *under Christ.* It says all things will be *in Christ.* If "all things" refers to" all creation" that means every saved person, every unsaved person (and there will be some in the Millennium), angels, demons, horses, cows, pigs, giraffes, 'possums, skunks, and rats will be *in Christ.* Sometimes people do not know what they are saying.

Context, Never Forget the Context

Having determined what a dispensation is and that "all things" can refer to, and certainly does include, people and "gathered together into one" is accurately translated and means exactly what it says and that the location of the gathering is "in Christ" and that the gathering includes people on earth and in heaven, we are ready to move on. We have also looked at what other people say and should have noticed something peculiar. No one is looking at the context of the Book of Ephesians. There is some cross referencing to a couple of verses in Ephesians and elsewhere, but there is not a close examination of the whole subject matter of the book to determine what, if any, light can be found.

We should start with the immediate context. In Eph. 1:1-14, the subject is God's blessings (1:3). The object of the blessings is "us." That is the blessings are for us Christians right now. Verse three says, "God hath blessed us," past tense. The blessings listed *have already been bestowed*. None of them are waiting until some future time. They have all been bestowed on Christians of the present dispensation. Although the inheritance is future, we are heirs *now* (1 Peter 1:3-4). The blessing that Ephesians one is focusing on is the *predestination* to the inheritance, which we *already have.*

In verse four He has chosen "us." In verse five He predestinated "us." In verse six, He made "us" accepted in the beloved one. In verse seven, "we" have redemption. In verse eight, God's grace has abounded toward "us." In verse nine, God's grace has made known to "us" the mystery, which, in verse ten, is the dispensation of the fullness of times. It makes sense that the mystery and the dispensation and the gathering are among the blessings and are items God has already given us as He says in verse three.

The dispensation of the fullness of times in Eph. 1:10 is the definition of the mystery mentioned in verse nine. The *mystery* is a major theme in the Books of Ephesians and Colossians. The word *mystery* mentioned in Eph. 1:10 is called "the mystery of His will." The word mystery is also mentioned in Eph. 3:3, 4, 9; 5:32; and 6:19. It is called "the mystery of Christ" (3:4) and "the mystery of the gospel" (6:19). In the remaining verses, it is simply called "the mystery." The fact that the mystery is described differently does not indicate there are three different mysteries. Our current dispensation is called by at least three different names as well (dispensation of the gospel-1 Cor. 9:17; dispensation of the grace of God-Eph. 3:2; and dispensation of God-Col. 1:25), but they each still refer to the same current dispensation in which we live. They are descriptive names rather than definitive titles. Much of chapter three explains the mystery and there it is defined in verse six.

1 For this cause I Paul, the prisoner of Jesus Christ for you Gentiles,
2 If ye have heard of the dispensation of the grace

of God which is given me to you-ward:
3 How that by revelation he made known unto me the mystery; (as I wrote afore in few words,
4 Whereby, when ye read, ye may understand my knowledge in the mystery of Christ)
5 Which in other ages was not made known unto the sons of men, as it is now revealed unto his holy apostles and prophets by the Spirit;
6 That the Gentiles should be fellowheirs, and of the same body, and partakers of his promise in Christ by the gospel:
7 Whereof I was made a minister, according to the gift of the grace of God given unto me by the effectual working of his power.
8 Unto me, who am less than the least of all saints, is this grace given, that I should preach among the Gentiles the unsearchable riches of Christ;
9 And to make all men see what is the fellowship of the mystery, which from the beginning of the world hath been hid in God, who created all things by Jesus Christ:
10 To the intent that now unto the principalities and powers in heavenly places might be known by the church the manifold wisdom of God ... (Eph. 3:1-10)

The mystery spoken of in these verses is that the Gentiles and Jews would be fellow heirs and members of the same body, one body, the body of Christ. This fellowship in the body is spoken of extensively in chapter two: "And that he might reconcile both (Jew and Gentile) unto God in **one body** by the cross, having slain the enmity thereby" (Eph. 2:16). In other words, the mystery of Ephesians chapters two and three is that God would **gather together** *saved Jews and Gentiles into* **one** *body* **in Christ**. Compare that with "he might gather together in one all things in Christ" (Eph. 1:10). The body is also defined. We find that in chapter one. "And hath put all things under his feet, and gave him to be the head over all things to the church, which is his body, the fulness of him that filleth all in all" (Eph. 1:22-23). If anyone insists that "head up" is in the meaning of the word *anakephalaiomai*, I refer them to verses 22-23 where Christ is said to be *right now* the Head over the body, the church, which is Jew and Gentile gathered together in Christ. The entire Book of Ephesians is about this mystery.

As the reader can no doubt already see, *the concept "gather together in one" is also a major theme in Ephesians*. In chapter two the Lord explains the relation of believing Jews and Gentiles. Eph. 2:14-18 clearly tells us that God has broken down the wall between Jews and Gentiles and has made believing Jews and Gentiles *one in Christ*. He has taken the two and made them "one new man." He has reconciled both to Himself "in one body" and "we both have access by one Spirit unto the Father."

Another major theme in Ephesians, that is mentioned in Eph. 1:10, is the phrase "in Christ." As mentioned before, the phrase "in Christ" is technical terminology in Paul's letters. Paul began right away addressing the Ephesian letter to "the faithful in Christ Jesus" (Eph. 1:1). Our spiritual blessings are in heavenly places "in Christ" (Eph. 1:3). Since He raised us up spiritually, He has made us sit together in heavenly places "in Christ" (Eph. 2:6). We have new life, because "we are his workmanship, created *in Christ Jesus* unto good works" (Eph. 2:10). In time past, we were sinners without Christ, but now we are made near to God "in Christ" (Eph. 2:12-13). The fact that believing Jews and Gentiles are now fellow heirs, of the same body, and partakers of the same promise is because they are "in Christ" (Eph. 3:6). In fact, God's eternal purpose is "in Christ" and we are partakers of it, not because of election, but because God has put us "in Christ" (Eph. 3:11). Every Christian is a member of His body. "For we are members of his body, of his flesh, and of his bones ... This is a great mystery: but I speak concerning Christ and the church" (Eph. 5:30, 32).

The whole emphasis of Eph. 1:10 is on a certain group of people who now occupy both heaven and earth being brought together into one group or one body and this group of people or body is "in Christ." There is absolutely nothing said in Eph. 1:7-12, explicitly or implicitly, about the entire creation being put under Christ as their head. Eph. 1:9-10 is a mini-definitive statement on the mystery that is the theme of the entire Book of Ephesians. Paul said in Eph. 3:3-4, "How that by revelation he made known unto me the mystery; (as I wrote afore in few words, Whereby, when ye read, ye may understand my knowledge in the mystery of Christ)." Paul said he had written about the ministry before in just a few words. The only time he mentioned the term "mystery" prior to chapter three was in Eph. 1:9-10 and it was in very few words. The mystery of chapters one and three is the same.

The Fullness of Times

Finally, we come to the point where we can discuss the meaning of the phrase "fullness of times." As we have seen, this phrase has been used to point to the final consummation of God's plan at the end of the millennium and it has been used to point to the millennium itself. One thing is certain. A casual reading of the text of Eph. 1:7-12 will give the clear impression that the "dispensation of the fullness of times" does not refer to anything in the Old Testament. The dispensation must be either the dispensation of the church or the dispensation of the kingdom in the millennium. These are the only two left before eternity begins. Most seem to lean toward the millennium. I believe the dispensation of the fullness of times is the dispensation of the church.

The Church is built upon a foundation that includes the fullness of a time. This fullness does not refer to the completion of all God's plans, but rather follows the completion of a part of them (Gal. 4:4-5). Fullness is a characteristic part of the dispensation of the church. Below is a list of some of the passages that reveal the fullness of being in Christ:

> John 1:16 And of his *fulness* have all we received, and grace for grace.
> Ephesians 1:23 Which is his body, the *fulness* of him that *filleth* all in all.
> Ephesians 3:19 And to know the love of Christ, which passeth knowledge, that ye might be *filled* with all the *fulness* of God.
> Ephesians 4:10 He that descended is the same also that ascended up far above all heavens, that he might *fill* all things.)
> Ephesians 4:13 Till we all come in the unity of the faith, and of the knowledge of the Son of God, unto a perfect man, unto the measure of the stature of the *fulness* of Christ:
> Colossians 1:19 For it pleased the Father that in him should all *fulness* dwell;
> Colossians 2:9 For in him dwelleth all the *fulness* of the Godhead bodily.

In Christ dwells all the fullness of the Godhead and we are to be filled with the fullness of Christ. We, above all other people, have a destiny to be conformed to the full image of Christ (Rom. 8:28-30). God has given this destiny to no one else. We are predestinated to it. The dispensation of the fullness of times ends with all things in Christ receiving an inheritance to which they are predestinated. "That in the dispensation of the fullness of times he might gather together in one all things in Christ, ... *In whom also we have obtained an inheritance, being predestinated ...* " (Ephesians 1:10). We experience fullness and are destined for fullness like no other people in history.

So, the dispensation of the church begins with a foundation of "fullness of time" (Gal. 4:4) and it ends with the fullness of Christ in us when we are conformed to His full image. The phrase "fullness of times" can easily mean *times characterized by fullness* and that would describe the dispensation of the church very well.

The dispensation of the church is a dispensation of times in many ways. The first "time" associated with it is in Gal. 4:4. Then there is *the time past*: "Wherefore remember, that ye being in *time past* Gentiles in the flesh ... *But now* (note: this is *times present*) in Christ Jesus ye who sometimes were far off are made nigh by the blood of Christ" (Ephesians 2:11, 13; see verse 3 also for the plural of time). There is *the time of repentance*. "And the times of this ignorance God winked at; but now (note: it is a new time) commandeth all men every where to repent" (Acts 17:30). Also, this is the *time of our walk with Christ.* A concordance search for time or times shows that the word *times* is used in just this way. The words *time* and *times* are also used to mean *years* (Dan. 4:32). There is definitely *fullness of times* associated with the dispensation of the church.

Anakephalaiomai (I Sum Up)

The dispensation of the fullness of times is more than a hope for the future; it is a wonderful present reality. It is a time described as a *mystery.* A subject explained in Ephesians 2 and 3 as the gathering together of Jew and Gentile in one body in Christ. The dispensation of the fullness of times is described as the gathering together of all things (all believers) in Christ. It is the same in its goals and effects as the mystery of Chapters 2 and 3. In the dispensation of the fullness of times, God gathers all things together which are in heaven and on earth. These things are put in Christ. Only saved people of the current dispensation are put in Christ. The Scriptures never described any person or any creature or object ever as being put in Christ except those who believe the gospel. Therefore, this includes saved people on earth and saved people who have died and gone to heaven. Our current dispensation consists of times that are characterized by fullness. The fullness of the Godhead dwells in Christ, the fullness of Christ dwells in us, and the church is the fullness of Him who fills all in all. The dispensation of the church is truly the dispensation of the fullness of times.

Ephesians 1:10 is the theme verse and the theme statement of the Book of Ephesians. It tells how that all believers are gathered together in one body in Christ. It is what the Book of Ephesians is all about.

CHAPTER FOUR

RECONCILIATION OF JEWS AND GENTILES IN THE CHURCH
Ephesians 2:1-22

**1 And you hath he quickened, who were dead in trespasses and sins;
2 Wherein in time past ye walked according to the course of this world, according to the prince of the power of the air, the spirit that now worketh in the children of disobedience:
3 Among whom also we all had our conversation in times past in the lusts of our flesh, fulfilling the desires of the flesh and of the mind; and were by nature the children of wrath, even as others. (Eph. 2:1-3)**

EPHESIANS CHAPTER TWO EXPLAINS the position of the Gentiles before and after the cross. This is necessary to let the Jews know that the Gentiles now have a standing with God that is equal to their own. Much of the Bible teaches that the Jews have a special place with God as a nation. They have had special blessings from God, such as, the Law of Moses and the Land of Palestine and the Old Testament (Rom. 3:1-2). In addition, they have special promises from God not given to the Gentiles, among which are the promises of the restoration of their land and being a nation special to God forever. However, regarding the matter of spiritual salvation, both the Jews and the Gentiles are equal: sinners in need of a savior (Rom. 3:9, 28-29; Gal. 3:22).

Therefore, Ephesians two begins with an explanation of this salvation.

The section on the topic of salvation (Eph. 2:1-10) can be sub-divided into three parts: the sin of mankind (Eph 2:1-3), the Savior of mankind (Eph. 2:4-7), and the salvation of mankind (Eph. 2:8-10). The first part, quoted below, is all about our condition and behavior prior to salvation.

The Sin of Mankind (Eph. 2:1-3)

In verse one, the word "quickened" means *made alive* and is the equivalent of being born again. The phrase "hath he quickened" is not in the Greek Received Text at this point, as shown by the fact that it is in italics. The phrase comes from verse five. The translators inserted it in verse one to smooth out the English translation. This is a legitimate translation technique. It is a true statement and highlights the fact that prior to being born again (John 3:3-6; Titus 3:5), we were dead in trespasses and sins.

What does it mean to be dead in sin? When we see someone who is physically dead, his body cannot move, see, hear, think, speak, reason, make decisions, or do anything else. This is the way some view the meaning of the phrase "dead in trespasses and sins." Augustine (354-430 A. D.), John Calvin (1509-1564 A. D.), and their followers teach that free will is included in this description and every individual is completely unable to make any spiritually good decision. The 1689 Baptist Confession of Faith, Chapter Nine paragraph three, puts it this way:

> Man, by his fall into a state of sin, has wholly lost all ability of will to any spiritual good accompanying salvation ... so as a natural man, being altogether averse from that good, and dead in sin, ... is not able by his own strength to convert himself, or to prepare himself thereunto. [54]

"Dead in sin," according to this statement means in part that man has "wholly lost all ability of will to any spiritual good accompanying salvation ..." In the Calvinistic/ Sovereign Grace system, this is called *Total Inability or Total Depravity*. On the other hand, there were those early Christian teachers who had a different opinion. The following quotes are from the early "church fathers" and show that many of them believed in free will, even Ignatius, whose life overlapped that of the Apostles Paul and John; he was a disciple of John. Emphasis in these quotes is mine, except for parenthesis.

> Seeing, then, all things have an end, and there is set before us life upon our observance [of God's precepts, but death as the result of disobedience, and every one, *according to the choice* he makes, shall go to his own place, let us flee from death, and *make choice of life*. - **Ignatius (35-107 AD)** [55]
>
> And again, unless the human race has the power of avoiding evil and choosing good by *free choice*, *they are not accountable for their actions*, of whatever kind they be. But that it is by *free choice* they both walk uprightly and stumble, we thus demonstrate... **Justin Martyr (110-165 AD)** [56]
>
> But this we assert is inevitable fate, that they who choose the good have worthy rewards, and they who choose the opposite have their merited awards. For not like other things, as trees and quadrupeds, which cannot act by choice, did God make man: for neither would he be worthy of reward or praise *did he not of himself choose the good*, but were created for this end; nor, if he were evil, would he be worthy of punishment, not being evil of himself, but being able to be nothing else than what he was made. **Justin Martyr (110-165 AD)** [57]
>
> This expression [of our Lord], "How often would I have gathered thy children together, and thou

wouldest not," set forth the *ancient law of human liberty, because God made man a free [agent] from the beginning*, possessing his own power, even as he does his own soul, to obey the behests (*ad utendum sententia*) of God voluntarily, and not by compulsion of God. For there is no coercion with God, but a good will [towards us] is present with Him continually. And therefore does He give good counsel to all. And *in man, as well as in angels, He has placed the power of choice* (for angels are rational beings), so that those who had yielded obedience might justly possess what is good, given indeed by God, but preserved by themselves. - **Iranaeus (120-202 AD)** [58]

Foolish heretic, who treat with scorn so fine an argument of God's greatness and man's instruction! God put the question with an appearance of uncertainty, in order that even here He might prove man to be the subject of a *free will* in the alternative of either a denial or a confession, and give to him the opportunity of freely acknowledging his transgression ... **Tertullian (145-220 AD)** [59]

Evil had no existence from the beginning, but came into being subsequently. *Since man has free will*, a law has been defined *for his guidance* by the Deity, not without answering a good purpose. For if man did not possess the *power to will and not to will*, why should a law be established? For a law will not be laid down for an animal devoid of reason, but a bridle and a whip; whereas to man has been given a precept and penalty to perform, or for not carrying into execution what has been enjoined. For man thus constituted has a law been enacted by just men in primitive ages. Nearer our own day was there established a law, full of gravity and justice, by Moses ... **Hippolytus (170-236 AD)** [60]

The Image of God and the Created Nature of Man

Mankind was made in the image of God (Gen. 1:27). The image is not a *physical* image, because "God is a spirit" (John 4:24). However, the term "image" indicates that mankind was made to resemble God in such a way that when people looked upon one another they saw things that revealed God's characteristics. Although 1 Cor. 11:7 says that man is still in the image of God, it is clear that the image of God was marred by the fall (Gen. 3) because of the presence of sin in human nature. Adam and Eve lost their innocence and righteousness was out of their reach.

The image of God means many things, but Colossians 3:10 indicates that part of that image is knowledge. We "have put on the new man, which is renewed in knowledge after the image of him that created him." So, knowledge is one thing God gave us as part of the image of God. Adam and Eve were created knowing God personally. Because of the fall, we no longer know God personally. Consider one thing very carefully. Mankind lost knowledge because of the fall, *but mankind never lost the ability to know!*

One thing the image of God certainly means is that man is a trinity like God is a trinity. "And the very God of peace sanctify you wholly; and I pray God your whole spirit and soul and body be preserved blameless unto the coming of our Lord Jesus Christ" (1 Thess. 5:23). Man has a body, a soul, and a spirit. Man is three parts, a trinity, just as God is a trinity. Each part of a human being has its own distinct functions. As we all know, the body has the functions of sight, touch, smell, hearing, and speech. The body enables us to relate to the world around us. There is a corrupt nature in man since the fall and it is connected with our flesh (Rom. 7:18, 23).

The soul of a person has the capacities of ***mind*** (Josh. 22:5; Ps. 119:20; 139:14; Prov. 16:24; 19:2; 24:14), ***emotion*** (Gen. 42:21; Deut. 13:3; Josh. 22:5; Jud. 16:16; 1 Sam. 1:10;

Job 10:1; Ps. 11:5; Ps. 35:9; Ps. 42:2; 138:3; Song 3:3; Jer. 31:25), and *will* (decision making ability) (Josh. 22:5; 1 Kings 2:4; Job 6:7; 7:15; Ps. 57:1; 63:8; 77:2). The Bible sometimes speaks of the soul in such a way that it gives the impression it is the body. For example, Leviticus 7:20 speaks of a soul eating of a sacrifice, like a body eats. We must remember that it is the *entire person,* body and soul and spirit, which commits an action. The soul considers it and makes the decision and the body does the action. The fact that the soul is a separate part of a human being is illustrated in 1 Kings 17:22, where a child is brought back to life when his soul enters into his body again.

Finally, the capacities of the human spirit are found in his relationship to God and his understanding of human life. Through his spirit a person senses and understands the spiritual. The term "spirit" from the Hebrew *ruach* is used in various ways in the Old Testament. It can mean breath (Jer. 14:6; Jud. 15:19), purposelessness or uselessness or vanity (Jer. 5:13; Job 16:3), wind (Ex. 10:13), direction (Jer. 49:36), life in man (Gen. 7:21-22), and mind-set or disposition (Ps. 32:2). [61] However, the term "spirit" is also used for the part of man that relates to God along with the soul (Is. 26:9). When a person dies his spirit returns to God (Eccl. 12:7).

Man was made in the image of God and the Bible says he is still in the image of God. "For a man indeed ought not to cover his head, forasmuch as *he is the image and glory of God*: but the woman is the glory of the man" (1 Cor. 11:7). Notice the use of the present tense. Upon extensive search, I have not found one word in Scripture to indicate that the capacities of the soul (mind, emotions, and will) have been in any way destroyed or removed by the fall of man. It is clear from Ephesians 2:1-3 that the soul is under the influence of the flesh, the world and the devil, but the *ability to choose*, which God gave Adam, remains in our nature.

So, in what way are we dead? Remember that God said to Adam, "But of the tree of the knowledge of good and evil, thou shalt not eat of it: for *in the day* that thou eatest thereof *thou shalt surely die* (Gen. 2:17). They ate and *that day* they died. In what way did they die? It certainly was not their bodies that died. Neither was it their souls. Their bodies and souls continued to function. They continued to have the ability to think, feel, and make decisions (mind, emotion, and will). We learn the answer in considering what part of a person is born again when they receive Christ by faith (John 3:6). Jesus said, *"That which is born of the Spirit is spirit."* So, it was Adam and Eve's spirits that died that day. In Eph. 2:1, it is the spirit of man that is dead, not his soul or his body. Man's ability to have a relationship with God is dead, but he can still think, feel, make choices, and perform actions.

Death is not the end of consciousness. Yes, the death of the body renders it completely inert, but the soul continues as a thinking being. This is clear from Jesus' story of the rich man and Lazarus (Luke 16:19-31). Death, in its basic concept, is separation. The death of the body is the separation of the body from the soul and spirit. Paul said, "We are confident, I say, and willing rather to be absent from the body, and to be present with the Lord" (2 Cor. 5:8). The death of the soul is separation from God in the Lake of Fire (Rev. 20:11-15). The current death of the spirit is separation from the life of God. All death is caused by sin (see Rom. 5; 6:23). That the spirit still has some ability to function is evident from 1 Cor. 2:11: *"For what man knoweth the things of a man, save the spirit of man which is in him?"* The spirit we have in us helps us understand our own life. So "death" does not mean a complete ceasing of function or an end of consciousness or an inability to make decisions, even spiritual ones. It means we are cut off from the life of God, eternal life, and we are separated from Him, without God, and without hope (Eph. 2:11-12).

When we were unsaved, we were under the domination of sin. Specifically, we were dominated by the flesh, the world (1 John 2:16), and the devil, the prince of the power of the air. The Bible says some harsh things about the condition of mankind. *"All have sinned"* (Rom. 3:23). The lists in Romans 3:10-18 and 1:18-32 present a very dark and bleak picture. By these lists, Paul intended to convey the utter corruption of the entire human race. Calvinists use these verses to teach that human beings are incapable of making any good decisions spiritually. However, the entire picture is a description of behavior *after birth*; it is not a depiction of man's basic fallen nature.

Humans are capable of positive decisions and positive actions, but they cannot be good enough to earn Heaven or match God's goodness. Compared to God's goodness, we are not good at all. Isaiah described this condition by saying, "But we are all as an unclean thing, and all our righteousnesses are as filthy rags" (Is. 64:6). On the other hand, Jesus said, "If ye then, being evil, know how to give good gifts unto your children, how much more shall your Father which is in heaven give good things to them that ask him" (Matt. 7:11)? To give a good gift to our children is an acceptable act. It does not displease the Lord. There are many such acts that are done every day.

What about spiritual decisions that accompany salvation? Acts 10 introduces Cornelius, a Roman centurion, who is said to be "a devout man, and one that feared God with all his house, which gave much alms to the people, and prayed to God always" (Acts 10:2). This man was not a saved man. He was a sincerely religious man, who did correct acts (giving alms). He believed in the God of the Old Testament, but not in Jesus Christ. He also feared God, showing that an unsaved person can have enough spiritual understanding to fear God. The Bible gives two evaluations of Cornelius' religious spirit. The first comes from the angel who told him to send for Peter. "And he said unto him, Thy prayers and thine alms are come up for a memorial before God" (Acts 10). God saw and took special positive notice of his actions and prayers. The second is from Peter after Cornelius got saved, "Of a truth I perceive that God is no respecter of persons: but in every nation he that feareth him, and worketh righteousness, is accepted with him" (Acts 10:34-35). These things were true of Cornelius in his unsaved condition. I am not saying that Cornelius got to the point he did without the work of the Holy Spirit in his life, but he was not saved; he had not been born again. Yet, he was able to do positive spiritual acts and he was able to make positive spiritual decisions.

People can make spiritual decisions. They can repent and come to Christ. The words of the Lord Jesus agree to this. There was a time when Jesus hid His words from a group who were under the judgment of God. Steve Jones, a former Calvinist, explains:

> Jesus himself did not seem to have been a believer in Total Inability. We read in Mark 4:11, 12 that he spoke in parables as a judgment against the obstinate Jews. The purpose of parables was to keep his message from entering their ears, "otherwise they might turn and be forgiven" (v.12). Had those stiff-necked people been allowed to hear the truth straight out, *they might have turned to receive it.* But how? Calvinism tells us that no one can turn and receive the forgiveness of sins because of Total Inability passed from Adam. There must first be an inward miracle of the heart, an "effectual call." [62]

The Failure of Human Nature

"*Wherein in time past ye walked according to the course of this world*" (Eph. 2:2). 1 John 2:16 tells us the world consists of the lust of the flesh, the lust of the eyes, and the pride of life. There are a lot of good things in the world, but the world is very hostile to living a moral and spiritual life.

The general spirit of the world influences unsaved people. They have very little defense against it. If they have had a moral upbringing, it helps, but doesn't completely insulate them from ungodly influences. God gives everyone a conscience that shows them right and wrong. This helps. But, the world is a very powerful influence. We are moved against God by the immorality around us, the philosophies we are exposed to on television, education, books, magazines, movies, video games, friends, relatives, and many other things in the world.

"Wherein in time past ye walked ... according to the prince of the power of the air, the spirit that now worketh in the children of disobedience" (Eph. 2:2). The prince of the power of the air is Satan. He is also called the prince of this world (John 14:30) and the god of this world (2 Cor. 4:4). He is the father of lies (John 8:44) and he blinds the minds of the unsaved to the gospel (2 Cor. 4:4). Just as Christians are led by the Spirit of God (Rom. 8:14), the unsaved are led about and guided by the satanic god of this world and they walk in accordance with him. The general culture around us, guided by the Devil, moves us toward rebellion against God. As one preacher commented:

> Further, the demoniac powers and principalities which control, drive, and guide the unsaved masses lead them to attack the Bible, imitate the Bible, ridicule the Bible, quote the Bible, and fulfill the Bible UNCONCIOUSLY. The briefest review of English literature, including magazines, newspapers, comic strips, political cartoons, feature articles, human interest stories, plays, dramas, movies, "soap operas," and essays, will reveal the "prince of the power of the air" working overtime in the "children of disobedience" and guiding their thoughts, brushes, pens, and typewriters against the revealed will of God in the Holy Bible. [63]

"Among whom also we all had our conversation in times past in the lusts of our flesh, fulfilling the desires of the flesh and of the mind" (Eph. 2:3). The primary word describing the fleshly nature is lust:

> **16 This I say then, Walk in the Spirit, and ye shall not fulfil the lust of the flesh**
> **19 Now the works of the flesh are manifest, which are these; Adultery, fornication, uncleanness, lasciviousness,**
> **20 Idolatry, witchcraft, hatred, variance, emulations, wrath, strife, seditions, heresies,**
> **21 Envyings, murders, drunkenness, revellings, and such like: of the which I tell you before, as I have also told you in time past, that they which do such things shall not inherit the kingdom of God. (Gal. 5:16, 19-21).**

Some have said that every person is not as bad as he could be, but all are as *bad off* as they can be. The lustful flesh is in everyone and everyone exercises sinful behaviors of the flesh. Nevertheless, the flesh shows up in different persons in different ways depending in part upon training, culture, and other influences. Bad behavior is present in all of us for *"all have sinned"* (Rom. 3:23) and this makes us all the "children of disobedience," but some are worse behaved than others.

This passage speaks of unsaved people as "children of disobedience" and "children of wrath." It says the unsaved are children of wrath "by nature." Jamieson, Fausset, and Brown in their commentary say this about our nature:

> He intentionally breaks off the construction, substituting "and we were" for "and being," to mark emphatically his and their *past* state by nature, as

contrasted with their present state by grace. Not merely is it, we had our way of life fulfilling our fleshly desires, *and so being* children of wrath; but *we were by nature* originally "children of wrath," and so consequently had our way of life fulfilling our fleshly desires. "Nature," in *Greek,* implies that which has *grown* in us as the peculiarity of our being, growing with our growth, and strengthening with our strength, as distinguished from that which has been wrought on us by mere external influences: what is inherent, not acquired (Job 14:4; Psa 51:5). [64]

The Savior of Mankind

4 But God, who is rich in mercy, for his great love wherewith he loved us,
5 Even when we were dead in sins, hath quickened us together with Christ, (by grace ye are saved;)
6 And hath raised us up together, and made us sit together in heavenly places in Christ Jesus:
7 That in the ages to come he might shew the exceeding riches of his grace in his kindness toward us through Christ Jesus. (Eph. 2:4-7).

When we were unsaved, our condition was as bad as it could get. Our destiny could not be worse; we were bound for Hell. But, God has the answer. It starts with the *"great love wherewith He loved us."* God knew that His created creatures had ruined themselves. His just nature moved Him to condemn and punish them. However, His great love moved Him to provide a way of escape for His creatures. He did just that. He sent His only begotten Son (John 3:16), who suffered the vicious death of the cross after having been whipped and scorned. Why was He eager and willing to do that? He did it for the *"great love wherewith He loved us."* Even though we were dead in sins, God had a way to regenerate us through the gospel. This new life was given by grace and His grace was given because of the *"great love wherewith He loved us."* The great preacher, Harry Ironside, expressed it this way:

> *"But God,"* how much that expression, *"But God,"* means. We have God coming in now. We were dead, helpless, unable to do one thing to retrieve our dreadful circumstances, but God came in ... and spoke the word of living power. "But God who is rich in mercy;" in what is He not rich? ... There are infinite resources of mercy for the vilest sinner. There is no one for whom there is no mercy ... Because we were dead, He sent Jesus to give us life; because we were guilty, He sent Jesus to be the propitiation by bearing our sins in His own body on the tree ... But now God comes in and works in power, and by the living Word He speaks to the dead Jews and to the dead Gentiles, and the Word brings life, and they believe it and are quickened together. [65]

The new life we have in Christ is a spiritual resurrection. We were dead, now we are alive. According to verse six, we have been raised and made to sit with Christ in Heaven. We are already in Heaven. It is sure and certain. Jamieson, Fausset, and Brown say:

> The Head being seated at God's right hand, the body also sits there with Him ... We are already seated there IN Him ("in Christ Jesus," Eph 2:6), and hereafter shall be seated *by* Him; IN Him already as in our Head, which is the ground of our hope; *by* Him hereafter, as by the conferring cause, when hope shall be swallowed up in fruition ... What God wrought in Christ, He wrought (by the very fact) in all united to Christ, and one with Him ... Believers are bodily in heaven in point of right, and virtually so in spirit, and have each their own place assigned there, which in due time they shall take possession of

(Phi 3:20, Phi 3:21). He does not say, "*on the right hand of God*"; a prerogative reserved to Christ peculiarly; though they shall share His throne (Rev 3:21). [66]

The Bible speaks of this spiritual resurrection in Christ in Romans 6:3-5. The Spirit of God baptized us into Christ and into His death. Because He rose from the dead, He also gave us newness of life. It is as Paul said in Galatians 2:20, "*I am crucified with Christ: nevertheless I live ...*" As He was crucified and then raised from the dead, we also are crucified and raised from the dead. Verse seven tells us that in the future God has prepared for us, we will be God's display. His kindness toward us through the salvation provided in Christ Jesus will show the entire universe just how great and rich His grace really is.

The Salvation of Mankind

8 For by grace are ye saved through faith; and that not of yourselves: it is the gift of God:
9 Not of works, lest any man should boast.
10 For we are his workmanship, created in Christ Jesus unto good works, which God hath before ordained that we should walk in them. (Eph. 2:8-10).

These are very clear verses. Grace gives us salvation. The means grace uses to save us is faith. The Pulpit Commentary says:

> He repeats what he had said parenthetically (Eph. 2:5), in order to open the subject up more fully. On the part of God, salvation is by grace; on the part of man, it is through faith. It does not come to us by an involuntary act, as light falls on our eyes, sounds on our ears, or air enters our lungs. When we are so far

enlightened as to understand about it, there must be a personal reception of salvation by us, and that is by faith. Faith at once believes the good news of a free salvation through Christ, and accepts Christ as the Savior. We commit ourselves to him, trust ourselves to him for that salvation of which he is the Author. In the act of thus entrusting ourselves to him for his salvation, we receive the benefit, and are saved ... faith indicates that attitude of men towards Christ in which it pleases God to save them, transferring to him all their guilt, imputing to them all his merit. [67]

The Pulpit commentary alludes to a disagreement among teachers about this verse. The verse says, "that not of yourselves." *What* is not of "yourselves?" Is it grace or is it faith? Many say it is both. At one time, I believed it was both. It could possibly even be salvation (a noun), which is implied by "are ye saved." It will help by looking closer at the grammar of the verse in both English and Greek. The word "that" ("that not of yourselves") is a pronoun. Pronouns refer to a noun, which is called its antecedent. What is the antecedent of "that?"

The pronoun "that" is singular. This is a very significant thing. It means that its antecedent must be singular. So, it can only refer to a *singular noun*. It cannot refer to *two nouns,* because it would need to be plural in that case. So, it cannot refer to both grace and faith. If it refers to one of these, it seems logical that it refers to "grace," because grace that saves us can only come from God.

However, this is one instance where the Greek New Testament might give us some insight. Why should we care what the Greek New Testament says? God originally inspired the New Testament in Greek and that has not changed. God preserved that Greek Text after he inspired it. The KJV translators had this text, because they said their version was "translated out of the original tongues." We also have the same Greek text they used, the Received Text. In other words, we have the original inspired words preserved by God in the Received Greek New Testament. A better question would be, "what is the justification for ignoring it, when it also is the Word of God and it might help us?" We are not looking at two *different* authorities, but at the *same authority* in two different languages.

In Greek, the word "that" (touto) is also a pronoun. In Greek pronouns also refer to a noun or another pronoun, as they do in English. The Greek pronoun *must agree with its antecedent in gender and number.* The pronoun, "that," is neuter singular in Greek. Therefore, its antecedent must also be neuter singular. The problem is that *neither* "grace" nor "faith" is neuter singular. They are both feminine singular. So, *neither* grace *nor* faith is the antecedent of "that" (touto). If they or one of them was the antecedent, then "that" would be feminine, not neuter. In fact, going back through the text, one must go all the way back to verse four to find a noun that is neuter singular. It is interesting that the word in verse four, which is "mercy," is related to salvation and grace, but it is not the antecedent we are seeking.

However, there is a noun in verse eight, itself, that fits. In the phrase, "it is the gift of God," the word "gift" is neuter singular. It's the only word that fits, according to the rules of grammar. Therefore, I conclude that "Gift" is the noun to which "that" refers.

Let's look at this a little more carefully. What is the *gift of God*? It's not grace, because God's grace gives you the gift. Also, *faith* is never said to be "the gift of God" anywhere in the New Testament. The first time the phrase "the gift of God" is used in the New Testament is in John 4:10, "Jesus answered and said unto her, If thou knewest the *gift of God*, and who it is that saith to thee, Give me to drink; thou wouldest have asked of him, and he would have given thee living water." John 7:38 defines living water as "the Spirit, which they that believe on him should receive." Next, it is used in Acts 8:20, referring to the Holy Spirit. The definitive verse is Romans 6:23: " For the wages of sin is death; but the **gift of God** is eternal life through Jesus Christ our Lord." So, the "gift of God" is the eternal life which is given by the Holy Spirit and which you receive when you believe on Christ. What is eternal life, but salvation? You get the gift of God because God's grace gives it to you when you trust in Christ and it is not of yourselves.

> **Verily, verily, I say unto you, He that heareth my word, and believeth on him that sent me, hath everlasting life, and shall not come into condemnation; but is passed from death unto life. (John 5:24)**

So, the phrase "the gift of God" in Ephesians 2:8 refers back to the salvation implied in the words "are ye saved." Eternal life is the gift of God and it is not of ourselves in any way. Nevertheless, we need to examine the elements of grace and faith a little closer.

It is easily understandable that the grace is God's grace, so it cannot in any way be from us, either. The salvation grace gives us is entirely of God, because we cannot save ourselves or do anything that earns salvation.

However, the Bible consistently speaks of faith as something you and I do. The Scriptures command us to believe and tell us that, when someone believes, *"his faith is counted for righteousness"* (Rom. 4:5). We hear the gospel and it results in faith. Therefore, human beings are involved. When you were saved, God showed you the truth from the Word of God and it was you who believed. Faith, however, is not a good work that earns salvation.

On the other side of the coin, God helps us with faith. The three helps He gives are the Word of God, the Holy Spirit, and "much assurance." The power of God works through and in all these to stimulate sinners to trust Christ. God works in you, but it is you who believes.

Romans 10:17 tells us, "So then, faith cometh by hearing, and hearing by the Word of God." Therefore, we must translate the Word of God into all the world's languages. There are over 3000 languages that have nothing of the Word of God published as far as is known. The Word provokes faith in the hearts of people. As we found earlier in chapter two, we are also called by the Gospel (2 Thess. 2:14). Therefore, the preaching of the gospel is necessary for people to be saved.

The Holy Spirit's ministry is to reprove the world. "And when he is come, he will reprove the world of sin, and of righteousness, and of judgment" (John 16:8). This reproving ministry shows the world that God is right and they are wrong. This ministry is to convince the world of the truth of the gospel. Coupled with the preaching of the Word of God, this ministry of the Holy Spirit will encourage faith.

Finally, Paul said, "For our gospel came not unto you in word only, but also in power, and in the Holy Ghost, and *in much assurance*; as ye know what manner of men we were among you for your sake" (1 Thess. 1:5). In this verse, we have all three elements: the Word, the Holy Ghost, and much assurance. The third is the assurance that comes when you see a true living example of faith. People see faith expressed in us and the change that has happened to us after we accepted the Gospel. People see the reality of faith in our lives. That encourages them to believe. Paul also said of the Corinthian believers, "Ye are our epistle written in our hearts, *known and read of all men*" (2 Cor. 3:2). Paul said this assurance came to the Thessalonians because of the manner of men they were as they lived their lives before the people of Thessalonica. He said they didn't use deceit, uncleanness, flattering words, or guile when they preached the gospel (1 Thess. 2:3-5). They sought to please God, not men (1 Thess. 2:4). They did not seek to make gain of them, as covetous men might do. They did not seek glory and honor from them, but rather sought to glorify God. They were humble, gentle, and affectionate (1 Thess. 2:5-8). People can see faith when it is real in our lives and we are trying to live according to it. They can also see hypocrisy.

Therefore, God makes provision to enable the sinner to respond to the gospel in faith. However, each of us has a personal responsibility to choose to believe.

Salvation is "not of works, lest any man should boast" (verse 9). If the grace of God that brings salvation is to abound to God's glory (Eph. 1:6; 2:7), then there can be nothing in salvation that can give man reason to boast. When God says this, He is specifically referring to "works." Romans 4:4 says, "Now to him that worketh is the reward not reckoned of grace, but of debt." If a person could work for salvation and earn it, God would owe it to him as a matter of debt. But no one can earn it. No one is good enough to deserve it. "But to him that worketh not, but believeth on him that justifieth the ungodly, his faith is counted for righteousness" (Rom. 4:5). The basis of salvation cannot be both works and grace through faith. "And if by grace, then is it no more of works: otherwise grace is no more grace. But if it be of works, then is it no more grace: otherwise work is no more work" (Rom. 11:6). "Where is boasting then? It is excluded. By what law? of works? Nay: but by the law of faith. Therefore we conclude that a man is justified by faith without the deeds of the law" (Rom. 3:27-28). Whether a person has the ability to make a decision or not, is not part of the question about boasting. God says that a person cannot work for salvation by keeping the Law and he cannot save himself, therefore he has no basis for pride or boasting.

This concept is also the reason you can be confident that you will never lose your salvation. If you cannot work to get saved, you cannot work to keep your salvation. Grace works both before and after salvation. You are "kept by the power of God through faith" (1 Peter 1:5). Grace saves you and grace keeps you.

So, let us try to bring this all together:

1. People are dead spiritually (Eph. 1:1-3)
2. They are dominated and influenced by the flesh, the world, and the devil.
3. However, humans still have the capacity of mind, emotions, and will.
4. Therefore, God had to bring influences of His own to people.
5. The influences from God include illumination (John 1:9), conviction from the Holy Spirit (John 16:7-11), drawing power (John 6:44), the gospel and calling by it (2 Thess. 2:14), the availability of faith through the preaching of the Word (Rom. 10:17), and the example of true believers.
6. These influences of God come through the Holy Spirit and the Word of God, making it immensely necessary that the Word of God be spread across the globe in every language.

Man cannot save himself or earn his salvation, but he can choose whether he will receive Christ or reject Him. "O Jerusalem, Jerusalem, thou that killest the prophets, and stonest them which are sent unto thee, how often would I have gathered thy children together, even as a hen gathereth her chickens under her wings, and **ye would not**" (Matt. 23:37). The Lord was completely sincere in His statement that they could and would have been accepted by Him. He was completely sincere that he wanted this. However, they refused. "Ye stiffnecked and uncircumcised in heart and ears, **ye do always resist** the Holy Ghost: as your fathers did, so do ye" (Acts 7:51). Here are people who had the work of the Holy Spirit going on in their hearts. Why did the Holy Spirit work on them if not to bring them to repentance? If so, they certainly could have repented. Yet, they refused. They rejected the work of the Holy Spirit.

"Search the scriptures; for in them ye think ye have eternal life: and they are they which testify of me. And **ye will not come to me**, that ye might have life" (John 5:39-40). God certainly meant what He said here. They could have come to Him. They could have had life. The fact that they did not come was because they *would not do it*. It was not because God refused to give them some mythical "effectual call" (which the Bible never speaks of). They rejected the power and influence of the Word of God.

"Come now, and **let us reason together**, saith the LORD: though your sins be as scarlet, they shall be as white as snow; though they be red like crimson, they shall be as wool" (Is. 1:18). "I call heaven and earth to record this day against you, that I have set before you life and death, blessing and cursing: therefore **choose life**, that both thou and thy seed may live" (Deut. 30:19). Could they all choose life or was God just lying? (Moses was speaking God's message under the inspiration of the Holy Spirit.) "And if it seem evil unto you to serve the LORD, **choose you this day** whom ye will serve ... but as for me and my house, we will serve the LORD" (Josh. 24:15).

Some point to John 1:12-13 to make the point that man's choice has nothing to do with salvation. "But as many as received him, to them gave he power to become the sons of God, even to them that believe on his name: which were born, not of blood, **nor of the will of the flesh, nor of the will of man**, but of God." These verses speak of "will," but they do not say that man's will has *nothing* to do with salvation. They say that your will did not and cannot save you, God alone can do that. Let's illustrate the matter. Let's suppose a man comes to me and says, "You have a mortgage on your home of $100,000, right?" "Yes," I answer. "Would you like to be free of that debt?" He inquires. Again, I answer, "Sure." The man smiles, "I'm going to pay your mortgage for you and you can still own the house." I could look at him, decide he is just teasing me, and decide to reject his offer; or, I could believe him and decide to accept his offer. The choice is mine. If I decide to accept the offer, the man pays my mortgage. Is my freedom from debt my doing? I certainly did not earn it. It was a free gift. Did my will accomplish it? Absolutely not! My freedom from debt was totally of the gracious offer and action of my benefactor. It was not of my will in any way. By refusing the offer, I could have prevented the man from paying my debt. However, my choice to accept the offer accomplished only one thing. It freed the man to do what he had determined to do in the first place, pay my debt. My will did not make me debt free. My will did not pay my debt. I could have willed all day and all night, and I would still have owed the debt. Only the gracious payment, which my benefactor conceived, offered, and provided, made me debt free. I have nothing to boast of. So, my will cannot save me. Only my Savior can do that. My choice to trust Him may free Him to do it, but my will cannot accomplish it.

The Necessity of Good Works

When a person gets saved, he is God's "workmanship, created in Christ Jesus unto good works" (Eph. 2:10). Good works are expected of a Christian. "Let your light so shine before men, that they may see your good works, and glorify your Father which is in heaven" (Mt. 5:16). Good works are one of the key ingredients of a godly life. Good works are part of the "much assurance" we were just thinking about. Women are encouraged to beautify themselves "with good works" (1 Tim. 2:10). Godly widows are praised if they are "well reported of for good works" (1 Tim. 5:10) among other things. One reason God gave the word of God is so that "the man of God may be perfect, throughly furnished unto all good works" (2 Tim. 3:17). The young minister is admonished to show himself "a pattern of good works" (Titus 2:7). In fact, the whole church is to be rich in good works because Christ "gave himself for us, that he might redeem us from all iniquity, and purify unto himself a peculiar people, zealous of good works" (Titus 2:14). "This is a faithful saying, and these things I will that thou affirm constantly, that they which have believed in God might be careful to maintain good works. These things are good and profitable unto men" (Titus 3:8). "And let ours also learn to maintain good works for necessary uses, that they be not unfruitful" (Titus 3:14). Go gives us the responsibility to encourage other believers to maintain good works: "And let us consider one another to provoke unto love and to good works" (Heb. 10:24).

All this Scriptural evidence proves that God wants the church to be full of good works. These are works of several types. The Bible doesn't specify what they all are, because the definition is flexible. It is certain God does not limit good works to telling others how to be saved. The works mentioned here include works that the world can see and know they are good works (Mt. 5:16). This is what leads the world to glorify God in us. The world is not likely to glorify God for hearing you preach the gospel. To them, the gospel is foolishness (1 Cor. 1:18). Good works are designed to *show* God's love to others, therefore they are meant to meet the needs of others.

Since these good works are plural, it is evident that the Great Commission is not the only good work we are to do. The primary purpose of the church is to fulfill the Great Commission, but the fruitful Christian life is not limited to that. It is true that anyone who does not fulfill the Great Commission and substitutes good works for it, is on a bad path, an unscriptural path. We often refer to this as a "social gospel." Nevertheless, we must be careful not to become unbalanced the other way by leaving off good works. God wants us to be involved in both mission work and in good works. Some of the benefits of good works include showing the world God's love and thereby glorifying Him, softening the hearts of people toward the gospel, and creating a genuine interest in them toward hearing the gospel.

The Reconciliation of the Gentiles

The rest of Ephesians chapter two explains why the gentiles are included in the body of Christ. The Jews held that the Gentiles were sinners (Gal. 2:15) and that Jews were not to fellowship with them (Acts 10:15; 11:1-3). It took a lot of work to prove to the Jewish Christians that God had accepted the Gentiles without commanding them to become Jews and keep the Law of Moses.

This kind of exclusiveness exists in our day. It is not so much Jew and Gentile anymore. Paul had a problem in Corinth that was much like the divisions of our day. "For it hath been declared unto me of you, my brethren, by them which are of the house of Chloe, that there are contentions among you. Now this I say, that every one of you saith, I am of Paul; and I of Apollos; and I of Cephas; and I of Christ. Is Christ divided? Was Paul crucified for you? Or were ye baptized in the name of Paul?" (1 Cor. 1:11-13). Some of our divisions today are based on doctrine and heresy. Some divisions cannot be avoided, as we will see later, but many divisions are as petty and unnecessary as those in Corinth. The question, "Is Christ divided," is very pertinent to the entire discussion in chapters two and three. That will become very clear when we get to our study of the "mystery."

The Past Estrangement of the Gentiles

11 Wherefore remember, that ye being in time past Gentiles in the flesh, who are called Uncircumcision by that which is called the Circumcision in the flesh made by hands;
12 That at that time ye were without Christ, being aliens from the commonwealth of Israel, and strangers from the covenants of promise, having no hope, and without God in the world: (Eph. 2:11-12).

The Jews called the Gentiles "uncircumcision," and God described the Jews as the "circumcision." God gave Abraham the practice of circumcision (Gen. 17:11) as a sign of the covenant He made between Him and them. It was to be a perpetual practice under the Law of Moses. To the Jews, it was a sign of their superior position with God. So, naturally, the Gentiles were strangers outside God's covenants and were hopeless sinners, because they were not circumcised.

The problem was that the Gentiles really were in a bad condition. Ephesians 2:12 describes that condition. They were without Christ and aliens from the common wealth of Israel and strangers from the covenants of promise-*in reality*. In the Old Testament, Israel was God's chosen people. No Gentile nation had any involvement in the covenants God made with the Jews. God made special promises to Israel. The Gentiles had no part in those promises. They were without hope and without God. Further, they were without excuse (Rom. 1:20) and without strength (Rom. 5:6).

The Present Equality of Jews and Gentiles

13 But now in Christ Jesus ye who sometimes were far off are made nigh by the blood of Christ.
14 For he is our peace, who hath made both one, and hath broken down the middle wall of partition between us;
15 Having abolished in his flesh the enmity, even the law of commandments contained in ordinances; for to make in himself of twain one new man, so making peace;
16 And that he might reconcile both unto God in one body by the cross, having slain the enmity thereby:
17 And came and preached peace to you which were afar off, and to them that were nigh.
18 For through him we both have access by one Spirit unto the Father. (Eph. 2:13-18)

The Gentiles were always far from God. God brought the Jews near to HIm through the covenant relationship He had with the nation. Now the blood of Christ, shed for Jews and Gentiles, has brought the Gentiles near. The gospel makes salvation available to everyone. The only thing He requires of them is to turn to God and believe (Rom. 3:25; 10:9-13). When it comes to salvation, there is no difference between Jew and Gentile. As a nation, the Jews still have their covenants and promises. However, as individuals they too are required to trust Christ.

The earlier passage (Eph. 2:11-12) used the word "ye" two times, referring to the Gentiles and their condition; that they are 1) Gentiles outside Israel and 2) without Christ, God, or hope. This passage (v. 13-18) uses the word "ye" one time in verse 13 to say that Christ has remedied that condition, "ye who sometimes were far off are made nigh by the blood of Christ." However, the main key word in Ephesians 2:13-18 is the word "both," which is used three important times: God has made both one (14), He has reconciled both (16), and both have access (18).

God Has Made Both One

First, He "hath made both one" (v. 14). The term *both* here and the other two times refers to both the Jews and Gentiles. He has united Jew and Gentile into "one," described as "one body" (v. 16), "one new man" (v. 15) and one "holy temple" (v. 21). To this we may add the statements of Peter in 1 Peter 2:5, 9, where he uses the word "a" to indicate *one* and to describe us as one "spiritual house," one "chosen generation," one "holy and royal priesthood," one "holy nation," one "peculiar people," and "the people of God." The point is that Jews and Gentiles are no longer separate in spiritual matters and Jews must no longer consider the Gentiles to be enemies. Christ, Himself, is the peace between Jew and Gentile.

Before the cross, God saw mankind as divided into *two* great categories: Jew and Gentile, which includes anyone who is not a Jew. *After the cross*, there are *three* great categories of mankind. "Give none offence, neither to the Jews, nor to the Gentiles, nor to the church of God" (1 Cor. 10:32). Now, we have the Jew, the Gentile, and the Church. The church consists of saved Jews and saved Gentiles. Each of these great divisions is a single unified group. God created this new category by putting saved Jews and Gentiles together in one body. So, the Bible says that God "hath made both one." God named this one new thing He made "the church" in 1 Corinthians 10:32. God made it *one* church.

It should be clear that this *body* is the same body spoken of in Ephesians 1:22-23, which is described as *His* body in v. 23 and as the body *of Christ* in Ephesians 4:12. The name He gave to this body in Ephesians 1:22, is "the church." The body of Christ consists of all saved Jews and Gentiles. Christ is its head (Eph. 1:22) and having both a body and a head, it is "one new man" (Eph. 2:15). Christ was crucified to create "one body" of saved Jews and Gentiles. Christ was crucified for *all* mankind; therefore, the body consists of *all* saved Jews and Gentiles. It is one body produced by one crucifixion.

The Lord did this by breaking "down the middle wall of partition between us" (v. 14). In Jesus' day, the Jewish temple illustrated this. There was a stone wall surrounding the inner courts and holy places of the Temple. On the outside of the wall was a huge court known as the Court of the Gentiles. No Gentile was allowed to pass the wall into the inner courts on penalty of death. That wall illustrates the wall that separated the Jews from the Gentiles.

The true wall was "the law of commandments contained in ordinances" (v. 15). The Old Testament Mosaic Law was the thing which separated us and now it has been "abolished." Christ did this "in his flesh," by His crucifixion. Colossians describes it this way: "Blotting out the handwriting of ordinances that was against us, which was contrary to us, and took it out of the way, nailing it to his cross" (Col. 2:14). The Law was the distinguishing characteristic of the Jewish nation. It hemmed the Jew in and any Gentile wanting to partake of the covenants and promises had to become a Jew and keep the Law. Moreover, the Law condemned the Gentiles and separated them from the covenants of God. All who seek to fulfill the Law, Jew or Gentile, are under a curse. "For as many as are of the works of the law are under the curse: for it is written, Cursed is every one that continueth not in all things which are written in the book of the law to do them" (Gal. 3:10) or, as James expressed it, "For whosoever shall keep the whole law, and yet offend in one point, he is guilty of all" (James 2:10). The Law requires perfect obedience. So, the Law was a difficult barrier to a Gentile.

No one, except Jesus Christ, could keep the Law perfectly. However, the Lord Jesus took care of that problem on the cross, because "Christ hath redeemed us from the curse of the law, being made a curse for us: for it is written, Cursed is every one that hangeth on a tree" (Gal. 3:13). Now the Law is abolished and the curse no longer exists for a believer.

There are those who object to the idea that God has abolished the Old Testament Law. However, He gave the Law for a specific purpose and that purpose has been fulfilled for those who have come to faith in Christ. The Law is holy, just and good, because it is God's Law (Rom. 7:12). However, the Law was against us (Col. 2:14). The Law revealed our sins to us (Rom. 7:7) and it condemned us (Rom. 7:10; 6:23; 2 Cor. 3:7-9), but it offered no way of perfect forgiveness or redemption (Rom. 8:3; Heb. 7:19); therefore, it became a burden neither the Jews nor the Gentiles could not bear (Acts 15:10). However, the Law fulfilled its purpose when it taught us that we need to be saved and we cannot save ourselves.

At that point, the Holy Spirit revealed to us that Christ alone gives eternal life. The Law became "our schoolmaster to bring us unto Christ, that we might be justified by faith" (Gal. 3:24).

In describing the status of the Law for Christians today, Paul uses definitive terminology, such as, "ye are **not under** the law" (Rom. 6:14); "that which is **done away**" (2 Cor. 3:11); "**Blotting out** the handwriting of ordinances" (Col. 2:14); "that which is **abolished**" (2 Cor. 3:13); and, "Having **abolished** in his flesh the enmity, even the law of commandments contained in ordinances" (Eph. 2:15). Done away, blotted out, and abolished is quite clear and definite language.

This also explains how John could write, "Whosoever is born of God doth not commit sin; for his seed remaineth in him: and he cannot sin, because he is born of God" (1 John 3:9). This verse has been a great difficulty for many of us, because we know that from time to time we do wrong and displease God. But, listen! God defines sin this way, "Whosoever committeth sin transgresseth also the law: for **sin is the transgression of the law**" (1 John 3:4). But, the law has been abolished, blotted out, and done away! For the believer, the Law has been fulfilled. The law is gone for a believer. The great truth is "where no law is, there is no transgression" (Rom. 4:15), because "sin is not imputed when there is no law" (Rom. 5:13). Oh, how great is the grace of God!

> Free from the law, O happy condition,
> Jesus has bled and there is remission,
> Cursed by the law and bruised by the fall,
> Grace hath redeemed us once for all.
> *Once for all, O sinner, receive it,*
> *Once for all, O brother, believe it;*
> *Cling to the cross, the burden will fall,*
> *Christ hath redeemed us once for all.*

> Now we are free, there's no condemnation,
> Jesus provides a perfect salvation.
> "Come unto Me," O hear His sweet call,
> Come, and He saves us once for all.
>
> "Children of God," O glorious calling,
> Surely His grace will keep us from falling;
> Passing from death to life at His call;
> Blessèd salvation once for all.
>
> *Once for all, O sinner, receive it,*
> *Once for all, O brother, believe it;*
> *Cling to the cross, the burden will fall,*
> *Christ hath redeemed us once for all.* [68]

Of course, the end of the Law for a Christian does not mean that a believer may do anything he wishes, good or evil, and still please God. The New Testament is very strong in its call to Christians to walk in obedience and holiness. For example, the Bible repeats seven of the Ten Commandments in Romans 13:9. Jesus said, "He that hath my commandments, and keepeth them, he it is that loveth me" (John 14:21). The difference between walking in the Law and walking in grace, as Paul said, is that we now "serve in newness of spirit, and not in the oldness of the letter" (Rom. 7:6). Obedience is no longer a matter of dry duty. It is the desire of our hearts and of our love for Christ. *It is the desire of our hearts to please Him.*

Both are Reconciled

We also find the word "both" in verse sixteen; "And that he might reconcile both unto God in one body by the cross, having slain the enmity thereby." So, Christ killed the enemy, the Law, and reconciled us to Himself and to one another (Jew and Gentile) by His death on the cross. The first use of "both" shows that God took saved Jews and Gentiles and united them into one *spiritual people.* This use of the word tells us that God took that people and created a peaceful relationship between Himself and them. "Therefore being justified by faith, we have peace with God through our Lord Jesus Christ" (Rom. 5:1).

Both have Free Access

Now "both have access by one Spirit unto the Father" (v. 18). Since we are saved by *one* Lord Jesus Christ and are united together with other believers in *one* body, we have access to *one* God by *one* Holy Spirit. In the Old Testament, only the High Priest could go into the presence of God once per year. Now, every believer can go into the holy of holies and enter the very presence of God. This access is unhindered. We do not have to wait for a special Day of Atonement to enter God's presence. We don't have to enter His presence with the blood of an animal nor become a Jew. We can freely come face to face with Him anytime every day. "Let us therefore come boldly unto the throne of grace, that we may obtain mercy, and find grace to help in time of need" (Heb. 4:16). "Come unto me, all ye that labour and are heavy laden, and I will give you rest" (Mt. 11:28). "Casting all your care upon him; for he careth for you" (1 Peter 5:7).

The Position of Gentile Believers

19 Now therefore ye are no more strangers and foreigners, but fellowcitizens with the saints, and of the household of God;
20 And are built upon the foundation of the apostles and prophets, Jesus Christ himself being the chief corner stone;
21 In whom all the building fitly framed together groweth unto an holy temple in the Lord:
22 In whom ye also are builded together for an habitation of God through the Spirit. (Eph. 2:19-22).

Through Jesus Christ, believing Gentiles have a new citizenship and a new family. They share these blessings with believing Jews. Jesus Christ has built all believers into a single building upon the foundational teaching of the apostles and prophets. Jesus Christ, himself, is the chief cornerstone. This building is a holy temple that is built for a habitation of God. The New Testament does not recommend or command a physical building or temple to house the church. All believers together are God's temple. Not only are we in Him, but He also dwells in us (John 17:26). This temple is a growing temple. It is continually receiving new members as people continue to believe on Christ. As parts of that building, God dwells in each of us.

All believers are fellow citizens with the saints (v. 19). The saints referred to are Jewish believers. This is clear because being "fellow citizens" is contrasted with the earlier mentioned condition of being "foreigners and strangers," or, in other words, Gentiles. Jewish believers are saints and so are Gentile believers. Every Christian is a saint. The word simply means "one who is holy to God" (see the Introduction). Jewish believers not only had the Law, the covenants, and the promises, they were also in Christ first, before the Gentiles (Acts 2). When God sent the gospel to the Gentiles, after Acts 9, Gentile believers joined the Jewish believers in the body of Christ.

All believers are also fellow citizens of the household of God (v. 19). Since we have been born again (John 3), we now have a new family. Galatians 6:10 mentions the household of God, "As we have therefore opportunity, let us do good unto all men, especially unto them who are of the *household of faith.*" Who are those today who would qualify to be in the "household of faith?" Obviously, it is those who have placed their faith in the gospel of the Lord Jesus Christ. Ephesians 2:13 and 16 says that we are made near to God by the blood of Christ and we are reconciled to God by the cross. Moreover, Romans 3:25 says that satisfaction for sins (propitiation) and forgiveness of sins comes through faith in His blood. So, then, all who have faith in Christ's blood are a part of the household of God, the household of faith. Every believer is equally accepted in the beloved One (Eph. 1:6). All the blessings and privileges of being in Christ are the same for everyone who believes

CHAPTER FIVE

THE MYSTERY OF THE CHURCH
Ephesians 3:1-13

1 For this cause I Paul, the prisoner of Jesus Christ for you Gentiles,
2 If ye have heard of the dispensation of the grace of God which is given me to you-ward:
3 How that by revelation he made known unto me the mystery; (as I wrote afore in few words,
4 Whereby, when ye read, ye may understand my knowledge in the mystery of Christ)
5 Which in other ages was not made known unto the sons of men, as it is now revealed unto his holy apostles and prophets by the Spirit;
6 That the Gentiles should be fellowheirs, and of the same body, and partakers of his promise in Christ by the gospel:
7 Whereof I was made a minister, according to the gift of the grace of God given unto me by the effectual working of his power.
8 Unto me, who am less than the least of all saints, is this grace given, that I should preach among the Gentiles the unsearchable riches of Christ;
9 And to make all men see what is the fellowship of the mystery, which from the beginning of the world hath been hid in God, who created all things by Jesus Christ:
10 To the intent that now unto the principalities and powers in heavenly places might be known by the church the manifold wisdom of God,
11 According to the eternal purpose which he purposed in

Christ Jesus our Lord:
12 In whom we have boldness and access with confidence by the faith of him.
13 Wherefore I desire that ye faint not at my tribulations for you, which is your glory. (Eph. 3:1-13)

THE MYSTERY OF THE CHURCH (called the mystery of His will in 1:9 and the mystery of Christ in 3:4) is the major theme of Ephesians. The first mention of the mystery was in 1:9, "having made known unto us the mystery," and was what Paul meant when he said he "wrote afore in few words" (Eph. 3:3). The mystery was *summarized* in 1:10, "that in the dispensation of the fulness of times he might gather together in one all things in Christ, both which are in heaven, and which are on earth; even in him." It is *defined* in 3:3, 10: "How that by revelation he made known unto me the mystery ... That the Gentiles should be fellowheirs, and of the same body, and partakers of his promise in Christ by the gospel..." The mystery was just *explained* in chapter 2:11-22.

The *key concept* in the mystery is in the word *ONE*. Ephesians two describes the union of Jewish and Gentile believers as *one* new man (2:15), *one* body (2:16), and *one* building, and *one* holy temple of God (2:21-22). The *one* body is Christ's body (1:22-23) and is called "the church." Therefore, the spiritual unity of all believers in Christ is one church. Those gathered together in Christ in Ephesians 1:9-10 are located both on earth and in heaven. They are certainly *not* all in one *local* church, but they are still ONE church in Christ. This may meet with a negative emotional reaction in some of my readers but bear with me a moment. I am not advocating one ecumenical church organization. I am teaching a *spiritual* reality.

To repeat, the key word all through what we studied in chapter two is *ONE*. Chapter four follows these thoughts with a list of the doctrines we must preserve as we are "endeavouring to keep the *unity* of the Spirit in the bond of peace" (4:3). These doctrines are all characterized by the word "one."

The Bible stresses that all this unity is *in Christ*. The unity of the body of Christ is not in a denomination. It is not in a fellowship or a convention. It is not in the World Council of Christian Churches. It is not in any other human organization. It is *in Christ*. When God saved us, He created us *in Christ* to good works (2:10). The blood of Christ brought the Gentiles near *in Christ* (2:13). The one new man exists only *in Christ* (2:15). The entire building is built only *in Christ* (2:21-22).

This truth of the church in the Book of Ephesians is God's answer to Christ's prayer in John 17. At His last supper, Jesus prayed for unity, that we would be one in Him and in the Father.

> 20 <u>Neither pray I for these alone, but for them also which shall believe on me through their word;</u>
> 21 That they <u>all may be one</u>; as thou, Father, art in me, and I in thee, that <u>they also may be one in us:</u> that the world may believe that thou hast sent me.
> 22 And the glory which thou gavest me I have given them; <u>that they may be one, even as we are one:</u>
> 23 I in them, and thou in me, <u>that they may be made perfect in one;</u> and that the world may know that thou hast sent me, and hast loved them, as thou hast loved me.
> 24 Father, I will that they also, whom thou hast given me, be with me where I am; that they may behold my glory, which thou hast given me: for thou lovedst me before the foundation of the world.
> 25 O righteous Father, the world hath not known thee: but I have known thee, and these have known that thou hast sent me.
> 26 And I have declared unto them thy name, and

will declare it: that the love wherewith thou hast loved me may be in them, <u>and I in them</u>.

It should be self explanatory that the Lord Jesus was praying for unity among believers, all believers. How do we know that He was praying for us also and not just praying for the apostles? It's because He said, "Neither pray I for these alone, but for them also which shall believe on me through their word" (verse 20). Who does this include? The apostles were the first to preach the gospel, beginning in Act 2 on Pentecost. Mark 16:20 informs us that "they went forth and preached everywhere." The apostles were the first gospel preachers. Their converts followed their example. Those referred to in the phrase "them also which believe on me through their word" includes everyone who has been saved or will be saved in the entire church age. That includes me, and it includes you, if you have believed the gospel. It includes us all regardless of which local church we belong to or which denomination we belong to or whether we belong to a local church at all or not. It includes those who were saved in the time of the Apostles. It includes those who were saved in the Middle Ages. It includes those saved in the Reformation, the early missionary movements from 1600 to 1900, and Billy Graham crusades. It includes people saved today. It includes Donatists, Waldensians, Lutherans, Anglicans, Puritans, Baptists, Calvinists, Arminians, and members of many other groups. The *only qualification* is to turn to God and believe on the Lord Jesus Christ (Acts 16:31). It includes every one of us who have trusted Christ. We are *all in Christ* and we are all *ONE in Christ*.

The importance of this truth cannot be overstated. It is our unity in Christ, our oneness in Christ, *that convinces the world that Jesus Christ is genuine*: "That they all may be one; as thou, Father, art in me, and I in thee, that they also may be one in us: *that the world may believe that thou hast sent me* (John 17:21).

Because Christ prayed for us all to be one in Him, it is a truth with an all-encompassing application. The Book of Ephesians is a perfect match to John 17 and describes God's answer to Jesus' prayer. The Book of Ephesians is teaching the same truth. Therefore, the teachings of Ephesians 1-3 are truths that apply to all believers. They are not limited to the Ephesian local church or to any other local church or to local churches in general. They apply to each and every individual Christian.

Paul also wrote of this in Galatians three. The distinction between Jew and Gentile is erased in Christ, but there is more than that. All natural distinctions are erased in Christ. Notice Galatians 3:27-29:

> **27 For as many of you as have been baptized into Christ have put on Christ.**
> **28 There is neither Jew nor Greek, there is neither bond nor free, there is neither male nor female: for ye are all one in Christ Jesus.**
> **29 And if ye be Christ's, then are ye Abraham's seed, and heirs according to the promise. (Gal. 3:27-29)**

Being in Christ is a spiritual reality and it is *only* spiritual. It cannot be seen with the eye. Paul said the things that are seen are temporal, but the things which cannot be seen are eternal (2 Cor. 4:18). The reality of being in Christ is spiritual, invisible, and eternal. In Christ, there are no earthly distinctions, such as race, national citizenship, or even gender. There certainly are no denominational differences or distinctions. In this world we have to maintain as much doctrinal purity as possible, but we should take heed that our cries, "I am a Presbyterian" or "I am a Baptist" or "I am a Lutheran," do not become simply fleshly proud distinctions like those in Corinth, "I am of Paul" and "I am of Apollos" and "I am of Christ" (1 Cor. 1:10-11).

There is only one application of this and it is not to compromise doctrinally or to make any ecumenical combination of denominations or any other organizations. The application is that all believers no matter their organizational affiliation must love one another: "A new commandment I give unto you, That ye love one another; as I have loved you, that ye also love one another. *By this shall all men know that ye are my disciples, if ye have love one to another*" (John 13:31-35). Spiritual unity is the way the world knows Christ is genuine and love is the way the world will know that we are genuine.

However, many have the concept that Jew and Gentile in one body refers to unity in the local church only. The Scriptures are not teaching that all Christians everywhere are one in only one body for all, right? That is exactly what the Scriptures teach. I am extremely strong regarding the importance of the local church and we will look at the local church in chapter seven of this commentary. However, it is not the local church that is in view here.

How We Get into the Body of Christ

How can we know that the statements about the body in Ephesians 1-3 speak of one body for all believers? First, we can answer that by asking, how does one get into Christ? We know it happens by grace through faith, but what spiritual operation does God perform to put you into Christ's body? We find that operation in 1 Corinthians 12:13:

> **For by one Spirit are we all baptized into one body, whether we be Jews or Gentiles, whether we be bond or free; and have been all made to drink into one Spirit.(1 Cor. 12:13)**

Three truths contained in this verse point out that the body referred to is not simply a Corinthian body. It is one body that transcends location. First, we get into the Body of

Christ by an operation called *baptism*. Second, it is the Holy Spirit that performs the operation that puts us into the body of Christ. It is not a preacher, priest, or church. Third, the little word "we" reveals the extent of this body, because it includes Paul.

God puts us into the Body of Christ by Baptism. This baptism is purely spiritual and is spoken of by John the Baptist in Matthew 3:11, "I indeed baptize you with water unto repentance: but he that cometh after me is mightier than I, whose shoes I am not worthy to bear: he shall baptize you with the Holy Ghost." The same operation that puts you into the body of Christ, also puts you into Jesus Christ. "For as many of you as have been *baptized into Christ* have put on Christ" (Gal. 3:27).

However, some have raised an objection to this. Typical of this group are the arguments made by Dr. Thomas Strouse. He uses the statements of John, the Baptist, about spiritual baptism, along with references such as that concerning Cornelius in Acts 10 and Peter's statement that their experience was like that of the Jews in Acts 2 (Acts 11:16) to say that spiritual baptism is something that happens after salvation. He further says that John paralleled water baptism with spirit baptism. Therefore, since John baptized in water after salvation. Jesus baptizes in the Spirit after salvation. [69]

The baptism of the Spirit is not connected with water baptism. They are separate operations and have different effects. The truth is that Spirit Baptism puts us into Christ. The effects of Spirit baptism can only happen at the time of salvation. Water baptism is merely an outward figure of Spirit baptism (1 Pet. 3:21; see Eph. 4).

Romans 6:3-4 Know ye not, that so many of us as were <u>baptized into Jesus Christ</u> were <u>baptized into his death?</u> 4 Therefore we are buried with him <u>by baptism into death:</u> that like as Christ was raised up

> from the dead by the glory of the Father, even so we also should walk in newness of life.
> Galatians 2:20 I am crucified with Christ: nevertheless I live; yet not I, but Christ liveth in me: and the life which I now live in the flesh I live by the faith of the Son of God, who loved me, and gave himself for me.
> Colossians 3:3 For ye are dead, and your life is hid with Christ in God.
> Galatians 3:27 For as many of you as have been baptized into Christ have put on Christ.
> Colossians 2:12 Buried with him *in baptism*, wherein also ye are risen with him through the faith of the operation of God, who hath raised him from the dead.

The baptism spoken of in these verses cannot be water baptism. This baptism puts us into Christ Himself, into Christ's death, gives us newness of life, causes us to put on Christ, and raises us spiritually to new life. It is impossible that water baptism could do any of this for us. The baptism mentioned in these verses cannot be other than Spirit baptism. Are we to believe that all these changes happen *after* salvation? There is not a chance of that. Salvation, regeneration, and being put into Christ are never depicted in Scripture as things you get in stages. Jesus prayed for every believer in John 17 that they would be in Him based on nothing but their faith. It is the baptism by the Spirit of God that places us into Christ. We get in Christ when we believe. Therefore, Spirit baptism happens when we believe. Furthermore, that same Spirit Baptism places us into the body of Christ at the same time that it accomplishes all the rest. It happens when we believe.

The second truth in 1 Corinthians 12:13 is that the baptism is performed by the Spirit of God. Dr. Strouse also objects to that. He says 1 Corinthians 12:13 is not talking about baptism by the Spirit at all. He says that the Greek construction in the verse, *en eni pneumati*, in or by one spirit, does not refer to the Holy Spirit. In the light of the divisions that were in the Corinthian church, he says it means "in one spirit" in the sense of the spirit of unity. From that, he concludes that the baptism of 1 Corinthians 12:13 is water baptism, which they experienced in a spirit of unity, and which put them into the Corinthian local church. [70]

One of the problems he raises is with the little Greek preposition "en," which means both "in" and "by" (among other things). One of these (in) has to do with location: such as, "in Christ" (Phil. 1:13) or "in their synagogues" (Mt. 4:23). The other (by) focuses on the means by which something is done. The context is the key to deciding which it is. Dr. Strouse says it should be translated "in" referring to unity in their spirits. So, even though Dr. Strouse professes to believe the King James is the Word of God, he is willing to alter the KJV translation to teach what he believes.

Which is it? The answer lies in one very small word: "we." Paul wrote. "For by one Spirit are **we** all baptized ..." Paul includes himself in this statement. This would mean, according to Strouse, that Paul was baptized by water into the Corinthian church along with everyone else mentioned in the verse. It never happened. You can look all day and all night and you will never find where this happened. Paul was water baptized in Acts 9, in Damascus. He was never baptized in water again after that. Therefore, with Paul included, it cannot refer to water Baptism. The correct translation is "by" and the word "spirit" refers to the Holy Spirit. This is confirmed by the final phrase of the verse: "and have been all made to drink into one Spirit." This phrase clearly refers to the Holy Spirit and the phrase ties back to the experience of baptism, indicating that "by the Spirit" means the Holy Spirit.

The third truth is also revealed by the little word "we." As said before, the use of the word "we" reveals that

Paul included himself when he wrote this verse. At the time he wrote 1 Corinthians, Paul was *not* a member of the church in Corinth. Paul's spiritual baptism took place when he was saved in Acts 9. The Corinthian church was started years later in Acts 18. Nevertheless, both Paul and the Corinthian believers were baptized by the same Spirit into the *same* body. Paul was baptized into that body many years before the Corinthian believers and at a location far away from Corinth. Paul was baptized into the same body that the Damascus Christians (Acts 9) were in and the body Barnabas was in and the body the other Apostles were in (Paul and Barnabas were apostles). They were all baptized into the same spiritual body as the Corinthian and Ephesian Christians; the one and only body of Christ. Every believer is baptized by the Spirit of God into the same spiritual body. Christ only has ONE body, not many.

What are we saying here? Let me be perfectly clear. I am *not* recommending ecumenicism. I am *not* recommending doctrinal compromise. There is nothing in this that says denominations or churches should join or combine with one another in any way at any time. There is nothing here that undermines the teaching that the local church is self-governing, self-sustaining, and self-propagating. There is no intent to teach any kind of organizational combination.

There are many churches, denominations, conventions, fellowships, and larger organizations with many names that claim to follow Christ. In these organizations, there may be both saved and unsaved individuals. However, above all these institutions, there is an invisible, purely spiritual body that incorporates only the saved people who are a part of those institutions and includes saved people who are not part of any local church. This body is completely spiritual in nature and its only members are saved individuals who are *in Christ*. Biblically, it is manifested in the world in local churches and individual Christians. Nevertheless, it exists in the spiritual world. It is eternal and, therefore, invisible; "While we look not at the things which are seen, but at the things which are not seen: for the things which are seen are temporal; but the things which are not seen are eternal" (2 Cor. 4:18). It is the body of Christ and is called "the Church." Christ is its only head. Since the Greek word for church means "assembly," it has been asked where this spiritual body assembles. That's easy. First, it assembles *in Christ*. Second, since Christ is seated in Heaven, the body assembles right now in heavenly places in Him.

The local church with its body of believers and the pastor as its head is a *picture* of the invisible spiritual body of Christ. However, every local church is seen; it is visible. Therefore, local churches are not eternal. When the rapture takes place and every Christian leaves the world, all local churches on earth will cease to exist (a local church is a fellowship of believers and cannot exist when there are no believers). Nevertheless, the local church is a God created institution and of vast importance. *In the comments on Ephesians 4, I will have more to say about the local church and its immense importance.*

When Did the Church Begin?

This question is very pertinent at this point and we should address it. However, it is also very controversial with people proposing different beginnings from Mark 3 (the calling of the disciples) to Acts 28 (the writing of the prison epistles). There are three major suggestions. The first two are Matthew 16 and Acts 2. The third has supporters suggesting Acts 9, 13, or 28. We will take each in turn.

Before looking at these three possibilities, we need to establish a principle. Whenever the church started, it has to have something to do with believers being baptized by the Spirit of God. 1 Corinthians 12:13 is a defining verse. The way anyone enters the body of Christ, the Church, is through the baptism by the Spirit. That did not happen in Mark 3 or Acts 9, 13, or 28. There is no defining event that marks a beginning for the church in those places. There is no mention of a baptism by the Spirit in Matthew 16 either, but we will deal with that passage at more length. So, whenever the church started, we will find some reference to being baptized by the Spirit of God. That should be the main thing we want to see.

Matthew 16:15-18 is a revelation and prophecy of the church, especially verse 18.

> **15 He saith unto them, But whom say ye that I am?**
> **16 And Simon Peter answered and said, Thou art the Christ, the Son of the living God.**
> **17 And Jesus answered and said unto him, Blessed art thou, Simon Barjona: for flesh and blood hath not revealed it unto thee, but my Father which is in heaven.**
> **18 And I say also unto thee, That thou art Peter, and upon this rock I will build my church; and the gates of hell shall not prevail against it. (Mt. 16:15-18)**

Some have taken Christ's words in verse 18 as a declaration that His church had already started. However, if you pay close attention to the actual words you will see something different. He said, "I *will* build my church." It is clearly future tense. He did not say He *had* built His church (past tense). He did not say He was building His church at that time (present tense). He said He *will* build it (future tense). In actuality, the verse constitutes a prophecy of the building of Christ's church sometime in the future. It is a confirmation that the church had not yet been built, but it would be.

A second reason that Matthew 16 cannot be the beginning of the Church is that nothing is said about anyone being baptized by the Spirit. In fact, the Scriptures say that the Holy Spirit had not yet been given. "But this spake he of the Spirit, which they that believe on him should receive: for the Holy Ghost was not yet given; because that Jesus was not yet glorified" (John 7:39). The Holy Spirit would not be given until after Jesus was glorified, that is, after He was crucified and risen. So, at the time of Matthew 16 (before the crucifixion and resurrection), the baptism by the Holy Spirit had not and did not take place. Therefore, Matthew 16 was not the time when the Church began.

Matthew 16:18 shows us something else. The Church Christ spoke of in verse 18 cannot be the local church. Why? Christ declared that "the gates of hell shall not prevail against it." That statement is certainly not true of the local church. We have already learned that the local church on earth is temporary, because it can be seen (2 Cor. 3:18). When the rapture takes place, all local churches on earth will cease to exist. Also, local churches have been attacked and destroyed by demonic forces. How many of us have seen church fights where the local church has been split? Churches have had to close their doors because of financial mismanagement or theft. Go to Turkey some day and look for the churches John wrote in the book of Revelation. They are no longer there. Nevertheless, the, body of Christ, the Church, is still here, having overcome everything hell has thrown against it.

Ultra-dispensationalists have suggested Acts 9 or 13 or 28. Acts 9 is where the conversion of Paul is described. Paul is called "the apostle of the gentiles" (Rom. 11:13). Therefore, the gentile church and the body of Christ today started with the conversion of Paul. In Acts 13, Paul declared that he and Barnabas would turn from the Jews to the Gentiles (Acts 13:48), therefore the body of Christ, which is mostly Gentile, started in Acts 13. In Acts 28, the same statement is made, "Be it known therefore unto you, that the salvation of God is sent unto the Gentiles, and that they will hear it" (Acts 28:28). One problem with all these ideas is that the Gentiles first received the gospel, not from the mouth of Paul, but from Peter (Acts 10). It was to Peter, Christ gave the keys of the kingdom (Mt. 16:19). The Jews first heard the gospel from Peter (Acts 2). The Samaritans received the Spirit when Peter and John laid their hands on them (Acts 8). And, the Gentiles first received the gospel from Peter. Even though the Spirit was mighty in Peter toward the Jews (Gal. 2:8), he still ministered to Gentiles. Also, even though Paul called himself the Apostle to the Gentiles, he still ministered to Jews (Rom. 1:16-17).

Another reason Acts 28 is suggested as the starting point of the church, is that Paul first received the revelation of the mystery in Acts 28. Additionally, the mystery was given only to Paul. However, both of these statements are false. Paul makes it clear that he was not the only one to receive the revelation of the mystery. He said the mystery "in other ages was not made known unto the sons of men, as it is now revealed unto his holy apostles and prophets by the Spirit" (Eph. 3:5). Paul was not the only apostle who laid the foundation of the church. He said others were involved. The Church was "built upon the foundation of the apostles and prophets, Jesus Christ himself being the chief corner stone" (Eph. 2:20). Paul understood the mystery long before Acts 28. When he told the Corinthians that mankind was made up of Jew, Gentile, and the Church (1 Cor. 10:32), he knew the Church was one body made up of both save Jews and saved Gentiles.

Finally, there is no mention of anyone getting baptized by the Spirit in Acts 9, 13, or 28. There is no new beginning for the church in any of those places. This is the key issue when examining any proposed beginning of the Church.

Acts 2 is a different case altogether. About one hundred twenty believers gathered in the upper room of a house. They waited there for ten days, spending much time in prayer. A few days earlier, the Apostles witnessed the Lord Jesus ascend into heaven after His resurrection (Acts 1:1-10). So, it was a time after the Father glorified Jesus in His crucifixion and resurrection. On the day of Pentecost, the sound of a mighty wind filled the place and tongues of fire appeared over each of their heads. They were all filled with the Holy Spirit and began to speak in tongues. The tongues were languages of the people gathered in Jerusalem. They all heard the message in their own language. About three thousand were saved and added to the church that day. In the days following, "the Lord added to the church daily such as should be saved" (Acts 2:47). I believe this was the beginning of the Church.

The day of Pentecost was clearly a beginning of some kind. In Acts 10, Peter went to preach the gospel to Cornelius and his household. When his Jewish colleagues demanded an explanation of why he entered the home of a gentile, he told them the details of the meeting. He included the fact that the Holy Spirit was given to them. He said, "And as I began to speak, the Holy Ghost fell on them, as on us *at the beginning*" (Acts 11:15). Peter was clearly referring to Pentecost. The experience there was a special *beginning* of some kind in distinction from any other event in the apostles' association with the Lord Jesus.

This event was the first time anyone was baptized with the Holy Spirit. Acts 2:4 says they were all "filled" with the Holy Spirit. It does not say there that they were baptized by the Spirit. However, in Acts 1 Jesus, "being assembled together with them, commanded them that they should not depart from Jerusalem, but wait for the promise of the Father, which, saith he, ye have heard of me. For John truly baptized with water; but *ye shall be baptized with the Holy Ghost* not many days hence" (Acts 1:4-5). Jesus clearly described the event at Pentecost as a baptism with the Holy Spirit and confirmed that it was the fulfillment of the prophecy John gave in Matthew 3:11. This was the first time anyone was baptized by the Spirit. Following this event, believers were routinely baptized "by one Spirit ... into one body" (1 Cor. 12:13).

A third reason this is the beginning of the church is because of what the event produced. Prior to the event of Pentecost, there were many assemblies in the Gospels, but none of them were called a "church." The disciples assembled often with the Lord. Many came together to hear the Lord preach or to get Him to heal them, but these gatherings were never called churches. The Greek word for "church," *ekklesia*, is used only twice in the Gospels. The first time is Matthew 16:18, where Jesus prophesied of His coming church. The second is Matthew 18:17, in a passage where Jesus outlined the disciplinary procedures to be used in His coming church. Otherwise, there is no mention of the church or churches in the gospels.

On the other hand, as soon as the events of Pentecost happened, the believers in Jerusalem were suddenly called a church. After those events, they were all praising "God, and having favour with all the people. And the Lord *added to the church* daily such as should be saved" (Acts 2:47). From that point on, the Book of Acts and the epistles are filled with references to the church and churches. Something changed from Pentecost on. Something was different. The church that Jesus had said He would build was suddenly on the scene. Before Pentecost there was only a rare use of the word "church" and then only as a future entity. After Pentecost, the term "church" and the reality of it was common place. The prophecy of Matthew 16:18 was fulfilled on Pentecost in Acts 2 and after. On Pentecost, the Lord created and began to build His church.

The Mystery

There are several important points about the mystery that are brought to light in Ephesians 3:1-13.

First, the passage points out that the source of the information is divine: "by revelation he made known unto me the mystery" (Eph. 3:3). It did not come from Paul's imagination. Paul was merely an ordinary man seeking to follow Christ and who was now in prison for the Lord's sake (Acts 28). In fact, in verse 3:8, he said he was "less than the least of all saints." Not only that, but the Spirit revealed these truths to other apostles and prophets (v. 5), so he was not alone in this knowledge. Paul had no special knowledge in himself and he had not learned it from any other apostle or prophet. Rather, his understanding came direct from the Spirit God. Therefore, he called it "the dispensation of the grace of God which is given me to you-ward" (3:2). God dispensed these truths to Paul so that he could give them to us in Holy Scripture.

The mystery was hidden before our current dispensation. Paul said the mystery "in other ages was not made known unto the sons of men, as it is now revealed unto his holy apostles and prophets by the Spirit" (3:5). He also said the mystery "from the beginning of the world hath been hid in God, who created all things by Jesus Christ" (3:9). In Colossians 1:26, Paul spoke of it as "the **mystery** which hath been hid from ages and from generations, but now is made manifest to his saints." The mystery of Christ has been hidden since creation, but is known in the church age, because it applies to the church age. God had it planned, but did not reveal it. Now, He has worked it out through Christ's redemptive work and has made it known to us.

The mystery specifically includes three benefits: "That the Gentiles should be fellowheirs, and of the same body, and partakers of his promise in Christ by the gospel" (v. 6). Membership in the "same body" was discussed above. The Jewish nation was always an heir of God, as a nation. Now, the Gentiles, who have been without God and without hope, join the Jews in being offered an individual inheritance from God through the gospel of the Lord Jesus Christ. Together we are "heirs of God, and joint-heirs with Christ, if so be that we suffer with him, that we may be also glorified together" (Rom. 8:17). The Scriptures themselves proclaim the glory of being heirs of God:

> Colossians 1:12 Giving thanks unto the Father, which hath made us meet to be partakers of the inheritance of the saints in light:
> Colossians 3:24 Knowing that of the Lord ye shall receive the reward of the inheritance: for ye serve the Lord Christ.
> 1 Peter 1:3-5 Blessed be the God and Father of our Lord Jesus Christ, which according to his abundant mercy hath begotten us again unto a lively hope by the resurrection of Jesus Christ from the dead, To an inheritance incorruptible, and undefiled, and that fadeth not away, reserved in heaven for you, Who are kept by the power of God through faith unto salvation ready to be revealed in the last time.

Furthermore, we are "partakers of his promise in Christ by the gospel" (3:6). What is "his promise in Christ?" There are many promises in the Scriptures, but this verse uses a singular word "promise." There is a particular promise that is the basis of our salvation. That was the promise of a seed made to Abraham and Galatians identifies the "seed. It was not just that God promised him a son which was fulfilled in Isaac. Rather, it was a seed that fulfilled God's promise to Abraham that he would be a blessing to all nations.

> 3:3 And the scripture, foreseeing that God would justify the heathen through faith, preached before the gospel unto Abraham, saying, <u>In thee shall all nations be blessed.</u>
> 14 That the blessing of Abraham might come on the Gentiles through Jesus Christ; that we might receive <u>the promise</u> of the Spirit through faith.
> 16 Now to Abraham and his seed were the promises made. He saith not, And to seeds, as of many; but as of one, And to <u>thy seed, which is Christ.</u>

> **17** And this I say, that the covenant, that was confirmed before of God in Christ, the law, which was four hundred and thirty years after, cannot disannul, that it should make <u>the promise</u> of none effect.
> **18** For if the inheritance be of the law, it is no more of <u>promise:</u> but God gave it to Abraham by <u>promise.</u>
> **19** Wherefore then serveth the law? It was added because of transgressions, till the seed should come to whom <u>the promise</u> was made; and it was ordained by angels in the hand of a mediator.
> **22** But the scripture hath concluded all under sin, that <u>the promise</u> by faith of Jesus Christ might be given to them that believe.
> **29** And if ye be Christ's, then are ye Abraham's seed, and heirs according to <u>the promise.</u>
> **4:23** But he who was of the bondwoman was born after the flesh; but he of the freewoman was by <u>promise.</u>
> **28** Now we, brethren, as Isaac was, are the <u>children of promise</u> (Gal. 3:8, 14, 16-19, 22, 29; 4:23, 28)

The promise summarized is that all nations will be blessed by the coming of Jesus Christ, who was the seed of Abraham, and His giving of the Holy Spirit to those who put their trust in Him. We are the children of the promise given to Abraham. We are the recipients of the blessing promised to him. That blessing comes only by faith and not by God's law. No one can gain anything of salvation from Christ by keeping the law. The Spirit is only given through faith.

Paul was made a minister of the mystery: as he said, "Whereof I was made a minister" (Eph. 3:7). Paul's calling was centered on this mystery. He was called to "make all men see what is the fellowship of the mystery" (Eph. 3:9). He preached the gospel to call men and women to come into that fellowship by trusting Christ. He taught the truths of the faith, which are all tied into this mystery of the church. He exhorted the saints to walk worthy of their calling (Eph. 4:1) and taught them how (Gal. 5). This is the calling of every pastor and evangelist today.

Paul was called to preach the unsearchable riches of Christ (Eph. 3:8). "Unsearchable" means something that "cannot be searched or explored; inscrutable; hidden; mysterious." [71] The human mind cannot discern God's riches. His gift is unspeakable (2 Cor. 9:15). God's love is unquenchable (Song 8:7). His peace is beyond understanding (Phil. 4:7). His joy is unspeakable (1 Pet. 1:8). His greatness is unsearchable (Ps. 145:3). His ways are past finding out and His judgments are unsearchable (Rom. 11:33).

> To those who were in the greatest spiritual poverty he proclaimed the possibilities of wealth beyond the power of human tongue to express, and he would have all men enter into the blessedness of this, and enjoy in reality the fellowship of the mystery ... [72]

God's intent in spreading the truth about the mystery is "that now unto the principalities and powers in heavenly places might be known by the church the manifold wisdom of God" (Eph. 3:10). God has put the church on display to make His great wisdom known (Rom. 11:33): "O the depth of the riches both of the wisdom and knowledge of God! How unsearchable are his judgments, and his ways past finding out!"

God's intended audience is the "principalities and powers." The two words, "principalities" and "powers", are used together in several places in the New Testament (Rom. 8:38; Eph. 3:10; 6:12; Col. 1:16; 2:15; Titus 3:1). The terms refer to two things. The first is civil governments (as in Rom. 13 and Titus 3:1). The second is what Paul describes as "the rulers of the darkness of this world ... spiritual wickedness in high places (Eph. 6:12). These are described as not being "flesh and blood" and they operate according to the "wiles of the devil" (Eph. 6:11). These are clearly demonic forces under the command of Satan. The church, the body of Christ, is God's example of His wisdom on display to this demonic audience. It shows them what they have rejected and how grand is the wisdom of His gracious plan. It is a wisdom they have rejected unnecessarily and to which they no longer have access. It also shows how He has rescued mankind from complete ruin and He has thwarted their plans. His wisdom has utterly defeated them. It is a wisdom that has condemned them and will ultimately destroy them in Hell.

This mystery is in accordance with "*the eternal purpose which he purposed in Christ Jesus our Lord*" (Eph. 3:11). What is God's eternal purpose? This verse is the only verse of the New Testament where that phrase is used. However, the term *purpose* is used by itself a number of other places. Predestination is according to God's purpose (Eph. 1:11). We saw in the discussion on that subject that we are predestinated to a glorious ultimate end, being conformed to the image of Christ. So, God's purpose includes bringing us to a state of complete maturity, holiness, and Christ-likeness. He will conform us to the image of Christ so that Christ "might be the firstborn among many brethren" (Rom. 8:29). When He saved us and called us, He did it "not according to our works, but according to his own purpose and grace, which was given us in Christ Jesus before the world began" (1 Tim. 1:9).

Another related aspect of the purpose for which Christ came is to "destroy the works of the devil" (1 John 3:8). God will make Christ preeminent in all things (Col. 1:18). All that He does will lead to "the praise of the glory of his grace" (Eph. 1:6).and to giving Him "glory in the church by Christ Jesus throughout all ages, world without end" (Eph. 3:21). "Now unto the King eternal, immortal, invisible, the only wise God, be honour and glory forever and ever. Amen" (1 Tim. 1:7). God is the only one who deserves this. "Thou art worthy, O Lord, to receive glory and honour and power: for thou hast created all things, and for thy pleasure they are and were created ... Worthy is the Lamb that was slain to receive power, and riches, and wisdom, and strength, and honour, and glory, and blessing" (Rev. 4:11; 5:12)!

Because of the greatness of the grace that has given us all these gifts and made us accepted in Christ (Eph. 1:6; 3:12), we now have complete access to Him. We come to Him with great boldness and confidence (Heb. 4:16).

"Wherefore I desire that ye faint not at my tribulations for you, which is your glory" (Eph. 3:13). Paul was in prison in Rome when he wrote Ephesians (Acts 28). He was concerned that his difficulties would discourage them. He reminded them that his troubles were for their good. As he told the Philippians, " But if I live in the flesh, this is the fruit of my labour: yet what I shall choose I wot not. For I am in a strait betwixt two, having a desire to depart, and to be with Christ; which is far better: Nevertheless to abide in the flesh is more needful for you" (Phil. 1:22-24). Prison was not the only tribulations Paul experienced for the sake of Christ. He listed several things he went through in 2 Corinthians 11:23-29 and 1 Thessalonians 2:1-2. Finally, he told Timothy, "Wherein I suffer trouble, as an evil doer, even unto bonds; but the word of God is not bound" (2 Tim. 2:9). When trouble rises for Christ's sake, we can be confident that God is using it for His glory. Remember, the trouble Joseph encountered when his brothers sold him into Egypt as a slave and after a while he ended up in Prison. God used the prison experience to exalt him to Pharaoh's right hand (Gen. 37-50). Joseph told his brothers, "But as for you, ye thought evil against me; but God meant it unto good, to bring to pass, as it is this day, to save much people alive" (Gen. 50:20). Paul said of his own imprisonment, "But I would ye should understand, brethren, that the things which happened unto me have fallen out rather unto the furtherance of the gospel" (Phil. 1:12). This is the perspective we should have when trouble threatens and our enemies rise up against us.

Testing Your Understanding

Now that we have spent a great deal of time on the subject of the Church, being in Christ, and how that we are all ONE in Christ, please indulge me a little further. I would like to test your understanding. Let's review some of the key verses in John 17, 1 Corinthians 1, and Galatians 3 and ask some pertinent questions. The verses are:

John 17:1 – 24
These words spake Jesus, and lifted up his eyes to heaven, and said, Father, ... Neither pray I for these alone, but for them also which shall believe on me through their word That they all may be one; as thou, Father, art in me, and I in thee, that they also may be one in us ... that they may be one, even as we are one ... I in them, and thou in me, that they may be made perfect in one ...

1 Corinthians 1:13
Is Christ divided? was Paul crucified for you? or were ye baptized in the name of Paul?

Galatians 3:27-28
For as many of you as have been baptized into Christ have put on Christ. There is neither Jew nor Greek, there is neither bond nor free, there is neither male nor female: for ye are all one in Christ Jesus.

On the following page, there is a list of questions that relate the foregoing verses. These questions are designed to bring out the import of the verses and test your understanding. This is for your own edification.

Regarding John 17:

If someone, anyone, is a saved person, is he IN Christ?
If a saved person is a Baptist, is he IN Christ?
If a saved person is in a Presbyterian Church, is he IN Christ?
If a saved person is in an Episcopal Church, is he IN Christ?
If a saved person is going to a Catholic Church, is he IN Christ?
If a saved person isn't in a local church at all, is he IN Christ?
Are all these saved people ONE IN Christ?
Are all these saved people ONE IN Christ, just as the Father and Christ are ONE?

Regarding 1 Corinthians 1:

Is Christ in any way divided?

Regarding Galatians 3:

Are there any Jews in Christ?
Are there any Greeks in Christ?
Are there any slaves (bond men) in Christ?
Are there any free men in Christ?
Are there any males in Christ?
Are there any females in Christ?
Are all saved people in Christ ONE?

Are there any divisions in Christ?
Are there any denominations in Christ?

So now, are you telling me that each local church is a SEPARATE body of Christ? There is only ONE body of Christ.
Some have the audacity to say that there are Baptists in Christ!
Even worse, some say that only Baptists are the bride of Christ!

This is nothing less than to DIVIDE Christ.

CHAPTER SIX

PAUL'S SECOND PRAYER FOR THE CHURCH
Ephesians 3:14-21

14 For this cause I bow my knees unto the Father of our Lord Jesus Christ,
15 Of whom the whole family in heaven and earth is named,
16 That he would grant you, according to the riches of his glory, to be strengthened with might by his Spirit in the inner man;
17 That Christ may dwell in your hearts by faith; that ye, being rooted and grounded in love,
18 May be able to comprehend with all saints what is the breadth, and length, and depth, and height;
19 And to know the love of Christ, which passeth knowledge, that ye might be filled with all the fulness of God.
20 Now unto him that is able to do exceeding abundantly above all that we ask or think, according to the power that worketh in us,
21 Unto him be glory in the church by Christ Jesus throughout all ages, world without end. Amen.

PAUL OFFERED TWO PRAYERS TO GOD for the Ephesians. This is the second. The first prayer, in Ephesians 1, is centered on requests for knowledge, understanding and wisdom. This second prayer centers on love of the saints for one another and issues related to that.

The first prayer is followed by the scope and panorama of doctrinal truth about the essential nature of the Church. The second prayer is followed by an application of those truths in our relationships with God and our brothers and sisters in Christ and in the local church. It is true that Ephesians 4 starts out with a list of doctrines that must be believed among us. However, the key point advanced by this list is *unity* among believers.

This prayer is short. In the KJV, it is 122 words long. The Bible gives us several examples of prayer in Paul's letters and all of them are short. However, some prayers in the Bible are very long. The Lord Jesus Himself prayed all night long (Luke 6:12). Nevertheless, long prayer is not necessary for effectiveness. Prayer depends on faith and continuing to ask when the answer doesn't come the first time (Mt. 21:22; Luke 18:1-8). A short prayer from a sincere heart is more effective than a thousand well prepared, long prayers. Jesus said, "But when ye pray, use not vain repetitions, as the heathen do: for they think that they shall be heard for their much speaking" (Mt. 6:7). While there is much to pray for and that may cause one to legitimately speak much, "much speaking" alone about the same request is worthless. Prayer doesn't require flowery phrases and long speeches to be effective.

Elijah challenged the Prophets of Baal to prepare a Bullock and call down fire from Baal to consume it (1 Kings 18:21-39). They prayed from morning to the time of the evening sacrifice over and over for Baal to send fire. He never did, of course, because he is a false god. Nevertheless, this is an example of prayer that is "much speaking." On the other hand, Elijah prayed a simple prayer of only sixty-three words and God sent fire that consumed the bullock and the altar. James, the brother of the Lord, made this comment on prayer:

> **16 ... The effectual fervent prayer of a righteous man availeth much.**
> **17 Elias was a man subject to like passions as we**

> are, and he prayed earnestly that it might not rain: and it rained not on the earth by the space of three years and six months.
> 18 And he prayed again, and the heaven gave rain, and the earth brought forth her fruit. (James 5:16-18).

The prayer begins with Paul bowing his knees (in humility and submission) and recognizing God's greatness (v. 14-15). It is typical that when Paul mentions his prayers for others, they are preceded by thanksgiving and praise to God. Notice the beginning of his prayer in Ephesians 1, "Wherefore I also, after I heard of your faith in the Lord Jesus, and love unto all the saints, cease not to *give thanks* for you, making mention of you in my prayers; that *the God of our Lord Jesus Christ, the Father of glory*, may give unto you ..." (Eph. 1:15-17). This procedure of putting praise and thanksgiving first in prayer is also in accord with the Lord's Prayer by focusing on God first. "Our Father which art in heaven, Hallowed be thy name. Thy kingdom come. Thy will be done in earth, as it is in heaven" (Mt. 6:9-10). Years ago, the mission organization, *The Navigators,* created the acronym A-C-T-S to remind people of the basic elements of prayer and the generally proper order. "A" stands for *adoration* or praise. "C" stands for *confession* of sin (1 John 1:9). "T" stands for *thanksgiving.* Finally, "S" stands for *supplication* (making requests). It is important to begin prayer by focusing first on God with praise and thanksgiving.

"*For this cause I bow my knees unto the Father of our Lord Jesus Christ, of whom the whole family in heaven and earth is named*" (Eph. 3:14-15). We must ask a question here. What is "the whole family" of God? This is the only place in the New Testament where this phrase is used. The Greek word for *family* is *patria* and is only used three times in the New Testament and translated three ways. It is translated *family* here. In Acts 3:25, it is translated *kindreds* and refers to the families of the earth. Lastly, it is translated *lineage* in Luke 2:4 and refers to a descendant of David. The basic meaning of the word is an individual or group descended from a common male ancestor. [73] It sounds like it includes all the saved from Genesis to Revelation. However, it is the saints of the church age who were the first to be born into God's family. Abraham was called "the friend of God" (James 2:23). Likewise, Moses was said to speak with God face to face as a man speaks to his friend (Ex. 33:11). John the Baptist is spoken of as the friend of the bridegroom (John 3:29). None of these, even though saved, are specifically spoken of as part of God's "family." The Children of Israel were God's people and God's chosen nation. The church is God's chosen spiritual people. It is only saved people of the church age that are called brothers of Jesus Christ (Rom. 8:29). It certainly seems true that all saved people in Heaven and on earth, whether saved in the Old Testament or the New, along with the holy angels, Seraphim, and Cherubim in heaven all are named of "the Father of our Lord Jesus Christ." The use of the word "whole" seems to imply more than just the church. However, the phrase "of whom" (v. 15) may refer to Jesus Christ in verse 14. Christians are the only group in the Bible specifically named for Jesus Christ (Acts 11:26). Also, the reference to people in heaven and earth elsewhere in Ephesians is a reference to Christians.

The prayer itself consists of four major requests and it closes with further praise to God (Eph. 3:16-21). Each request is separated by semicolons in the KJV text. The first request is for *endowment* of God's strength (v. 16). The next is the *enthronement* of Christ in our hearts (v. 17). The third request is for *enlightenment* (vv. 17-18). The last request is for our *enlargement* (v. 19)

First Request: Endowment (Eph. 3:16)

Paul's first request is that "he would grant you, according to the riches of his glory, to be strengthened with might by his Spirit in the inner man" (v. 16). This request is that we would be endowed with God's strength. Paul also makes this request for the Colossians (Col. 1:11). To be strong in the Lord is a continual theme in the New Testament. "Finally, my brethren, be strong in the Lord, and in the power of his might" (Eph. 6:10). "Thou therefore, my son, be strong in the grace that is in Christ Jesus" (2 Tim. 2:1). This strength has nothing to do with your own strength or with physical strength. It is strength "in the inner man." The strength comes by the grace of God through prayer and faith. It comes by the inner working of the Holy Spirit. I can only be strong if my strength is "the power of his might." Zechariah 4:6 says, "Not by might, nor by power, but by my spirit." The Lord made this clear when He said in 2 Corinthians 3:5, "Not that we are sufficient of ourselves to think anything as of ourselves; but our sufficiency is of God." WE have NO sufficiency in ourselves. HE is our sufficiency and our strength. We cannot face the temptations and trials and challenges of life with our own resources. Every time we attempt to do so, we fail. However, "I can do all things through Christ which strengtheneth me" (Phil. 4:13). God even promises to make a way to escape temptation: "there hath no temptation taken you but such as is common to man: but God is faithful, who will not suffer you to be tempted above that ye are able; but will with the temptation also make a way to escape, that ye may be able to bear it" (1 Cor. 10:13).

How, then, do we become strong in the power of His might? Strength is something God can provide at a moment's notice in the heat of spiritual battle, but it is also something that grows. Even though Jesus was God and had strength from the Father, He also grew in spiritual strength over time: "And the child grew, and waxed (grew) strong in spirit, filled with wisdom: and the grace of God was upon him" (Luke 2:40; see Acts 9:22). God has given us mighty weapons to fight our spiritual warfare against Satan and the flesh. "For the weapons of our warfare are not carnal, but mighty through God to the pulling down of strong holds" (2 Cor. 10:4).

The first thing that ought to be mentioned is *prayer*. This should be clear since Paul prayed for the strength of believers (as we have seen) in Ephesians and Colossians. Ask God for strength. On one hand, it is true that if you ask you will receive (Mt. 7:7). On the other hand, it is also true that "ye have not, because ye ask not" (James 4:2).

We are also strengthened by *sound preaching*. Jesus told Peter: "when thou art converted, strengthen thy brethren" (Luke 22:32). Jesus also told him, Feed my sheep (John 21:16). Peter's method to strengthen and feed the brethren included preaching. We need to regularly listen to preaching and teaching. However, the greater key is to go beyond merely hearing the preaching, but also to obey the taught Word of God. Moses told Israel, "Hear therefore, O Israel, *and observe to do it*; that it may be well with thee, and that ye may increase mightily" (Deut. 6:3).

Fellowship is a very powerful tool to gain strength. "And let us consider one another to provoke unto love and to good works: not forsaking the assembling of ourselves together, as the manner of some is; but exhorting one another: and so much the more, as ye see the day approaching" (Heb. 10:24-25). Fellowship is one Christian helping and encouraging another. This requires developing relationships. Church meetings are key opportunities to have fellowship. There have been many discussions about how to promote this in churches. It's clear that the program of traditional church meetings does not encourage or allow for much fellowship. Small group Bible studies are one effective method some churches use.

"Man shall not live by bread alone, but by every word that proceedeth out of the mouth of God" (Matt. 4:4). When we consider this, it is evident that *the Word of God is essential to strength.* Paul told the Ephesian elders, "I commend you to God, and to the word of his grace, which is able to build you up" (Acts 20:32). The Word puts spiritual muscle on us. The Word builds our faith (Rom. 10:17). It is imperative that Christians have a strong and regular intake of the Word of God. Which of us would fail to eat regularly? Job said, "Neither have I gone back from the commandment of his lips; *I have esteemed the words of his mouth more than my necessary food*" (Job 23:12). Colossians 3:16 puts it this way, "Let the word of Christ dwell in you richly in all wisdom." Methods helpful to "let the word of Christ dwell in you" include hearing the Word (Rom. 10:17), reading the Word (Col. 4:16; 1 Tim. 4:13; Rev. 1:3), memorizing (Ps. 119:9, 11), studying (2 Tim. 2:15), and meditating (Josh. 1:8).

One of the most powerful tools to gain strength is *an attitude of weakness and trust in God*. When Paul needed God's help, he prayed about it. God's answer was, "My grace is sufficient for thee: for my strength is made perfect in weakness" (2 Cor. 12:9). Paul followed this up by declaring "when I am weak, then am I strong" (2 Cor. 12:10). This attitude moves us from trusting in ourselves to relying in faith on God and that makes all the difference. "Jesus said unto him, If thou canst believe, all things are possible to him that believeth ... And Jesus looking upon them saith, with men it is impossible, but not with God: for with God all things are possible" (Mark 9:23; 10:27). "I can do all things through Christ which strengtheneth me" (Phil. 4:13).

Second Request: Enthronement of Christ

Paul's second request is that "Christ may dwell in your hearts by faith (Eph 3:17). This may look like an unusual request, at first. Doesn't Christ already dwell in us who are saved? Yes, He certainly does. Christ is in us from the moment we put faith in Him. So why ask for this to occur, since he was praying for people who were already saved? It is possible that Paul was thinking of some who were not saved and praying that they all would be. However, since most of those Paul was praying for were people who had been saved for some time, there is more to it than that. Perhaps it refers to Christ being enthroned in our hearts as Harry Ironside thought. [74]

We can make some definite observations and perhaps come to some conclusions. First, the word *dwell* means in Greek what it means in English. It means to inhabit a place permanently or temporarily. Sometimes, though, the word indicates that the inhabitant is making *his home* in a certain place. "Making a home" implies settling down, becoming comfortable, having a sense of belonging, establishing ownership over a certain place, taking charge, and such like. When one considers a certain place to be his home, he feels that this is where he belongs and this is where he is *supposed* to be. In the case of Christ in us, it is Christ who takes charge and we give over our hearts to Him so that He feels at home there and we feel comfortable and happy to have it so. To do this, one must be in submission to Christ as his Lord and Master.

Beyond that, it is significant that Paul uses the term *heart*. Recall our discussion of the structure of a human being under Ephesians 2:1-3. A human being consists of three parts: body, soul, and spirit. The Spirit is the part that is born again when we believe (John 3:1-6). Christ comes to live within us when our spirits are born again. Our souls have three functions: mind, emotions, and will. The term *heart* is most often used in Scripture to refer to two of those functions, sometimes one and sometimes the other. It is used to describe emotions (Gen. 6:6; Lev. 26:6; Deut. 15:10; 28:28; Prov. 16:5; 12:25; 13:12; 14:13; 17:22; etc.) and it is used to refer to the mind and thoughts (Gen. 6:5; 8:21; 17:17; Deut. 8:17; Prov. 15:14, 28; 23:7; and more). It also refers to attitudes, which often are a combination of both emotions and thought (Prov. 11:20; 12:8; 16:5; 17:20; 22:15; etc.).

Christ is in our spirits by virtue of the new birth, but it is in the *heart* where He must dwell at home and be in control. Our hearts must become His *home*. That is, He must be at home in our thoughts, attitudes, and feelings. This does not automatically happen. It has a definite beginning that is described in Romans 12:1-2: "I beseech you therefore, brethren, ... that ye present your bodies a living sacrifice ... And be not conformed to this world: but be ye transformed by the renewing of your mind." The *presenting* is a single act, but the renewing of the mind is a *process* of growth. Paul further speaks of that process as "bringing into captivity every thought to the obedience of Christ" (2 Cor. 10:5). Wouldn't you want the Lord Jesus Christ to be comfortable and at home in your thoughts and feelings? Fill your heart with the Word of God.

Third Request: Enlightenment (v. 17, 18)

Paul's third prayer request in verses 17 and 18 is "that ye, being rooted and grounded in love, may be able to comprehend with all saints what is the breadth, and length, and depth, and height." This prayer request is hard to understand, mainly because it does not say the "breadth, and length, and depth, and height" *of what*. It assumes that the comprehension occurs in the context of love, but it does not say that we are to comprehend the magnitude of love. The objects of this comprehension that have been suggested include the love of Christ, mystery of calling the Gentiles and the Jews, the temple of Ephesus, the church, and other things. In fact, one could make nearly anything the object of this knowledge, if he divorced verse eighteen from the context. At least love is in the context and it is clear that love is involved. However, the love mentioned is not the love of Christ *for us* because that is the subject of the next prayer request (v. 19).

The major context of Ephesians 1:20 through 3:13 is the nature of the church. Christ is the head of that church (v. 22) and God raised Him from the dead and placed Him at

God's right hand in Heaven (v. 20). There are three heavens (2 Cor. 12:1-4): The heaven where the birds fly (Gen. 1:20-21), the heaven where the stars are (Gen. 1:14-16), and the heaven where God's throne is (Paul called *Paradise* in 2 Corinthians 12). Christ is physically in the third heaven, past the edge of what we call "the universe." Every Christian believer is also there spiritually in Christ (Eph. 1:3; 1:20; 2:6; 3:10). However, in a physical sense some believers are alive on earth and others have died, leaving their bodies behind and their souls relocating to heaven. That makes us part of a body that stretches from heaven to earth and includes every believer in heaven and on earth. It includes any believer who leaves earth in a spaceship and circles the moon or goes to Mars. It includes all without exception. We must get that comprehension. There are no physical limitations to the church. Wherever the church is found, it is still one body and the same body. It is still unified in Christ. Although the local church is the outward visible manifestation of the "church" on earth, the local church is not the sum total of what the church is.

The love in which we are to be "rooted and grounded," is our love for one another. We must love every Christian believer, regardless of who they are or where they are. We may not agree with them on everything. We may not wish to "go to church" where they go. But, we must love them regardless, because "he that loveth not his brother whom he hath seen, how can he love God whom he hath not seen" (1 John 4:20)? Love for our brothers and sisters in Christ has been commanded and it carries many benefits (1 John 2:10; 3:11-18, 23; 4:7-21; 5:1-3). It is to be extended to every believer in Christ without exception and without qualification. It is to be a practical love as well. "But whoso hath this world's good, and seeth his brother have need, and shutteth up his bowels of compassion from him, how dwelleth the love of God in him? My little children, let us not love in word, neither in tongue; but in deed and in truth"

(1 John 3:17-18). There is coming a day when we will be "going to church" in Heaven with people we would never have fellowshipped with in this life. We will not only be joining the Apostles there. We will worship with Martin Luther (a Lutheran and former Catholic), John Wesley (a Methodist), William Carey and Adoniram Judson (Baptists), Carl McIntire (a Presbyterian), John Knox (a Scottish Presbyterian and associate of John Calvin), David Wilkerson (a charismatic), and so on. We don't have to go to their churches in this life, but we have to love them. "We know that we have passed from death unto life, because we love the brethren. He that loveth not his brother abideth in death" (1 John 3:14).

The Fourth Request: Enlargement (v. 19)

The final request in Paul's prayer is that we "know the love of Christ, which passeth knowledge, that ye might be filled with all the fulness of God" (Eph. 3:19). This prayer request is as strange as the last one was hard to understand. It is a request that God will enable us to do something that is apparently impossible. He prayed that we will know something that is unknowable, the love of Christ which "passeth knowledge." How can we know something that passes knowledge? We can express it, but only in an incomplete way. We can tell what God has done to love us, but how can we make others to truly know it? It is something that can only be truly known by experiencing it. We can know it by seeing and feeling the love of God in our lives and hearts. That's why Paul speaks of being filled with all the fullness of God. How great and wonderful is such an experience, but it cannot be fully expressed or known by words. It is something God does for us inwardly and it helps us understand the love of God for us.

Being filled with the fullness of God is also something that must be experienced. How can one be filled with God?

The Book of Ephesians

When Solomon built the first temple in Jerusalem, he said, "But will God indeed dwell on the earth? behold, the *heaven and heaven of heavens cannot contain thee*; how much less this house that I have builded" (1 Kings 8:27)? Yet, God came to dwell and show His glory in that house. God said, "Do not I fill heaven and earth" (Jer. 23:24)? Yet, Christ come to us to dwell in us lowly finite and limited creatures leading Paul to say, "But we have this treasure in earthen vessels, that the excellency of the power may be of God, and not of us" (2 Cor. 4:7). In my home, the master bedroom has a sky light. On a sunny day, sunlight that shines brightly over the entire earth enters my bathroom illuminating it by natural light. I can say that my bathroom is filled with the fullness of the sunlight. Although the sunlight is spread over the earth and in space, it can also be contained in my bathroom. Though God fills heaven and earth he can also fill me.

We are filled with the fullness of God's love. This is a love that led God to sacrifice His own son for sinful wretched men and women. It led Christ to suffer a horrible death for us. It is a love that redeemed us and gave us forgiveness. It is a love that cleans us up and transforms us. It is a love that fills us with "love, joy, peace, longsuffering, gentleness, goodness, faith, meekness, temperance" (Gal. 5:22-23). It is a mercy filled love that endures forever. It is a greater love than any other. God, Himself, puts it in our hearts; "the love of God is shed abroad in our hearts by the Holy Ghost which is given unto us" (Rom. 5:5).

> The love of God is greater far
> Than tongue or pen can ever tell.
> It goes beyond the highest star
> And reaches to the lowest hell.
> The guilty pair, bowed down with care,
> God gave His Son to win;
> His erring child He reconciled
> And pardoned from his sin.

O love of God, how rich and pure!
How measureless and strong!
It shall forevermore endure
The saints' and angels' song.
Could we with ink the ocean fill,
And were the skies of parchment made;
Were every stalk on earth a quill,
And every man a scribe by trade;
To write the love of God above
Would drain the ocean dry;
Nor could the scroll contain the whole,
Though stretched from sky to sky. [75]

The Conclusion of the Prayer

Finally, the prayer ends with the most reassuring benediction: "Now unto him that is able to do exceeding abundantly above all that we ask or think, according to the power that worketh in us, unto him be glory in the church by Christ Jesus throughout all ages, world without end. Amen" (Eph. 3:20-21). God can work for us and in us according to His great power: "the exceeding greatness of his power to us-ward who believe, according to the working of *his mighty power*, which he wrought in Christ, *when he raised him from the dead*, and set him at his own right hand in the heavenly places" (Eph. 1:19-20). The life giving power that raises the dead is the power God employs in our lives. So, God is well able to answer our prayers far above what we ask or think. He answers prayer for two purposes. The first is to transform us to be like Christ (Rom. 8:28-30). Second, that we may glorify Him. God's greatest glory comes from the grace and power He bestows upon the church. To Him be the glory! He alone deserves it!

4:11 Thou art worthy, O Lord, to receive glory and honour and power: for thou hast created all things,

and for thy pleasure they are and were created ...
5:12 Worthy is the Lamb that was slain to receive power, and riches, and wisdom, and strength, and honour, and glory, and blessing.
13 And every creature which is in heaven, and on the earth, and under the earth, and such as are in the sea, and all that are in them, heard I say, Blessing, and honour, and glory, and power, be unto him that sitteth upon the throne, and unto the Lamb for ever and ever. (Rev. 4:11; 5:12-13)

CHAPTER SEVEN

THE DOCTRINAL UNITY OF THE CHURCH
Ephesians 4:1-6

1 I therefore, the prisoner of the Lord, beseech you that ye walk worthy of the vocation wherewith ye are called,
2 With all lowliness and meekness, with longsuffering, forbearing one another in love;
3 Endeavouring to keep the unity of the Spirit in the bond of peace.
4 There is one body, and one Spirit, even as ye are called in one hope of your calling;
5 One Lord, one faith, one baptism,
6 One God and Father of all, who is above all, and through all, and in you all. (Eph. 4:1-6).

SO FAR, IN THE BOOK OF EPHESIANS, we have been studying the unity of the church in Christ. This unity is entirely spiritual. One cannot walk around and see the fact of being *one in Christ* with your eyes. It is an invisible reality, and therefore, it is eternal. "While we look not at the things which are seen, but at the things which are not seen: for the things which are seen are temporal; but the things which are not seen are eternal" (2 Cor. 4:18). If there is no invisible church, there is no eternal church.

There is an eternal church. The writer of Hebrews, speaking to his audience, said that they will not come to a physical Mount Sinai seeking the law (Heb. 12:18-21). Rather, they are come to Mount Zion, the city of God, the heavenly Jerusalem. When they arrive, they will find there "the general assembly and church of the firstborn" (Heb. 12:22-23).

Because Jesus said this spiritual oneness and unity is important "that the world may believe that thou hast sent me" (John 17:21), we must apply these truths to our daily lives. Your love for other Christians shows the world that you are a genuine disciple of Christ (John 13:34-35). Unity among believers shows the world that Jesus Christ is genuinely sent from God. The practical demonstration of these things, that the world can see, takes place in the local church.

Ephesians 4 begins to apply these truths in a practical way to Christians in the world. It is all about the unity of love and truth among Christians. It's about how we live in love and unity among ourselves and in our churches.

The Local Church

How can we show these things to the world? How can the world see this love and unity? The body of Christ is invisible. It cannot be seen. The love between two people can be seen, but more than that is necessary to show the unity and love of those who follow Jesus Christ. It requires a whole community of believers. The local church is that community.

The reality is that all believers are members of one spiritual body in Jesus Christ. However, the practical application of the work and life of that body is in the local church. In fact, as we shall see, the local church is a visible illustration of the body of Christ openly displayed to the world. This is where the love of the body is practiced and this is where the fight for doctrinal purity takes place.

I will start with a basic statement of what the Bible teaches about the local church. *There are only two God made earthly Christian organizations described in the Book of Acts and spoken of in the epistles. The first is the local church and the other is produced by the local churches.* The second organization is the ministry team. The example of this is the missionary team Paul built, which started in the local church at Antioch, but whose daily operations were independent.

It's necessary to understand what the local church is. The term "church" comes from the Greek word *ekklesia*, which means *a called-out assembly*. It was a common term in Paul's day of any assembly of people called together for a purpose. It is used in Acts 19:32, 39, 41 to describe the assembly called together by the silversmiths to stop Paul's ministry in Ephesus. Every other time it is used in the New Testament it is translated *church* or *churches*.

The term *local* is never used of the church in Scripture, but the concept is clearly there. However, the term "church" is applied to different settings. The term refers to *groups of people*, not *buildings*. William Tyndale translated the first English New Testament from the Greek Textus Receptus. He translated *Ekklesia* as *congregation*.

Ekklesia or church is applied to different groups of Christians. All Christians in any particular city were considered to be one and the same church, such as the church in Philippi or the church in Ephesus or the church in Thessalonica (Phil. 1:1; Eph. 1:1; 1 Thess. 1:1). This was not true for a region, however. In provinces such as Galatia or Judea, we find references to churches. All Christians in a city were called a single church, even if they met in different locations in the city. Beyond that, it was churches.

Very often they did not meet in one place in the city. In fact, many times meetings were in homes and each assembly that met in a separate location was also called a church. An example of this was the home of a gentleman named Nymphas "and the church which is in his house" (Col. 4:15). Of Priscilla and Aquila, the Roman Christians were told to "greet the church that is in their house" (Rom. 16:5).

Elders, Pastors, and Bishops are names for the same office described in 1 Timothy 3. Each name designated an aspect of that ministry. The term "pastor" speaks of the office as a shepherd of sheep and the necessity to feed the sheep. The word "bishop" means overseer and speaks of the Bishop as one who watches over the flock of God. As an "elder," he is spiritually mature and capable of leadership. The only other office mentioned in the New Testament is that of the Deacon, also described in 1 Timothy 3. Elders in a city-wide local church are always described in the plural. There were several elders in each city-wide church. The reason for this is most likely because each assembly meeting in its own location had an elder, or Pastor. Since there were no doubt several assemblies meeting separately in each city, there would have been at least an equal number of elders.

Elders in a city seem to have been equal to one another. The New Testament does not mention nor does it recommend Metropolitan Bishops, District Bishops, Archbishops, Cardinals, Popes, or any such thing. From all indications each assembly was in charge of its own affairs and normally supported its own ministers. They were individually independent, but they were in fellowship and cooperation with all the other assemblies in the city. They gathered at conferences, such as the one in Jerusalem in Acts 15.

Even though all Christians are one in Christ, the New Testament does not describe or recommend any *universal church organizations* that encompass all local churches. There are no organizations described or recommended that are greater than the local church. It is clear in the New Testament that churches can fellowship with one another and loving Christian relationships can and should be practiced between individuals in different churches. However, the local church is the primary context in which Christian love and unity is learned and practiced. In the New Testament times, it was the local church that trained Christians in discipleship and ministry, as well. Training took place in independent ministries like Paul's also, but his ministry began in the local church (Acts 13:1-4) and consistently reported back to the originating local church (Acts 14:26-28).

New Testament local churches are the visible practical expression and testimony of the spiritual body of Christ in several ways. When the world sees a local church, they are supposed to be able to see the reality of that body and the reality of Christ.

> 1. The body of Christ has one head, Jesus Christ, and one body. The local church that has one head, the senior pastor, and a unified body is a picture of Christ and his body.
> 2. The local church is where Christians express the love of Christ toward one another. This love, which is supposed to be in word, deed and truth (1 Jn. 3:18), shows the world that we are true disciples of Jesus Christ (Jn. 13:34-35).
> 3. The local church is the place where the battle for truth takes place. We "endeavor" to maintain the unity of the Spirit in doctrine, as we will shortly see.
> 4. The local church must be unified (of the same mind) in at least the following ways: love, purpose, truth, humility, obedience, and judgment (Phil. 2:2, 5-8; 1:27; Eph. 4; 1 Cor. 1:10). This will go a long way toward showing the world the unity which will convince them that God sent Jesus (Jn. 17:21).

In the Book of Acts, all the churches were unified in love and doctrine. This is God's ideal. Nevertheless, even in that day there were those who challenged the truth (see Acts 15) and battles took place. However, in today's world this kind of unity among the churches does not exist. There are also divisions inside the local church and these are inexcusable and absolutely against God's will. "Now I beseech you, brethren, by the name of our Lord Jesus Christ, that ye all speak the same thing, and that there be no divisions among you; but that ye be perfectly joined together in the same mind and in the same judgment. For it hath been declared unto me of you, my brethren, by them which are of the house of Chloe, that there are contentions among you" (1 Cor. 1:10-11).

After the events on Pentecost, the body of Christ had begun, and the first local church had come into existence. The benefits and activities of the local church quickly became evident in Acts 2:42-47. Several activities are listed in these verses that became continuing activities in every local church:

> 1. The teaching and preaching of the Word of God (v. 42).
> 2. Fellowship, exhorting, encouraging, and edifying one another (v. 42; Heb. 10:24-25).
> 3. Prayer together (v. 42).
> 4. Evangelism (v. 47)

The other activities narrated in Acts 2:42-47 are not mentioned later in the New Testament as common or required. Teaching, fellowship, prayer, and evangelism are necessary activities in the local church.

The fact that all believers are one in Christ does not take away from the importance of the local church in any way. The local church is a part of God's over-all plan. In fact, the local church is **the key** to the fulfillment of God's plan in this dispensation.

Walk Worthy of Your Calling

Chapter four starts out with an exhortation to "walk worthy of the vocation wherewith ye are called" along with a list of the attitudes necessary to do that. *Walking worthy is the theme of the final three chapters of the Book of Ephesians.* The focus of chapter four is on the things necessary for unity of doctrine and proper function within the church and among Christians. It gives God's plan for the application of the truths of unity in the church and in individual Christian relationships. Following this section of chapter four, the Bible describes the unity that is brought about through the loving use of spiritual gifts and the result of that in relationships. Chapter five speaks of moral behavior, being filled with the Spirit, and marriage. Chapter six follows with more instruction about family and ends with a discussion of spiritual warfare.

What is the vocation "wherewith we are called?" Let's start with some definitions. Since the King James Bible is a good concordance and lexicon for Greek words, we will start there. The KJV translates the Greek word *klesis*, used here, once as *vocation* and ten times as *calling*. One of the definitions of the English word *vocation* is "a calling by the will of God; or the bestowment of God's distinguishing grace upon a person or nation." [76] So, our vocation is not just a job. It is a special calling. However, it is not a calling which we have chosen. It is the calling God has chosen to give us (Rom. 11:29). Our calling is a holy calling (2 Tim. 1:9). It is a high calling (Phil. 3:14). This calling produces hope (Eph. 4:4). It is a heavenly calling (Heb. 3:1). It is a calling for all Christians and there is a prize given for pleasing God in its pursuit (Phil. 3:14).

Specifically, the vocation or calling is one which is common to all Christians. It is a calling which is unchangeable: "For the gifts and calling of God are without repentance" (Rom. 11:29). It is not a calling to a job, such as, witnessing, preaching, teaching, or using your gift. Notice 1 Corinthians 1:23-24, "But we preach Christ crucified, unto the Jews a stumblingblock, and unto the Greeks foolishness; but unto them **which are called**, both Jews and Greeks, Christ the power of God, and the wisdom of God." There is a contrast in Ephesians 4:1 between the verb *called* and the noun *calling*. Many are *called*, but only those who accept the call by faith have the *calling*. "For many are called, but few are chosen" (Mt. 22:14).

This calling is the call to salvation and it comes through the gospel (2 Thess. 2:13-14). Those who believe the gospel have the calling and the benefits of the gospel. It comes as a free gift by faith, but it is a calling that carries responsibilities.

"I ... beseech you that ye walk worthy of the vocation ... " Our response to the free gift of the gospel should be to seek to please God, to be worthy of our calling. How are we to do that? In general, it requires submission to God and obedience to Him. The word worthy means, "Suitable." [77] The Greek word, *axios*, also means the same. A synonym for suitable is *becomes*, which means (in this context) "to suit or be suitable; to be congruous; to befit; to accord with, in character or circumstances; to be worthy of, decent or proper." [78] Philippians 1:27 says we are to conduct ourselves in a manner that *becomes* the gospel, using the same Greek word. The same Greek word is also used in combination with the word "God" in 3 John 6, where it is translated "after a godly sort." So, to walk worthy of the Lord (Col. 1:10) or to walk worthy of your calling means *to conduct yourself in a godly manner that pleases God*. It is a "holy calling" and, therefore, requires holiness in living (2 Tim. 1:9; 1 Peter 1:15-16). To do this, we are advised to look forward, not backward (Phil 3:13-14). To walk worthy one must keep his eyes on our future hope (Eph. 1:18; 1 Thess. 1:10; Titus 2:13; Heb. 12:1-2).

The Unity of the Spirit (Eph. 4:2-3)

**2 With all lowliness and meekness, with longsuffering, forbearing one another in love;
3 Endeavouring to keep the unity of the Spirit in the bond of peace.**

Walking worthy of our calling includes a responsibility for maintaining unity in the church and that requires certain attitudes and actions: lowliness, meekness, longsuffering, and forbearing one another (Eph. 4:2).

Lowliness means, "Humility, lowliness of mind, the esteeming of ourselves small, inasmuch as we are so, the correct estimate of ourselves." [79] "For I say, through the grace given unto me, to every man that is among you, not to think of himself more highly than he ought to think; but to think soberly, according as God hath dealt to every man the measure of faith" (Rom. 12:3). Paul expressed it to the Ephesian elders, "Serving the Lord with all humility of mind ..." He explained it to the Philippian Church, "Let nothing be done through strife or vainglory; but in lowliness of mind let each esteem other better than themselves. Look not every man on his own things, but every man also on the things of others" (Phil. 2:3-4). Humility does not exalt oneself but focuses on the needs of others. It is other-centered rather than self-centered.

Meekness has often been misunderstood and confused with weakness. It can be defined as "softness of temper; mildness; gentleness; forbearance under injuries and provocations." [80] A meek person controls himself and does not easily lose his temper. It also requires trust in God to accept His will and the circumstances God has allowed into one's life. The Word Study Dictionary explains it this way:

> Primarily it does not denote outward expression of feeling, but an inward grace of the soul, calmness toward God in particular. It is the acceptance of God's dealings with us considering them as good in that they enhance the closeness of our relationship with Him. However, *praótēs* encompasses expressing
> wrath toward the sin of man as demonstrated by the Lord Jesus ... who indeed was called meek but expressed His anger toward those who were chiding

Him because He had done good on the Sabbath day [Mar. 3:5]. This meekness does not blame God for the persecutions and evil doings of men. It is not the result of weakness, and in the third Beatitude it expresses not the passivity of the second Beatitude, but the activity of the blessedness that exists in one's heart from being actively angry at evil. [81]

Meekness is a necessary characteristic to maintain the unity of the spirit in the bond of peace in the local church and in personal relationships. The Bible reveals to us that "only by pride cometh contention: but with the well advised is wisdom" (Prov. 13:10). Meekness is the opposite of prideful action. Pride is the source of many divisions in local churches. This is especially true if something insulting or harsh is said (out of pride) to someone who reacts explosively because of wounded pride. Meekness is the spirit that responds gently. Proverbs 15:1 contrasts the reaction of meekness with the reaction of pride, "A soft answer turneth away wrath: but grievous words stir up anger."

Longsuffering means what it sounds like, *to suffer a long time*. Other words that help explain what it means are patience, endurance, and slowness to avenge wrongs. [82] It is defined in Webster's Dictionary as "bearing injuries or provocation for a long time; patient; not easily provoked." [83] The Bible speaks many times about God's longsuffering toward us. Any Christian who has struggled a long time with a difficult fault knows God's longsuffering well. Longsuffering is indispensable to peace and unity in the local church and between churches. When people wrong one another, longsuffering enables one or both parties to follow the steps of Matthew 18:15-17. Longsuffering can lead to the resolution of conflicts and opens the door to forgiveness.

Finally, there is *forbearing*, which is very similar to longsuffering. However, longsuffering is more the attitude while forbearing is more of an action. It involves patience and endurance, but it means to withhold oneself from harmful or hurtful response to difficulty or wrong. Forbearing "one another" also implies helping restrain others from harmful actions; a thing that is usually done gently and patiently. The Scriptures are our guide as to what we should do and what we should abstain from doing in relationships. John Gill described it this way.

> **Forbearing one another in love**; overlooking the infirmities of one another, forgiving injuries done, sympathizing with, and assisting each other in distressed circumstances, the spring of all which should be love; by that saints should be moved, influenced, and engaged to such a conduct, and which should be so far attended to, as is consistent with love; for so to forbear one another, as to suffer sin to be on each other, without proper, gentle, and faithful rebukes for it, is not to act in love. [84]

All these attitudes and actions tie together. We can see that when we pay attention to the prepositions in verse 2. We are to walk worthy *with* an attitude of lowliness and meekness and *with* an overall attitude of longsuffering. "Forbearing" is a participle and is the action resulting from these attitudes.

The Bond of Peace

The foregoing and the doctrinal unity that follows will help us in "endeavouring to keep the unity of the Spirit in the bond of peace" (Eph. 4:3). God's blessings give a wealth of peace: peace with Him, peace in our hearts, often peace with our enemies (Prov. 16:7), and peace between ourselves. Jesus is called the "son of peace" (Luke 10:6). A church characterized by peace, as well as unity, is of great price. Peace with love is the glue that bonds us together in. Life and peace spring from being spiritually minded (Rom. 8:6). "Let us therefore follow after the things which make for peace, and things wherewith one may edify another" (Rom. 14:19). "And let the peace of God rule in your hearts, to the which also ye are called in one body; and be ye thankful" (Col. 3:15). "Follow peace with all men, and holiness, without which no man shall see the Lord" (Heb. 12:14).

The Unity of Doctrine - Ephesians 4:4-6

**4 There is one body, and one Spirit, even as ye are called in one hope of your calling;
5 One Lord, one faith, one baptism,
6 One God and Father of all, who is above all, and through all, and in you all. (Eph. 4:4-6)**

We have just been discussing the fact that unity of heart and love among believers is extremely important to God. Unity of doctrine is just as important. There are *rare* circumstances when a fellow believer is to be rejected by other believers. Two instances stand out. Paul told the Corinthian church to deliver a man to Satan "for the destruction of the flesh," because he was involved in an immoral relationship with his father's wife (1 Cor. 5:1-6). Unrepentant immoral behavior is a cause for separating someone from the local church. Another instance of rejection is found in Titus 3:10, "A man that is an heretick after the first and second admonition reject." A heretic can be legitimately ousted from the church *only* after he has been admonished at least two times. A heretic is not someone who has an honest misunderstanding or difference in opinion. He is one who is teaching falsehood and causes division as a result (1 Cor. 11:18-19). A true heretic usually wants others to believe as he does, so he will usually try to convince others of his views. This inevitably leads to division. Such a one is to be admonished at least two times and then kicked out of the church, if there is no repentance. However, the local church is not permitted to reject someone as a heretic if they have not admonished him at least twice. One church cannot reject a heretic from another church unless someone has admonished him. The hope is always to restore the one who is in error, whether it is moral failure or heresy.

In evaluating when a heretic is worthy of being dispelled from the church, what doctrinal standards do we use? We can't kick someone out of the church simply because he disagrees that the Antichrist will have a bad right arm, can we? There are seven doctrines listed in verses four through six. They all follow the statement "Endeavouring to keep the unity of the Spirit in the bond of peace" (v. 3). The admonitions of verses one through three are the foundation of maintaining the unity of peace and love in the church and the doctrines of verses four through six are the foundation of doctrinal unity. Each of these doctrines is characterized by the word "one."

One Body

There is one body. There are not two or three or a hundred or a thousand. There is only one. This is the same body we have been studying in chapters one through three. It is called the church in Ephesians 1:22-23 and is said to be Christ's body. It is composed of only saved people, washed clean by the blood of Christ. There are no unsaved people in this body. It is a single body that the Spirit of God has made perfectly unified. It is this unity of the Spirit that is to be worked out practically in the relationships between Christians. John Gill put it this way.

> It is called "one" with relation to Jews and Gentiles, who are of the same body, and are reconciled in one body by Christ, and are baptized into it by the Spirit; and with respect to saints above and saints below, who make up one general assembly; and with regard to separate societies; for though there are several

particular congregations, yet there is but one church of the firstborn, whose names are written in heaven; and saints of different ages, places, states, and conditions, are all one in Christ Jesus, who is the one, and only head of this body: and this is an argument to excite the saints to unity of Spirit; since they are, as one natural body is, members one of another, and therefore should not bite and devour one another; they are one political body, one kingdom, over which Christ is sole King and lawgiver, and a kingdom divided against itself cannot stand; they are one economical body, one family, they are all brethren, and should not fall out by the way. [85]

One Spirit

Obviously, the reference is to the Holy Spirit. Each member of the Trinity is listed in verses 4-6; Spirit (v. 4), Lord (v. 5), and Father (v. 6). First off, we are not speaking of three Gods here: Father, Son, and Spirit. Verse six clearly says that there is one God, and this is true. "Hear, O Israel: The LORD our God is one LORD" (Deut. 6:4). We have one God consisting of three parts or, as some say, three persons. This is a very difficult concept for some people to understand. It is doubtful that anyone really understands it fully. Nevertheless, God has given us a perfect illustration by making human beings a trinity also (1 Thess. 5:23). Human beings are one person with three parts: body, soul, and spirit. This was explained in detail in chapter four of this commentary.

You may have noticed that we are often in conflict with ourselves. Your body wants to eat something, but your mind (a function of your soul) knows that it is unhealthy. Your soul and body are in conflict. Different parts of you want different things. However, God, being perfect is never in conflict with Himself. He is always in perfect agreement. In addition, humans are limited, but God is infinite. God is all powerful, and God is everywhere (Jer. 23:24). He can manifest himself to us in whatever way He chooses, and He has chosen to manifest Himself as the Father, the Son, and the Holy Spirit. He can manifest each part of Himself in a different way.

So, how do we know the Holy Spirit is God? First, the Holy Spirit is a person. He has intellect (Rom. 8:7, 27; 1 Cor. 2:10, 11; Is. 11:3; 1 Pet. 1:11), emotion (Eph. 4:30), and will (1 Cor. 12:11). The Spirit has names that indicate He is inseparable from God. He is the *Holy* Spirit (Luke 11:13), the Spirit of grace (Heb. 10:29), the Spirit of burning (Is. 4:4), the Spirit of truth (John 14:17; 15:26; 16:13; 1 John 5:6), the Spirit of life (Rom. 8:2), the spirit of wisdom and knowledge (Is. 11:2; 61:1-2), the Spirit of promise (Eph. 1:13), the Spirit of glory (1 Peter 4:4), and the Spirit of God and of Christ (1 Cor. 3:16; Rom. 8:9). In Acts 5, He is called God. In verse three, Ananias was told that he lied to the Holy Spirit and in verse four he is told that he lied to God. The Holy Spirit possesses divine attributes. He is eternal (Heb. 9:14). He is everywhere present (Ps. 139:7-10). He is all-knowing (1 Cor. 2:10-11). The Spirit of God was actively engaged in creation and is said to have made man (Gen. 1:2; Job 33:4). [86]

The Holy Spirit has a very active ministry in the world in general. The Scriptures themselves are the best commentary on this. "And when he is come, he will reprove the world of sin, and of righteousness, and of judgment: of sin, because they believe not on me; of righteousness, because I go to my Father, and ye see me no more; of judgment, because the prince of this world is judged" (John 16:8-11). He is also called "the spirit of truth" because he testifies of Christ in the World (John 15:26). Peter preached that we are the Lord's witnesses, but so also is the Holy Spirit (John 15:27; Acts 5:32). The Holy Spirit works as our team mate in witnessing. [87]

The Holy Spirit was sent into the world by the Father and by the Lord Jesus to take the Lord's place on earth after His resurrection and ascension (John 14:16; 16:7). This was fulfilled in Acts 2. He teaches us truth (John 16:13-15; 1 John 2:20, 27; 1 Cor. 2:9-14). He gives the new birth to the believer (John 3:3-5). The Spirit lives permanently within us (1 Cor. 6:19). The Spirit of God seals us (Eph. 1:13-14). The Holy Spirit fills the believer (Eph. 5:18). The Spirit empowers the believer to have success in life and service (Rom. 8:2, 9-13; Gal. 5:17). The Spirit of God is our guide (Rom. 8:14). He enables us in service (Acts 1:8). [88]

The emphasis on "one" Spirit highlights the fact we may have to deal with more than one spirit, but there is only one Holy Spirit who is God. The Corinthians were warned of a false spirit and false teachers (2 Cor. 11:4); "For if he that cometh preacheth another Jesus, whom we have not preached, or if ye receive another spirit, which ye have not received, or another gospel, which ye have not accepted, ye might well bear with him." Satan is one of these spirit beings, a former cherub, now a dragon and serpent, who pretends to be an angel of light (Ezek. 28:14; 2 Cor. 11:14; Rev. 12). Satan is a deceiver and so are his demonic angels (John 8:44). "Beloved, believe not every spirit, but try the spirits whether they are of God: because many false prophets are gone out into the world" (1 John 4:1).

One Hope

Christians have an eternal hope and it is not hope in this world or in this life. "If in this life only we have hope in Christ, we are of all men most miserable" (1 Cor. 15:19). Our hope involves the resurrection. That will take place at the coming of the Lord Jesus Christ. We should always be "looking for that blessed hope, and the glorious appearing of the great God and our Saviour Jesus Christ" (Titus 2:13). This is our hope; it is the one hope. It is described again in 1 Thessalonians 4:15-17.

> **15** For this we say unto you by the word of the Lord, that we which are alive and remain unto the coming of the Lord shall not prevent them which are asleep.
> **16** For the Lord himself shall descend from heaven with a shout, with the voice of the archangel, and with the trump of God: and the dead in Christ shall rise first:
> **17** Then we which are alive and remain shall be caught up together with them in the clouds, to meet the Lord in the air: and so shall we ever be with the Lord.
> **18** Wherefore comfort one another with these words. (1 Thess. 4:15-17)

This hope is a practical thing. The Lord didn't promise us such a glorious future to challenge us intellectually or to provide us a mystery to solve. He did not intend to give us an interesting puzzle. Neither did he intend to simply distract us from the rotten decay of society and the horrible events that take place in the world around us. No. He gave us a hope of a better place; a hope of a wonderful eternal future that is just as real (or more real) than the world we live in now. He has given us the assurance of ultimate victory in our battle against sin and Satan. That's why he said, "Wherefore comfort one another with these words" (1 Thess. 4:18).

> **16** The Spirit itself beareth witness with our spirit, that we are the children of God:
> **17** ¶And if children, then heirs; heirs of God, and joint-heirs with Christ; if so be that we suffer with him, that we may be also glorified together.
> **18** For I reckon that the sufferings of this present time are not worthy to be compared with the glory which shall be revealed in us.

> **19** For the earnest expectation of the creature waiteth for the manifestation of the sons of God.
> **20** For the creature was made subject to vanity, not willingly, but by reason of him who hath subjected the same in hope,
> **21** Because the creature itself also shall be delivered from the bondage of corruption into the glorious liberty of the children of God.
> **22** For we know that the whole creation groaneth and travaileth in pain together until now.
> **23** And not only they, but ourselves also, which have the firstfruits of the Spirit, even we ourselves groan within ourselves, waiting for the adoption, to wit, the redemption of our body. (Rom. 8:16-23).

The event of 1 Thessalonians 4, which we call the rapture, is not the only event of the second coming of Christ. The Bible mentions this in 2 Timothy 4:1.

> **I charge thee therefore before God, and the Lord Jesus Christ, who shall judge the quick and the dead at his appearing and his kingdom ...**

There are two events listed in 2 Timothy 4:1, the Lords "appearing" and His "kingdom." The "appearing" is the event we call the rapture and the "kingdom" is the second coming where the Lord establishes His rule over the earth from Jerusalem. The Rapture of the church is pictured in Revelation 4:1-2. Following that, the tribulation period is described in Revelation 6-18 (see also Mt. 24:21). Finally, Jesus will return visibly and appear to the world (Rev. 1:7) to establish His Kingdom on earth for one thousand years (Rev. 19-20).

One Lord

We have one Lord who is obviously the Lord Jesus Christ. He is the one who is "God ... manifest in the flesh" (1 Tim. 3:16). The same Word became flesh, dwelt among us, and was the only begotten of the Father (John 1:14), proving that the "Word" refers to Jesus Christ. The Word is said to be God in John 1:1 and is the creator of all things in John 1:2-3. He is life and the light of men and He lights every person who comes into the world (John 1:3, 4, 9). There can be no doubt that Christ is God and equal to the Father.

The work of the Lord Jesus Christ on our behalf spans the entirety of time, beginning with creation. We often say He is a prophet and priest and king. As a prophet, He came to earth as a man, born of a virgin (Is. 7:14; Mt. 1:23; Luke 1:26-38). As a priest, He offered Himself as a perfect sacrifice. He died on the cross, paying for all our sins, so that we could gain forgiveness of our sins (John 1:29; Rom. 5:8). Three days later, He rose physically from the dead (Mt. 17:23; 28:1-6). He is a priest forever after the order of Melchizedek (Heb. 7:21). He took His blood and presented it to the Father in the heavenly temple (Heb. 9:20-28). He sat down on the right hand of God the Father and now makes intercession for us (Rom. 8:34). As a king, He will return and establish His Millennial Kingdom (Rev. 19, 20).

How is it that the Lord Jesus Christ is both God and the only begotten Son of God? Luke 1:35 is the key verse that answers that question. The angel, Gabriel, appeared to a virgin, Mary, and told her she would have a son. Mary inquired how that could happen without the involvement of a man. Gabriel replied, "The Holy Ghost shall come upon thee, and the power of the Highest shall overshadow thee: **therefore** *also that holy thing which shall be born of thee shall be called the Son of God.*" Adam had been created by God and was called a son of God because of it (Lk. 3:38). However, he was not a *begotten* son. According to John 1:12-13, we also are the sons of God by virtue of the new birth, but we are not *begotten* sons. Jesus was born physically because the Holy Ghost by the power of God created a pregnancy in the womb of a virgin. *He was literally begotten of God.* It is for this reason that Jesus is called the *only begotten* Son of

God. The virgin birth is that reason. In His spirit, He is God (Lord). As a man (Jesus), He is the Son of God.

However, some will object to this assessment. Since the mid-third century AD, the doctrine of the eternal begetting of the Son of God has been taught. This is the idea that the Son of God was begotten in eternity before creation. It was affirmed in the Nicene Creed in 325 AD, where God the Son was said to be "eternally begotten of the Father." Several reasons have been given for believing this.

> 1. It was the Son who created all that is (Col. 1:13-16; Heb. 1:2). He is said to be the Son in those passages implying that He was already the Son when He created.
> 2. Several passages state that the Father sent the Son to redeem the world (John 20:21; Galatians 4:4; 1 John 4:14; 1 John 4:10), implying that He was the Son before He was sent.
> 3. 1 John 3:8 says the Son of God was manifested to destroy the works of the Devil. Again this implies that he was the Son previous to His manifestation.
> 4. Hebrews 13:8 teaches that the Son is the same yesterday, today, and forever. Therefore, He must have been the Son forever.
> 5. The triune nature of God indicates an eternal relationship between Father, Son, and Holy Spirit. [89]

There are some serious problems with these arguments. The first four arguments rely entirely upon perceived *implications*. That is, these implications are *assumed* to be true. The Bible never *states explicitly* that the Son of God was begotten of God in eternity before creation. For example, 1 John 3:8 says, "He that committeth sin is of the devil; for the devil sinneth from the beginning. For this purpose the Son of God was manifested, that he might destroy the works of the devil." The Son of God was first manifested at the virgin birth, but it does not necessarily follow that he was the Son before the virgin birth. He could have become the Son of God through the virgin birth, just as Luke 1:35 says He did. The same is true for each of the first four arguments. There is no clear statement that He was the Son in eternity past and the so-called implications are mere assumptions.

It is interesting that the assumed implication of all these verses is accepted over the plain statements of Luke 1:35 and Psalm 2:7 (quoted in Hebrews 1:5). We have already discussed Luke 1:35, which *explicitly states* that Jesus is called the Son of God *because* of the virgin birth. Psalm 2:7 says, "I will declare the decree: the LORD hath said unto me, Thou art my Son; this day have I begotten thee." This verse is used to teach the eternal sonship of Jesus, because of the belief that all God's decrees are eternal. The Bible never says that either. The real significance of this verse is that God begat the Son on a "day." This proves beyond doubt that the begetting of the Son of God did not take place in eternity past. *There were no days in eternity past. There were no days until creation (Gen. 1:5).* The begetting took place in time, not eternity.

The final argument regarding the relationship of the trinity to itself is a bit different. It does, however, seem to stem from a misunderstanding of the Trinity. God has manifested Himself to us with the appearance of three different individual persons with individual tasks. This may have been done for our sakes, because of the difficulty of understanding the Trinity. However, in reality the three are not individual persons at all, but they are parts of the same person. There is only one God. He is one person in three parts, just as each of us is one person with three parts: body, soul, and spirit. God fills heaven and earth (Jer. 23:24) and can manifest Himself where He will and in any way He will.

Our Trinitarian formula of Father, Son, and Holy Spirit does not seem to have been the formula in eternity. In John 1:1, the Lord Jesus is called the "Word" in connection to creation. The formula in 1 John 5:7 reads, "For there are three that bear record in heaven, *the Father, the Word, and the Holy Ghost*: and these three are one." The reference to the second person of the Trinity in eternity appears not to be "the Son," but, rather, "the Word."

One Faith

Here we enter into some confusion. Some will say that "the faith" mentioned here is the great body of doctrine of Christianity or the body of Christian truth. If this is so, "the faith" would include the doctrines mentioned before and after it here and would be redundant, except to point out that there is only one faith. There must be something more particular about it.

Let's look at the first time the phrase "the faith" is used in the Bible. "And his name through faith in his name hath made this man strong, whom ye see and know: yea, *the faith* which is by him hath given him this perfect soundness in the presence of you all" (Acts 3:16). This is about the man who was healed in the temple when Peter and John went there during the hour of prayer. "The faith" is something the healed man had and it is defined as "faith in His (Christ's) name." Faith is a noun, but it is used here as if it was an action. However, once I put my faith in some object, that object is what I believe in; it is "the faith" to me. If I put my faith in Christ's name, then His name is what I believe in. So, what is the object of my faith? What is the distinct truth that makes me a Christian? What is the thing that I believed that began my spiritual life; that made me a child of God? Is it not the gospel? Therefore, "the faith" is the gospel. Does this idea stand up elsewhere in the New Testament?

Acts 6:7 says, "And the word of God increased; and the number of the disciples multiplied in Jerusalem greatly; and a great company of the priests were obedient to the faith." Here the Bible speaks of *obedience* to the faith;

likewise, Romans 1:5. How does one *obey* the faith? Once again Paul explains it: "And how shall they preach, except they be sent? ... But they have not all *obeyed the gospel*. For Esaias saith, Lord, who hath *believed* our report" (Rom. 10:15-16)? Look at this carefully. To obey the gospel is to *believe* the gospel. Philippians 1:27 speaks of "the faith of the gospel." Philippians 3:9 tells us of "the faith of Christ." Finally, in Acts 13:8, Elymas, the sorcerer, tried to turn the Roman official away from *the faith*. What faith was it that Paul and Barnabas were teaching? Did they put the governor in catechism classes so he could learn and believe the whole body of Christian truth? That's nonsense. They preached the word of God to him, but clearly it was not *all* of the word of God. They preached the gospel to him, because he needed to know about the death, burial, and resurrection of Christ to be saved (1 Cor. 15:1-4). *The faith* is Christ and the gospel of Christ. There is only one gospel, one faith that saves, no more (2 Cor. 11:1-4; Gal. 1:6-9).

One Baptism

Once again, we are faced with a doctrine that is not only confusing, but also controversial. For centuries, people have argued about the meaning and mode of water baptism. Sometimes the controversy has been widespread and bitter.

All the fighting has been over *water* baptism. The forgotten truth is that there is more to baptism than *water*. Baptism by water is not the only kind of baptism. In fact, there are at least *seven baptisms* in Scripture. Some of these involve water and some do not. All of them involve some type of immersion. The first is the *baptism to repentance* practiced by John the Baptist (Mt. 3:11; Mk. 1:4). It was a water baptism performed in the Jordan River (Mt. 3:6; Mk. 1:5). It was done in connection with repentance and confession of sins.

When John spoke of Jesus, he said that Jesus would give two other types of baptism: *the Holy Spirit and fire*

(Mt.3:11; Mk. 1:8; Lk. 3:16). We have mentioned the baptism of the Holy Spirit before and will bring it up again a bit later. Although the Apostles received the baptism of the Holy Spirit in Acts 2 and it was associated with "cloven tongues of fire" (Acts 1:5; 2:3), it is likely that the Baptism of fire is separate from that of the Spirit. Indeed, there is coming a day in which the unsaved will be baptized with fire, when they are cast into the lake of fire (Rev. 20:15). The Bible says that it will be Jesus who is judge at that time (John 5:25-30).

The fourth type of baptism is the *baptism of suffering.* After James and John requested a special place in Christ's kingdom, He answered them (Mark 10:38), "Ye know not what ye ask: can ye drink of the cup that I drink of? And be baptized with the baptism that I am baptized with?" He had already been baptized in water, so the only baptism He had left involved the scourge and the cross, suffering (Lk. 12:50).

Next, we have *Christian water baptism.* "Go ye therefore, and teach all nations, baptizing them in the name of the Father, and of the Son, and of the Holy Ghost" (Mt. 28:19). This is the baptism that has caused much confusion and conflict throughout Church history. Some believe it is necessary for salvation and others do not. Some believe children or infants should be baptized to bring them into the Christian Covenant. Others are convinced that only those who have made a conscious decision to trust Christ are fit subjects for baptism. Many confuse Romans 6 and 1 Corinthians 12:13 with Christian water baptism.

A sixth baptism mentioned in the Scriptures is the *baptism to Moses.* "Moreover, brethren, I would not that ye should be ignorant, how that all our fathers were under the cloud, and all passed through the sea; and were all baptized unto Moses in the cloud and in the sea" (1 Cor. 10:1-3). This experience of the Israelites coming out of Egypt, going through the Red Sea and the cloud, identified them as part of the nation and under the leadership of Moses.

Finally, there is the Baptism of Christ Himself (Mt. 3:13-17). John performed it, but it was not the same as his other baptisms. Jesus had no need for repentance or confession of sin, so His baptism was not for that purpose. His baptism made Him known to the Jews. It was the time of His first showing to Israel. It was also a time when God the Father proclaimed Christ to be His Son (John 1:30-31).

So, we have seven baptisms, but there is only one real baptism for us Christians. Which can it be? It is not John's Baptism, because that's over. The baptism of Jesus was His own personal experience and occurred only once. We will never be baptized with fire, because we will never go to Hell. It is not the baptism of suffering, although we generally suffer for our faith to one degree or another. It is not the baptism unto Moses, because that was for the Jews in the Old Testament. That leaves just two candidates for the "one baptism:" Christian water baptism or the baptism of the Holy Spirit.

There have been things on this earth that seem real to us but are described in the Scriptures as merely shadows of the true items. Hebrews 9:1-27 addresses this in detail regarding the first tabernacle, its furniture and sacrifices, which were built and used when Israel came out of Egypt. The Scripture calls these real solid touchable items merely "a figure for the time then present (Heb. 9: 9). There is "a greater and more perfect tabernacle, not made with hands" (Heb. 9:10). The comparison is between the tabernacle on earth and the tabernacle in Heaven: "It was therefore necessary that the *patterns* of things in the heavens should be purified with these (animal sacrifices); but the heavenly things themselves with better sacrifices than these" (Heb. 9:23). He calls the earthly tabernacle and its furniture mere patterns purified with animal sacrifices (see Heb. 9:19-22). However, the tabernacle in heaven required a better sacrifice, the blood of Christ (Heb. 9:12-18). The things on earth are nothing more than the *figures* of the true things in

Heaven. "For Christ is not entered into the holy places made with hands, **which are the figures of the true**; but into heaven itself, now to appear in the presence of God for us (Heb. 9:24).

In the same manner, water baptism is not the true baptism, but merely a figure. It is called "**the like figure** whereunto even baptism doth also now save us (**not** the putting away of the filth of the flesh, **but the answer of a good conscience toward God**,) by the resurrection of Jesus Christ" (1 Pet. 3:21). Baptism does not save us in reality, but only in a figure. In other words, it is a picture of our salvation. It does not cleanse away the sinful filth of the flesh. It is only the answer of a conscience already made clean by the blood of Christ. Just as Hebrews 9 says, the blood of sacrificial animals cannot make the conscience clean, neither can baptism. The blood of Christ and only His blood can make the conscience clean (Heb. 9:9, 14; 10:1-2, 10).

If water baptism is the figure, what is the true? The only baptism left is the baptism of the Holy Spirit. The baptism of the Spirit accomplishes many things that cannot be accomplished by water. As we have said, the baptism of the Spirit places us into the body of Christ and it places us into Christ (1 Cor. 12:13; Rom. 6:3). Water can never do that. Romans 6 speaks about what baptism does for us, but never specifies whether it is water or Spirit.

> **3 Know ye not, that so many of us as were baptized into Jesus Christ were baptized into his death?**
> **4 Therefore we are buried with him by baptism into death: that like as Christ was raised up from the dead by the glory of the Father, even so we also should walk in newness of life.**
> **5 For if we have been planted together in the likeness of his death, we shall be also in the likeness of his resurrection:**
> **6 Knowing this, that our old man is crucified with**

> him, that the body of sin might be destroyed, that henceforth we should not serve sin.
> 7 For he that is dead is freed from sin.(Rom. 6:3-7)

As we have noted before, in Romans 6, baptism causes us to die and gives us new life (Rom. 6:4). In fact it says, "Our old man is crucified with him, that the body of sin might be destroyed" (Rom. 6:6). Therefore, we are now "dead to sin" (Rom. 6:2) and "he that is dead is freed from sin" (Rom. 6:7). The result of this is that we are no longer enslaved to the flesh but are free to live an obedient life in Christ. "Likewise reckon ye also yourselves to be dead indeed unto sin, but alive unto God through Jesus Christ our Lord. Let not sin therefore reign in your mortal body, that ye should obey it in the lusts thereof." (Rom. 6:11-12). Spiritual baptism has made us free to live a godly life. Believe it or not, some people think *water did all this.* Baptism did it, but it wasn't water. It was the Spirit of God.

So why did Paul use the word *baptism*, but not define whether it was water or Spirit? It is because there is a connection between water baptism and the baptism of the Spirit. Spiritual baptism puts us into real death *in the likeness of His death* (Rom. 6:5). Spiritual baptism gives us real new life *in the likeness of His resurrection* (Rom. 6:5). Water Baptism by immersion clearly pictures a death and burial (immersed in the water) and a resurrection (rising out of the water). The baptism of the Spirit creates the reality. Baptism in water pictures that reality. Water baptism is *the figure*; the baptism of the Spirit is the *reality*. Being baptized by the Spirit of God is the one true baptism.

One God and Father of All

> One God and Father of all, who is above all, and through all, and in you all. (Eph. 4:6).

Paul's declaration here is reminiscent of Moses' declaration to Israel, "Hear, O Israel: The LORD our God is one LORD" (Deut. 6:4).

God is above all. He is over and above everything. Unlike the teaching of Pantheism that says God is identical with the creation, God is above the creation. He is the Creator of all things, so He is greater than the creation. "To whom then will ye liken me, or shall I be equal? saith the Holy One. Lift up your eyes on high, and behold who hath created these things, that bringeth out their host by number: he calleth them all by names by the greatness of his might, for that he is strong in power; not one faileth" (Is. 40:25-26). God is distinct from His creation. He is a person distinct from us. God is all knowing (Is. 40:28; Prov. 15:3), almighty (Gen. 1:1-3; Eph. 1:19-20), everywhere present (Jer. 23:23-24), eternal (Hab. 1:12), and unchanging (Mal. 3:6). God has perfect character. He is holy (Is. 57:15; Ps. 99:9; Hab. 1:13; 1 Pet. 1:15-16), righteous and just (Ps. 116:5; 145:17; merciful, (Ps. 103:8; Is. 55:7), and God is love (Jn. 3:16; 1 Jn. 4:8-16).

God is "through all, and in you all." The use of the word "you" shows this doesn't apply to the unsaved. Even though God is everywhere and in that sense "in him we live, and move, and have our being" (Acts 17:28), Paul is applying this to the saints in Ephesus and therefore, to us. We have a special relationship with God. He is our Father. We have the Spirit of the Father, the Spirit of Adoption and in our hearts we cry "Abba, Father!"

CHAPTER EIGHT

UNITY OF LOVE IN THE CHURCH
Ephesians 4:7-32

THE REMAINDER OF EPHESIANS CHAPTER FOUR brings up several subjects, but throughout them all there is a central theme of Christian love and service.

First, gifts are given to men and they are used so that all may profit together (Eph. 4:9-10; 1 Cor. 12:7). As a result, the saints are equipped, the ministry is done, and the whole body is edified (Eph. 4:11-12). God's purpose in this method is to bring the whole body into the unity of faith and knowledge of the Son of God (Eph. 4:13-16). This can only be accomplished if every part of the body, the members, supply that which God has given them (Eph. 4:16). We must all work together as a spiritual team. Every part is necessary.

Verses 17-32 are about maintaining unity through serving one another and treating one another right.

This whole chapter is about walking "worthy of the vocation wherewith ye are called." The recommended way to do that per this chapter is by "endeavoring to keep the unity of the Spirit in the bond of peace." The church is unified doctrinally in the matters we have just covered. It is unified through edification by "the whole body fitly joined together and compacted by that which every joint supplieth" (v. 16). And it is unified in "peace" through right relationships.

Gifts Given to Men (Eph. 4:7-16)

**7 But unto every one of us is given grace according to the measure of the gift of Christ.
8 Wherefore he saith, When he ascended up on high, he led captivity captive, and gave gifts unto men.
9 (Now that he ascended, what is it but that he also descended first into the lower parts of the earth?
10 He that descended is the same also that ascended up far above all heavens, that he might fill all things.)(Eph. 4:7-16)**

These few initial verses open up some profound truths that go far beyond just the fact that God gives men a measure of grace by imparting gifts to them. The references to ascending and descending are clearly references to Christ. However, the text throws in this enigmatic statement "he led captivity captive" and the declaration that He descended into the "lower parts" of the earth.

We know He ascended after His resurrection. That's referenced in Acts 1:6-11. What does it mean that He descended into the lower part of the earth? Matthew 12:40 says, "For as Jonas was three days and three nights in the whale's belly; so shall the Son of man be three days and three nights in the *heart of the earth*." Does the reference to the heart of the earth only refer to the grave? The Lord was buried in a cave. One might think it strange that a *cave* would be called the *heart* of the earth. When Jesus died, the Scriptures say He gave up the ghost (John 19:30). What did He do for three days?

There is more to it. Acts 2:31 explains it a bit further: "He seeing this before spake of the resurrection of Christ, that his soul was not left in hell, neither his flesh did see corruption." If we take this to mean what it says and believe it, Jesus Christ went to Hell after He died on the cross. Why in the world would He do that? It looks like Christ not only redeemed us with His blood, but He also suffered Hell in our place. Also, think what Christ actually did on the cross. Christ "his own self bare our sins in his own body on the tree, that we, being dead to sins, should live unto righteousness: by whose stripes ye were healed" (1 Pet. 2:24; cf. Heb. 9:28). Our sins were on His body and His very soul was an offering for sin (Is. 53:10). When John the Baptist first saw Christ, he declared, "Behold the Lamb of God, which taketh away the sin of the world" (John 1:29). What did Jesus do with all our sins, after He paid for them on the cross? I suggest that He left them in Hell. He entered there and when He left, He left victorious with "the keys of hell and of death" in His possession (Rev. 1:18). It is certain:

> **9 He will not always chide: neither will he keep his anger for ever.**
> **10 He hath not dealt with us after our sins; nor rewarded us according to our iniquities.**
> **11 For as the heaven is high above the earth, so great is his mercy toward them that fear him.**
> **12 As far as the east is from the west, so far hath he removed our transgressions from us. (Ps. 103:9-12).**

The location of Hell has long been a matter of discussion and disagreement. Following the law of first mention, the first place Hell is mentioned in the Bible is Deuteronomy 32:22, "For a fire is kindled in mine anger, and shall burn unto the lowest hell." From this very first mention, we learn that Hell is associated with God's anger, burning, and depths. It has levels, some lower than others (see Ps. 86:13). The second mention, 2 Samuel 22:6 tells us that sorrow is a part of Hell: "The sorrows of hell compassed me about." Job 11:8 reveals that Heaven is high and Hell is deep. Psalm 55:15 and Proverbs 15:24 point to Hell as being *down* and *beneath*.

Job 11:8 It is as high as heaven; what canst thou do? deeper than hell; what canst thou know?
Psalms 55:15 Let death seize upon them, and let them go down quick into hell: for wickedness is in their dwellings, and among them.
Proverbs 15:24 ¶The way of life is above to the wise, that he may depart from hell beneath.

To get to Hell, Isaiah 5:14 says you must *descend* and it is located in "the nether parts of the earth" (Ezek. 31:16-17). "Nether" means "in the lower part." [90] In fact Isaiah 14:15, describes the Devil's defeat this way: "Yet thou shalt be brought **down** to hell, to the sides of the **pit**." Hell is down, in the lower parts of the earth, a pit with sides, but there is no mention of a bottom. This is verified in Revelation 20:1-3, "And I saw an angel come down from heaven, having the key of the bottomless pit ... And he laid hold on ... Satan, and bound him a thousand years, and cast him into the bottomless pit." How could a bottomless pit be downward in the heart of the earth (where Jesus went), unless it is a donut shaped pit with sides, but no bottom? If a living human would get to Heaven, he must *climb*, but to get to Hell, he must *dig* (Amos 9:2). Hell is always described as being down (Mt. 11:23; Rev. 1:18). It has gates and keys (Mt. 16:18; 2 Peter 2:4; Rev. 1:18).

The idea that Hell is downward in the heart of the earth is actually not so far-fetched. Heaven is clearly upward. Paul called it the third heaven. First, there is the atmosphere, then what we call space, and finally the third Heaven where God's throne is.

Why is it so hard to accept the idea that Hell is downward? The truth is that the structure of the earth is conducive to this idea. See the diagram on the next page. The earth is surrounded by a crust which ranges from 5 miles (8 kilometers) in the oceans to 25 miles (40 Kilometers) thick. Next is the earth's mantel, which is about 1,800 miles (2,900 kilometers) thick. Below this is the earth's core. The core is divided into two parts. The outer core is 1,400 miles (2,250 kilometers) thick. The outer core is entirely made of molten metal. It is literally a furnace about 6,700 to 7,800 degrees Fahrenheit. The inner core is about 1,600 miles (2,600 kilometers) diameter. The "the inner core may reach 12,600 degrees F (7,000 degrees C), hotter than the surface of the sun. Only the enormous pressures found at the super-hot inner core keep it solid." [91] The outer core of earth, with a solid center, is a round shaped pit with no bottom. All the Biblical references combined point to the possibility that this is the location of Hell.

The story Jesus told of the rich man and Lazarus, recorded in Luke 16:19-31, reveals some interesting things about the state of the saved and the unsaved before the death and resurrection of Christ. Lazarus died and went to something called Abraham's Bosom (Lk. 16:22), while the rich man went to Hell (Lk. 16:23). The inhabitants of Abraham's

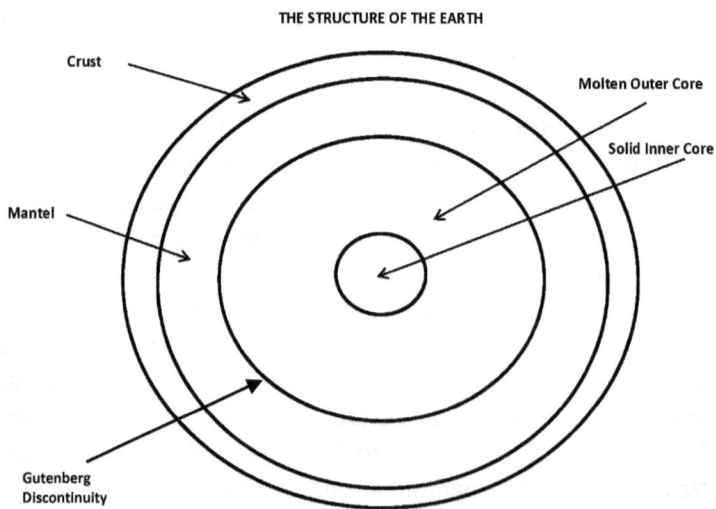

Bosom, which included Abraham, were comforted while the rich man was tormented in the *flames* of Hell (Lk. 16:24-25). It is interesting to note that Abraham and the other inhabitants of the place of comfort could see and communicate with the inhabitants of Hell. Therefore, Abraham's Bosom was definitely not in Heaven.

Referring back to the diagram of the structure of earth, there is a distinct thin layer between the mantel and the molten outer core. It is sometimes called the "Gutenberg Discontinuity" after Beno Gutenberg, who discovered it. Not much is known about it at this time. It was discovered by the way seismic waves behave when passing through it. [92] I am not declaring that this is definitely the location of Abraham's Bosom, but I think it probable. It is intriguing to find a separate layer at this spot.

It is reasonable to deduce from Luke 16 that all the Old Testament saints were in Abraham's Bosom at that time, not in Heaven, although they were certainly saved. How could this be? Why were they not in Heaven? Remember, that the Old Testament saints were justified by faith in God's current revelation as Abraham was. However, the blood of Christ had not yet been shed and, therefore, they could not be truly clean from their sins. "For it is not possible that the blood of bulls and of goats should take away sins" (Heb. 10:4). All they had was the blood of bulls and goats and lambs. This was important as a temporary measure, because "without shedding of blood is no remission" (Heb. 9:22).

God brought in the Law through Moses to show man their sinfulness (Gal. 3:21-24) and to drive them to faith. Justification could not be gained by keeping the law, because none of them could do it. Peter and Paul both said this (Acts 15:7-11; Rom. 7:7-13). The law could not give life, because of the weakness of men (Rom. 8:3). The nature of the Law was the same before the cross as it is after the cross. In the final analysis, all they had was faith in the revelation God gave them at that time, just like Abraham (Rom. 4:3-5, 13-22).

This included faith in the sacrifices for sin. In regard to that, God said, "For the law having a shadow of good things to come, and not the very image of the things, can never with those sacrifices which they offered year by year continually make the comers thereunto perfect. For then would they not have ceased to be offered? because that the worshippers once purged should have had no more conscience of sins" (Heb. 10:1-2). Yet, they did have conscience of sin. "But in those sacrifices there is a remembrance again made of sins every year" (Heb. 10:3). Not only that, but their sins were not taken away (Heb. 10:4). Old Testament saved people were forgiven and they were justified as Abraham had been. Nevertheless, they were not perfect, their conscience was not clean, and their sins were not taken away. Therefore, they went to Abraham's Bosom when they died, not Heaven.

However, when the sacrifice of Christ took place on the cross it was a perfect and complete sacrifice (Heb. 10:7-14). Christ "offered one sacrifice for sins for ever" and "we are sanctified through the offering of the body of Jesus Christ once for all" and "by one offering he hath perfected for ever them that are sanctified" (Heb. 10:10, 12, 14). As a result, the way was made for the Old Testament saints in Abraham's Bosom to enter Heaven.

Finally, we come to the phrase he "led captivity captive." Verse eight is a quote from Psalm 68:18. The phrase is used in Judges 5:12 in reference to the victory of Deborah and Barak over Jabin, king of Canaan (Judg. 4 and 5): "Awake, awake, Deborah: awake, awake, utter a song: arise, Barak, and lead thy captivity captive, thou son of Abinoam." Israel had been held captive by Jabin and Sisera, the Captain of his army. Some say that God captured the one who had held Israel captive and, therefore, Jesus captured the one who had held us captive, the devil. However, this does not fit the facts in the case of Barak and Jabin nor in the case of the Devil. The evil one is still free to do much mischief. Sisera was killed (Judg. 4:21) and Jabin was destroyed (Judg. 4:24). Nothing was said about either of them being taken captive. Deborah and Barak actually took the Israelite captives captive in the sense that they took control and led them to freedom.

Jesus did the same thing. After He died, He went to Hell and at some point He entered into Abraham's bosom. There, He took control of all the captives who had been waiting a long time for complete redemption and led them out of their captivity into the glorious presence of God in Heaven. He led "captivity captive," He ascended up on high, He received gifts for men (as Ps. 68:18 says), and He gave those gifts to men.

Gifts given to the Saints

> 11 And he gave some, apostles; and some, prophets; and some, evangelists; and some, pastors and teachers;
> 12 For the perfecting of the saints, for the work of the ministry, for the edifying of the body of Christ:
> 13 Till we all come in the unity of the faith, and of the knowledge of the Son of God, unto a perfect man, unto the measure of the stature of the fulness of Christ:
> 14 That we henceforth be no more children, tossed to and fro, and carried about with every wind of doctrine, by the sleight of men, and cunning craftiness, whereby they lie in wait to deceive;
> 15 But speaking the truth in love, may grow up into him in all things, which is the head, even Christ:
> 16 From whom the whole body fitly joined together and compacted by that which every joint supplieth, according to the effectual working in the measure of every part, maketh increase of the body unto the edifying of itself in love. (Eph. 4:11-16).

"And He gave some:" To whom did He give these gifts? Verse eight says He "gave gifts unto men." "Some" in verse eleven refers to the "men" of verse eight.

This section of Ephesians Four should be cross-referenced and correlated with 1 Corinthians 12, the great gifts chapter. Ephesians 4:11 lists apostles, prophets, evangelists, and pastor-teachers. All of these are among the gifts listed in 1 Corinthians 12. They are also the most vocal and easily seen gifts.

The Apostles and prophets of the early church had a specialized ministry. "Now therefore ye are no more strangers and foreigners, but fellowcitizens with the saints, and of the household of God; and are **built upon the foundation of the apostles and prophets**, Jesus Christ himself being the chief corner stone" (Eph. 2:19-20). The Lord Jesus Christ is the founder of the church, the foundation, and the chief cornerstone of the building. The Apostles and the prophets have laid the foundation of the building by establishing the gospel and doctrinal truth from the Lord Jesus Christ.

We no longer need these to lay a foundation. That is done. What we need now are builders to build the building, "in whom all the building fitly framed together **groweth** unto an holy temple in the Lord: in whom ye also are **builded** together for an habitation of God through the Spirit" (Eph. 2:21-22). Paul warned, "According to the grace of God which is given unto me, as a wise masterbuilder, I have laid the foundation, and another buildeth thereon. But let every man take heed how he buildeth thereupon" (1 Cor. 3:10). The purpose of the evangelists and the pastor-teachers is to build upon the foundation laid by the Apostles and prophets. It is a blessing beyond telling that all the foundation and truth we need to do that in any age is contained in God's written, inspired, and preserved Word. The Word of God was given that the man of God may be perfect, throughly furnished to every good work (2 Tim. 3:16-17).

There are three basic goals for the use of these four gifts (Eph. 4:12). These goals are not four goals that are reached simultaneously although all are ongoing activities in the church. They are progressive. Each leads to the next.

"For the perfecting of the saints:" This involves an in depth ministry of teaching the word of God and exhorting the saints to put it into practice (2 Tim. 4:2). The Word of God is that which perfects the saints, as stated above. The Word instructs believers in righteous living and helps keep them straight. "All scripture is given by inspiration of God, and is profitable for doctrine, for reproof, for correction, for instruction in righteousness" (2 Tim. 3:16). The Word is good for "doctrine." It teaches us what to believe and what manner of living is right in God's eyes. It shows us what path to walk on. The Word is good for "reproof." It makes it clear when we have gotten off the right path. It rebukes us, sometimes severely. Third, the Word is good for "correction." It tells us how to get back on the right path. Finally, the Word is good for "instruction in righteousness." It gives us clear instruction on how to stay on the right path. "Thy word is a lamp unto my feet, and a light unto my path" (Ps. 119:105).

"For the work of the ministry:" the saints, who are in the process of being perfected by the evangelists and pastor-teachers, are responsible to do the work of the ministry. The word "ministry" is *diakonia* and means service, "*Diakonía* involves compassionate love towards the needy within the Christian community (Acts 6:1, 4; 2Cor. 8:4; 9:12-13; Rev. 2:19)." [93] Paul expressed the attitude involved in service to others: "For we preach not ourselves, but Christ Jesus the Lord; and ourselves your servants for Jesus' sake" (2 Cor. 4:5) and "I will very gladly spend and be spent for you; though the more abundantly I love you, the less I be loved" 2 Cor. 12:15). His instruction on it was equally clear: "As we have therefore opportunity, let us do good unto all men, especially unto them who are of the household of faith" (Gal. 6:10).

As the saints do the work of ministry, the result is "the edifying of the body of Christ." The word *edify* (Greek=*oikodome*) has to do with construction. It is the same word translated "building" in Ephesians 2:21. It is to build one another up spiritually and morally. It means "to instruct and improve the mind in knowledge generally, and particularly in moral and religious knowledge, in faith and holiness." [94] The work of the ministry and the edifying of the body are not only for the preacher or the teacher or the evangelist. They do not perfect the saints so that they can sit down in their comfortable homes and do nothing, feeling no responsibility for the ministry. The work of the ministry is for all to do. It is the responsibility of all to build up the body of Christ. They do this through the use of their spiritual gifts motivated by love and desire for the glory of God.

How long are we carry on this work of the ministry and of edifying the body of Christ? How long are our spiritual leaders to give themselves to the work of perfecting the saints? We are to do it "till we all come in the unity of the faith, and of the knowledge of the Son of God, unto a perfect man, unto the measure of the stature of the fulness of Christ" (Eph. 4:13). This is a process that is never finished in this life, but we can get closer and closer. We as individuals are always seeking to grow ever closer to the image of Christ, who is the express image of God (Heb. 1:3).

Once again this brings us back to the necessity of unity. First, we are all to be unified in the faith. Not all who profess to be Christians truly believe the faith of the gospel. Many so-called churches are preaching a false gospel. We need not be concerned about unity of faith with anyone who is preaching a false gospel. However, there may be those, whether members of our church or another, who are confused about this doctrinal point or that. We should love them enough to perfect their knowledge, if they will listen. On the other hand, we may be the one who is confused or in error. We should be humble enough to listen to instruction that will perfect our understanding, being careful to be sure that we are listening to Biblical teaching.

The same is true of our knowledge of Christ, which covers a lot of ground theologically. When Paul departed from Ephesus, Apollos came into the city to preach. He was a sincere man of faith, but all he knew was the baptism of John. Aquila and Priscilla, friends of Paul, took Apollos under their wing and "expounded unto him the way of God more perfectly" (Acts 18:24-28). Go and do ye likewise!

The more we know the Word and the truth therein, the more we will become "no more children, tossed to and fro, and carried about with every wind of doctrine, by the sleight of men, and cunning craftiness, whereby they lie in wait to deceive" (Eph. 4:14). There are many deceivers in the world. Many are as subtle as Satan in their presentation of falsehood (Gen. 3:1). How are we to remain pure in our understanding of truth? I have been told that the Secret Service has a special way to detect counterfeit bills and whether it is true or not, it would be very wise. They do not study all the different kinds of counterfeit currency. What they do, and it is the best way, is to learn the real thing so well that they can detect a counterfeit bill when it shows up. Each of us should know the truth of the Word of God so well that when a false doctrine presents itself, we will immediately spot it as untrue or, at least, suspect. We really have no excuse not to do this. When I was a fairly young Christian I read a biography of Dawson Trotman who started the Navigators. When he was challenged by others, he determined that he would never be stumped on the same question twice. The Bible has all the truth we need and we are responsible to learn it. The only possible excuse for anyone anywhere in the world not to know his Bible thoroughly is if they have no well translated Bible in their language or cannot get one. At the time of this writing there are about 3800 languages with no Bible. This is inexcusable as well. The body of Christ should be one hundred percent committed to translating the Bible into all languages as soon as possible.

The alternative to being tossed about with falsehood and deception is "speaking the truth in love" (Eph. 4:15). The cure for error is truth. It is absolutely necessary that we speak truth with one another. We should not hold back the truth, sugar coat the truth, or keep our mouths shut. I will say it once again. The "truth" is not everyman's opinion. The "truth" is the Word of God, the Bible (John 17:17). The Bible is the only source of truth that is eternal and that causes us to "grow up into him in all things, which is the head, even Christ." Albert Barnes had this to say about speaking the truth in love:

> The second thing is that the truth should be spoken "in love." There are other ways of speaking truth. It is sometimes spoken in a harsh, crabby, sour manner, which does nothing but disgust and offend. When we state truth to others, it should be with love to their souls, and with a sincere desire to do them good. When we admonish a brother of his faults, it should not be in a harsh and unfeeling manner, but in love. Where a minister pronounces the awful truth of God about depravity, death, the judgment, and future woe, it should be in love. It should not be done in a harsh and repulsive manner; it should not be done as if he rejoiced that people were in danger of hell, or as if he would like to pass the final sentence; it should not be with indifference, or in a tone of superiority. And in like manner, if we go to convince one who is in error, we should approach him in love. We should not dogmatize, or denounce, or deal out anathemas. Such things only repel. "He has done about half his work in convincing another of error who has first convinced him that he loves him;" and if he does not

do that, he may argue to the hour of his death and make no progress in convincing him. [95]

The body of Christ is edified by "that which every joint supplieth." So far there has been an emphasis in this passage on the fact that every believer is involved with ministering to other saints. There are many other gifts other than the prominent gifts listed in verse eleven. In 1 Corinthians 12 and 14, there are two types of gifts: sign gifts and what may be called edifying gifts (1 Cor. 14:12). The sign gifts are tongues and interpretation of tongues, miracles, and healings. Others are listed in Mark 16 where God's purpose in sign gifts is also given. "And they (the Apostles) went forth, and preached every where, the Lord working with them, and confirming the word with signs following" (Mark 16:20). Sign gifts were useful for confirming the preached word at a time when the New Testament had not yet been written. After the New Testament was available the sign gifts were not needed so much. Historically, after about 100 A.D. when the Book of Revelation was finished, the sign gifts faded off the historical scene.

However, the edifying gifts are Paul's focus in verse sixteen. In 1 Corinthians 12 these include word of knowledge (which is synonymous with teaching), word of wisdom (exhortation), faith, discerning of spirits, helps, and governments. The list in Romans 12 includes ministry, teaching, exhortation, ruling, showing mercy, and giving. The purpose of the gifts is the edifying of the body and every gift is necessary (1 Cor. 12:12-26). The church cannot do without any of the gifts. Every Christian is given at least one gift (1 Cor. 12:7). Your gift is necessary. You are necessary. You have a ministry and your ministry is needed. The body can only be built up properly by the use of every gift and every ministry.

The Walk We Have Learned From Christ

**17 ¶This I say therefore, and testify in the Lord, that ye henceforth walk not as other Gentiles walk, in the vanity of their mind,
18 Having the understanding darkened, being alienated from the life of God through the ignorance that is in them, because of the blindness of their heart:
19 Who being past feeling have given themselves over unto lasciviousness, to work all uncleanness with greediness. (Eph. 4:17-19)**

So far, we have looked at doctrinal unity (vv. 4-6) and the internal unity of the organism itself and how it is knit together into one unit. Now, in verses 17-32, we turn to the unity and the bond of peace produced when relationships within the church are based on love.

The basic principle in verses 17-19 is that: 1) you were gentiles and, as such, you were in terrible condition spiritually, 2) you are no longer in that spiritual condition, and 3) do not live like you are still in that condition. "How shall we, that are dead to sin, live any longer therein" (Rom. 6:2)?

If we add what the Lord tells us here to what He said in chapter two, we get a very dark picture of the spiritual condition of the world around us. Galatians 1:4 calls the present world *evil*.

    1. The mind is vain (4:17),
    2. The understanding is darkened (4:18),
    3. Alienated from the life of God (4:18),
    4. Ignorant (4:17),
    5. Blind of heart (4:17),
    6. Past feeling (4:18),
    7. Given to lasciviousness, to work all uncleanness with greediness (4:19),
    8. Without Christ (2:12),

9. Aliens from the commonwealth of Israel (2:12),
10. Strangers to the covenants of promise (2:12),
11. Without God in the world (2:12), and
12. Without hope (2:12).

Is it any wonder that God says do not live like they live? Is it any wonder our world in the early twenty-first century is in the corrupt shape in which we see it? Do not follow their path. Do not follow their advice. "Blessed is the man that walketh *not* in the counsel of the ungodly, *nor* standeth in the way of sinners, *nor* sitteth in the seat of the scornful. But his delight is in the law of the LORD; and in his law doth he meditate day and night" (Ps. 1:1-2).

The "vanity of their mind" does not mean that they are proud. It means their minds are *empty*. The word means "emptiness; want of substance to satisfy desire; uncertainty; inanity." [96] It also means, "1) ... devoid of truth and appropriateness 2) perverseness, depravity, 3) frailty, want of vigour." [97] Their minds are empty of Biblical truth and, instead, filled with depraved and worthless thought. When God looked at men before the flood, he saw that "every imagination of the thoughts of his heart was only evil continually" (Gen. 6:5). These are general statements and are not to say that unsaved people do not sometimes have meaningful thoughts. But, let's face it. There is a lot of worthless and depraved thinking that goes on in the best human mind. When those thoughts and imaginations take place in a mind that is empty of God's thoughts from the Bible, the result is corrupt actions and foolish decisions. If you want proof of this, listen to a news telecast and compare it to the thoughts of God in the Bible.

"Having the understanding darkened" can be coupled with "ignorance" and "blindness of their heart." Many of us have seen the cartoon illustration of a light bulb turning on over the head of someone who suddenly understands. That is the picture here, except the light bulb is off and there is no understanding. An astronomer may "understand" the composition of a star or the immense distances in the universe yet have no concept of a creator. Instead he will believe that all things evolved by chance from simple to complex. He would never believe his wrist watch could have come into being without a designer and a watch maker. However, he will look at something as vastly more complex as a human body or the movements of planets in relation to the path of the sun and the galaxy, and he will believe it all happened accidently without design. Could there be a creator and a designer? He just cannot see it. He cannot see it, because his heart is blind, and his understanding is darkened. Therefore, he is ignorant. This ignorance keeps him from getting saved because he has no understanding of the gospel. They can only believe through knowledge and understanding of the gospel. No matter how highly a person has been educated, if he is unconverted, he still has a darkened understanding of the truth of God (1 Cor. 2:14). Romans 1:21 explains, "Because that, when they knew God, they glorified him not as God, neither were thankful; but became vain in their imaginations, and their foolish heart was darkened."

    They are "past feeling." That is, their feelings are dead or subdued. It is the result of having given "themselves over unto lasciviousness, to work all uncleanness with greediness." If a person is raised with strong moral teaching, he will have an active conscience. But if he frequently violates that conscience, eventually it will be dead and all feelings of guilt will also die. Past inhibitions against sin will weaken to the point where one can do many things he never thought he would. "Lasciviousness" means "Loose; wanton; lewd; lustful." [98] "Uncleanness" is "Moral impurity; defilement by sin; sinfulness" or "lewdness; incontinence." [99] This kind of behavior produces deadness inside. "But she that liveth in pleasure is dead while she liveth" (1 Tim. 5:6) and it is not limited to women. Finally, the more you get of sin and uncleanness, the more you want. Indulgence begets a desire for more indulgence. [100] You become a slave to it (Rom. 6:16). "Hell and destruction are never full; so the eyes of man are never satisfied" (Prov. 27:20). One eventually begins "to work all uncleanness with greediness." It is an addiction to sin.

But ye have not so learned Christ (Eph. 4:20-21)

> 20 But ye have not so learned Christ;
> 21 If so be that ye have heard him, and have been taught by him, as the truth is in Jesus (Eph. 4:20-21).

We certainly did not learn any of the items in verses seventeen to nineteen from Christ. We may have learned it from teachers, TV, internet, books, magazines, friends, and relatives, but we did not learn any of it from Christ. When Paul speaks of Christ, he is thinking of the risen and living Lord Jesus Christ, who opens our eyes and communicates with us in the midst of our daily lives, through the Holy Spirit (John 14:16-17) and the Word of God. The Lord Jesus Christ has redeemed us and given us a new birth (John 3:3-6). He has made us a brand new creature (2 Cor. 5:17). He has changed us and freed us from sin (Rom. 6:1-13). We do not have to yield to the temptations of that old life described in verses seventeen through nineteen.

The Process of Growth (Eph. 4:22-24)

> 22 That ye put off concerning the former conversation the old man, which is corrupt according to the deceitful lusts;
> 23 And be renewed in the spirit of your mind;
> 24 And that ye put on the new man, which after God is created in righteousness and true holiness.(Eph. 4:22-24)

The picture presented here is similar to changing clothes. You take off one set and put on another. It is not, however, a one-time change. It is more like changing one garment at a time. It is a process of putting off certain characteristics and habits of life and replacing them with new characteristics and habits. God doesn't just ask us to quit being a certain way or stop doing certain things. This could leave empty places in our lives and feelings that could end up being filled with worse things (cf. Lk. 11:24-26). No, He does not just ask us to quit and stop; He asks us to start and build. He wants us to start new behaviors, establish new attitudes, and build new habits and character in place of the old ones. Paul repeats this concept in Colossians 3:8, 12 where he says, "But now ye also put off all these; anger, wrath, malice, blasphemy, filthy communication out of your mouth ... Put on therefore, as the elect of God, holy and beloved, bowels of mercies, kindness, humbleness of mind, meekness, longsuffering." New things are modeled after the new man, Jesus Christ, who abides within us.

    Christian living and growth are not dependent on you and me alone. The Lord reminds us that we are not sufficient for these things; He alone is sufficient and we must find our sufficiency in Him (2 Cor. 3:5; 12:9). It is a joint effort, but left to ourselves it would be impossible.

    God also advises you in Ephesians 4:23 that you must "be renewed in the spirit of your mind." When I was in the Army, I ran across a booklet titled, "Your Mind Matters," by John Stott. I do not remember much of its contents, but it opened my eyes to realize that the *mind* is one of the chief keys to an obedient Christian life. You can either be carnally minded or you can be spiritually minded. To be spiritually minded is life and peace (Rom. 8:5-9). Whichever kind of mind you have, your thoughts determine your character; "as he thinketh in his heart, so is he" (Prov. 23:7). The great Romans 12 passage, where we are told to present our bodies to God as a living sacrifice (Rom. 12:1), also tells us to not be conformed to world, but "be ye transformed by the renewing of your mind" (Rom. 12:2). The renewing of our minds is the key to having our lives transformed.

So, if the renewing of our minds is a great key, how can we do this? We cannot. It can only be done by the sufficiency and the grace of God. To accomplish this, we have two things from God: the Spirit of God, along with His great power, and the Word of God. "Now the Lord is that Spirit: and where the Spirit of the Lord is, there is liberty. But we all, with open face beholding as in a glass the glory of the Lord, are changed into the same image from glory to glory, even as by the Spirit of the Lord" (2 Cor. 3:18). Who is the glory of the Lord? It is Jesus Christ (2 Cor. 4:6; Heb. 1:3). What is the glass in which we behold the glory of the Lord? It is the Word of God (James 1:23-24). As a man fills his heart with the Word of God and the Spirit helps him understand and apply it his life, his mind will be progressively renewed and he will be transformed.

> **23** For if any be a hearer of the word, and not a doer, he is like unto a man beholding his natural face in a glass:
> **24** For he beholdeth himself, and goeth his way, and straightway forgetteth what manner of man he was.
> **25** But whoso looketh into the perfect law of liberty, and continueth therein, he being not a forgetful hearer, but a doer of the work, this man shall be blessed in his deed. (James 1:23-25).

Transformation Applied to Relationships
Eph. 4:25-32

> **25** Wherefore putting away lying, speak every man truth with his neighbour: for we are members one of another.
> **26** Be ye angry, and sin not: let not the sun go down upon your wrath:
> **27** Neither give place to the devil.

28 Let him that stole steal no more: but rather let him labour, working with his hands the thing which is good, that he may have to give to him that needeth.
29 Let no corrupt communication proceed out of your mouth, but that which is good to the use of edifying, that it may minister grace unto the hearers.
30 And grieve not the holy Spirit of God, whereby ye are sealed unto the day of redemption.
31 Let all bitterness, and wrath, and anger, and clamour, and evil speaking, be put away from you, with all malice:
32 And be ye kind one to another, tenderhearted, forgiving one another, even as God for Christ's sake hath forgiven you. (Eph. 4:25-32)

This passage applies the growth principles of *putting off and putting on* to personal relationships, particularly relationships with other Christians. I nearly wrote "in the church," but these instructions apply across churches. I am to act this way, not just to the members of my own local church, but also to Christians who are outside my church. The passage covers quite a lot of ground: lying, speaking truth, being angry, but not sinning, not giving place to the devil, not stealing, laboring, giving, bad communication, good communication, bitterness, wrath, clamor, evil speaking, malice, kindness, tenderheartedness, and forgiveness. Some of these are to be put on and some are to be put off.

"Wherefore putting away lying, speak every man truth with his neighbour: for we are members one of another" (v. 4:25). This verse should be mostly self-explanatory. We are to quit lying to one another. We are to tell the truth. If I could make it any plainer, I would say that the Greek word for lying is the word that gives us *pseudo*, false. Other words that say the same are: false witness (see the Ten Commandments Ex. 20:16), deceit, slander, misleading, double-dealing, fibbing, misrepresenting, half-truth, misstating, deceptive, guileful, false, prevaricating, treacherous, untruthful, two-faced, dissimulating, tricky, etc. [101] Lying can cause great harm and hurt. "A lying tongue hateth those that are afflicted by it; and a flattering mouth worketh ruin" (Prov. 26:28). "The instruments also of the churl are evil: he deviseth wicked devices to destroy the poor with lying words, even when the needy speaketh right" (Is. 32:7). A churl is a scoundrel. [102] It is no wonder "lying lips are abomination to the LORD" (Prov. 12:22).

"Be ye angry, and sin not: let not the sun go down upon your wrath" (v. 4:26). This is a verse that I have struggled to understand. It is in the imperative, that is, command form in both English and Greek. Sometimes, we are supposed to be angry. Anger is not always wrong. There are several times that Jesus was angry. One time was when a man wanted to be healed and it was the Sabbath. The people in the synagogue watched Him to see if He would heal the man on the Sabbath. Jesus healed him, but not until "he had looked round about on them with anger, being grieved for the hardness of their hearts" (Mark 3:1-5). It is right to be angry at man's rebellion against God or against blasphemy. It is right to be angry at sin when other people are being hurt and harmed. There is a lot in society to be angry at in the best of times. Child abuse, spousal abuse, murder, terrorism, young women kidnapped from college and murdered, and so on ought to stir our blood. This is one way to be angry and "sin not;" to have the right motivation and object of your anger. One preacher wrote the following.

> The Christian is to get angry at times (Titus 1:13, Matt 23:15, 2Cor 13:2), but he is not to "sin" when he gets angry, for **"the wrath of man worketh not the righteousness of God"** and **"anger resteth in the bosom of fools"** (Ecc 7:9). Jesus was angry at nothing

but sin and angry at no one but the religious leaders of the ecumenical council of His day. His words to harlots (John 4:4-20) and beggars (Mark 10:52) were much more charitable than His words to Doctors of Law and Rabbis (Matt 23:3-30). [103]

How can we be angry and, yet, avoid sin? Perhaps it would be well to see the ways you can sin when you get angry. When Jesus exhibited righteous anger, He gave them straightforward clear truth. Look at what He told them in Mark 3:1-5. He never allowed His anger to get out of control and He rarely struck at His opponents with vicious words. He occasionally used the word "hypocrite" and one time He gave the Pharisees and Scribes a tough dressing down (Mt. 23). May God give us the wisdom when to use such words. The guide for how to deal with opponents to truth is "in meekness instructing those that oppose themselves; if God peradventure will give them repentance to the acknowledging of the truth" (2 Tim. 2:25). Sometimes the instruction must be tough.

Often, we fail to maintain the proper motive for anger. Most of our anger is directed toward someone who has wronged us (or we think they have). Most of our anger is based on personal pride. This should be avoided as much as possible. You may be angry, but you must not exacerbate the issue by hurting someone else by your anger. "There is that speaketh like the piercings of a sword: but the tongue of the wise is health" (Prov. 12:18). Self-control or temperance is a fruit of the Spirit (Gal. 5:23). To control your temper is to control your tongue, which unleashes a mighty fire (James 3:5) that can deeply wound people. The Scriptural guidelines for anger in interpersonal relationships are clear:

> **Proverbs 14:17 He that is soon angry dealeth foolishly: and a man of wicked devices is hated.**
> **Proverbs 15:1 A soft answer turneth away wrath:**

but grievous words stir up anger.
Proverbs 15:18 A wrathful man stirreth up strife: but he that is slow to anger appeaseth strife.
Proverbs 16:32 He that is slow to anger is better than the mighty; and he that ruleth his spirit than he that taketh a city.
Proverbs 19:11 The discretion of a man deferreth his anger; and it is his glory to pass over a transgression.
Proverbs 20:2 The fear of a king is as the roaring of a lion: whoso provoketh him to anger sinneth against his own soul.
Proverbs 21:14 A gift in secret pacifieth anger: and a reward in the bosom strong wrath.
Proverbs 21:19 It is better to dwell in the wilderness, than with a contentious and an angry woman.
Proverbs 22:8 He that soweth iniquity shall reap vanity: and the rod of his anger shall fail.
Proverbs 22:24 Make no friendship with an angry man; and with a furious man thou shalt not go:
Proverbs 25:23 The north wind driveth away rain: so doth an angry countenance a backbiting tongue.
Proverbs 27:4 Wrath is cruel, and anger is outrageous; but who is able to stand before envy?
Proverbs 29:22 An angry man stirreth up strife, and a furious man aboundeth in transgression.
James 1:19 Wherefore, my beloved brethren, let every man be swift to hear, slow to speak, slow to wrath:

The next statement is "let not the sun go down upon your wrath." If you are angry at someone, you have to deal with it before it robs you of a good night's rest. First confess your sin of anger and ask the Lord's help. If someone has made statements that hurt you, you need to try to solve it before the day closes (Mt. 5:23-24). If you have made someone mad and spoken hurtful words, you still ought to go to them and solve it (Mt. 18:15-18). If it is impossible to do either of these or if you are filled with anger, the verses that follow in chapter four give some advice regarding the proper attitudes. It may also help to follow the advice of the beloved preacher, Harry Ironside:

> But he said, "I am not going to sleep tonight until all that indignation is quieted down – 'Stand in awe, and sin not: commune with your own heart upon your bed, and be still.'" Just get quietly into the presence of God and you will be able to look at things from a right standpoint, and as you think of your own failures, of the many, many times that God in grace has had to forgive you, it will make you very lenient as you think of the failure of others, and instead of getting up on the judgment-seat and judging another believer, it will lead you to self-judgment and that will bring blessing, whereas the other is only harmful to your own spiritual life. [104]

The final instruction about anger is "Neither give place to the devil" (v. 4:27). Why does he say this? When we hold on to anger and nurse it, it leads to a whole list of other things like bitterness, malice, and hatred. It poisons a person's soul and the resulting attitude makes others around him miserable. When anger is allowed to fester in a church, it is easy for the devil to get in and pit people against one another. He causes angry division. Perhaps you have seen what this does in a church. I have seen it, and it is not pretty. It can make men and women, who are usually wise, look like foolish children. I once saw a church meeting (that was called to solve interpersonal problems) in which a preacher threw his Bible to the floor in anger (or utter frustration). Anger unchecked can cause the destruction of a church or a life, especially when the devil walks into the opportunity.

"Let him that stole steal no more: but rather let him labour, working with his hands the thing which is good, that he may have to give to him that needeth" (v.28). The alternative to stealing is labor, hard work. The alternative to poverty is hard work, "that he may have to give to him that needeth." The solution for those who fall into hard times is another Christian who gives. Hard times come for various reasons. It may be a lay off. It may be that no work is available. It may be that God has called you to full time service and your work is entirely ministry. You need the help of others who give. Hard times may come because of physical injury or disease. The fact is that hard times do come and any of us may fall into them. Therefore, labor so that you will have resources to give. Some of us have great excess of resources, because we have been especially wise and hard working in business. Therefore, "Charge them that are rich in this world, ... that they do good, that they be rich in good works, ready to distribute, willing to communicate" (1 Tim. 6:17-18). "If a brother or sister be naked, and destitute of daily food, and one of you say unto them, Depart in peace, be ye warmed and filled; notwithstanding ye give them not those things which are needful to the body; what doth it profit" (James 2:15-16)? "But whoso hath this world's good, and seeth his brother have need, and shutteth up his bowels of compassion from him, how dwelleth the love of God in him" (1 Jn. 3:17)?

"Let no corrupt communication proceed out of your mouth, but that which is good to the use of edifying, that it may minister grace unto the hearers" (v.29). There are two primary types of vocal communication listed here: corrupt speech and edifying speech. In the past, when I have thought of *corrupt speech,* I have thought of cussing and other foul or dirty speech. I have often wondered why there are so many professing Christians who seemingly aren't bothered by cussing.

However, corrupt speech takes in a great deal more territory than just cussing and dirty talk. Since good speech is edifying and ministers grace to the hearers, corrupt speech does just the opposite. Corrupt speech includes lying, false witness, slander, insults, rudeness, hurtful words, grievous words (Prov. 15:1), gossip, and such like. Corrupt speech can be very hurtful. "There is that speaketh like the piercings of a sword: but the tongue of the wise is health" (Prov. 12:18). Corrupt speech causes hurt, discouragement, anger, confusion, deception, and much more.

Corrupt speech even includes some "good words and fair speeches." This kind of talk can be the worst of all. "For they that are such serve not our Lord Jesus Christ, but their own belly; and by good words and fair speeches deceive the hearts of the simple" (Rom. 16:18). For an example, listen to a politician or a prosperity preacher (give to me and God will give a lot more back to you, but you have to give to *me first*). Whenever a deceiver wishes to convince people of a lie, it is almost always with a beautiful speech. The message is often filled with enough truth to make it sound plausible and true. This is the worst kind of deception. It may sound true, but it is merely half truth. *Half truth* makes it *all lie*. No matter who speaks, you must make sure it is true according to the Scriptures. Do not believe anyone unless the Scriptures verify what they say. "These were more noble than those in Thessalonica, in that they received the word with all readiness of mind, and searched the scriptures daily, whether those things were so" (Acts 17:11). God commended the Bereans, because they would not even accept the word of the great Apostle Paul at face value. They checked him out against the Scriptures.

Edifying speech is something entirely different. Edifying speech ministers "grace unto the hearers." Grace involves benefits given to a person as a free gift. Therefore, edifying speech is beneficial speech. This is a high goal. No one is perfect in their speech and they will make mistakes

(James 3:2). That doesn't mean we shouldn't try. It is a joy to speak words that build people up, encourage people, and strengthen people, impart wisdom and knowledge, and motivate. "A word fitly spoken is like apples of gold in pictures of silver" (Prov. 25:11). Edifying speech is more than preaching and teaching. It is also a kind word here or an understanding word there. Sometimes it is even a rebuke given in love. "For the commandment is a lamp; and the law is light; and reproofs of instruction are the way of life" (Prov. 6:23).

"And grieve not the holy Spirit of God, whereby ye are sealed unto the day of redemption" (v. 4:30). Since the Holy Spirit is a person with a mind, will, and feelings, He can be grieved. It causes grief to the Spirit when we do the wrong things listed in this passage. But, the things that cause Him grief are not limited to what is listed here. What we do touches the heart of God whether it is good or bad. We can grieve the Spirit, but Paul makes it clear we cannot drive Him away: "whereby ye are sealed unto the day of redemption." The Holy Spirit is the Comforter sent by the Father and the Son. "And I will pray the Father, and he shall give you another Comforter, that he may abide with you for ever" (John 14:16).

"Let all bitterness, and wrath, and anger, and clamour, and evil speaking, be put away from you, with all malice: and be ye kind one to another, tenderhearted, forgiving one another, even as God for Christ's sake hath forgiven you" (v. 4:31-32). We are all familiar with anger, wrath (excessive anger), and bitterness (deep continuing pain). These emotions are progressive. What starts out with anger becomes wrath. The more you think about *what someone did to you*, the greater your anger grows. In some cases wrath breaks out in violence. However, when no apology comes and there is no way to satisfy the anger, angry frustration grows and burrows its way deeply in the heart where it is transformed into bitterness. When there is contact, there is no good and helpful communication; there is just *clamor*. Arguing, shouting, sometimes cussing, talking over one another, that is, clamor causes great confusion. In other words, there is much evil communication. The clamor Paul is speaking of is a result of anger and bitterness of heart.

Evil speaking is from the Greek word *blasphemia*. It is a type of blasphemy against other people. In 1 Tim. 6:4, the word is translated *railing*, which means reproachful or insulting words or accusations. [105] It is lying about others or verbally wishing them to come to harm (Ps. 41:5; 1 Peter 3:6) or trying to hurt them with words. The term *verbal abuse* describes one aspect of evil speaking.

The solution to such actions, feelings, and confusion is *kindness, tenderheartedness, and forgiveness.* Two statements in Scripture help explain the situation. First, Proverbs 13:10 says, "Only by pride cometh contention: but with the well advised is wisdom." The source of anger, wrath, and bitterness is usually pride. That is, the source is self-centeredness; a heart centered on itself. Conversely, Paul tells us in Philippians 2:2-4, "Fulfill ye my joy, that ye be likeminded, having the same love, being of one accord, of one mind. Let nothing be done through strife or vainglory; but in lowliness of mind let each esteem other better than themselves. Look not every man on his own things, but every man also on the things of others."

The answer lies in a general change of attitude. Philippians 2:2-4 describes Christians who love one another. That is why there is such an emphasis in the New Testament on love. "And above all things have fervent charity among yourselves: for charity shall cover the multitude of sins" (1 Pet. 4:8). This attitude will cause us to be tenderhearted toward one another and, so, be kind in our speech and actions. Kindness will stop much anger and bitterness. "A soft answer turneth away wrath: but grievous words stir up anger" (Prov. 21:1). Only God can give us a heart that prefers others, even strangers, above ourselves. It is a divine gift.

However, I remind the reader that if you know Jesus Christ as your Savior, you have the Spirit of God within you. His power is so great that He can create the universe and raise the dead, as He did with Christ. He can change *your* heart. "The king's heart is in the hand of the LORD, as the rivers of water: he turneth it whithersoever he will" (Prov. 21:1).

The final piece of the puzzle that reconciles bitter relationships is *forgiveness*. The definition of forgiveness is "to pardon; to remit, as an offense or debt; to overlook an offense, and treat the offender as not guilty." [106] You must not focus on God changing the heart of the other person. Rather, focus on God changing your heart. Peter asked the Lord Jesus how many times he had to forgive his brother when that brother offended him and apologized. Peter suggested seven times. "Jesus saith unto him, I say not unto thee, Until seven times: but, Until seventy times seven" (Mt. 18:22). There is no limit on how many times we forgive another. Someone said, "Why should I forgive you? You'll just do it again." You forgive because the Lord said to forgive, and you forgive because the Lord forgave you.

It is certainly possible to forgive people when they are sorry and sincerely apologize. But, what if they do not apologize and they are not sorry? Should we forgive then? Of course, we should. Part of the prayer Jesus taught the disciples says, "And forgive us our sins; for we also forgive every one that is indebted to us" (Lk. 11:4). Jesus taught them to ask God for forgiveness based on how they forgive others. If you do not want God's forgiveness, then you do not have to forgive. Otherwise, forgive them regardless of their attitude. It is not easy. It takes an act of the will, confession of bitterness and anger as sin (1 Jn. 1:9), and the help of the Holy Spirit, but it is something we must have.

Perhaps one of the keys to forgiveness is found in the prayer as stated in Luke 11:4 and in Matthew 6:12, "And forgive us our debts, as we forgive our debtors." Luke asks God to forgive our *sins* as we forgive those *indebted to us*.

Matthew used the word *debt* for both sides of the ledger. If we equate the idea of sin with indebtedness, we can see that we feel someone who hurts us owes us. They owe us sorrow, shame, an apology, suffering, or other things. We are forbidden to give them suffering, because God said, "Vengeance is mine; I will repay" (Rom. 12:19). Still, we feel they owe us. Forgiveness is a release of debt. There was a time in the not too distant past, when four people banded together to hurt and harm a certain man in a worse way than anyone else had. They accomplished their goal. He felt they owed him some of the things listed above. Nevertheless, he had to forgive them and he knew it. The Lord, using prayer and Scripture, helped him a great deal. When he realized that he had to release them from any debt to him, he sought to do so. He had tried to open a door to reconciliation, but it appeared to be closed. So, He frankly released them from anything they owed him; apology, sorrow, shame, restoration, or whatever. It was not easy and was only accomplished by the inner working of the Holy Spirit. The result was relief in his soul.

    God Himself has forgiven us completely. He has released us from *our* debt to pay for *our* sins by *our* going to Hell. He loved us and Christ paid the sin debt for us. For your own sake and your future happiness, you must forgive *as He forgave you*. If God has been so merciful to you, and He has forgiven you all your debt to Him, and He has forgiven your brother for all his sins, even those he committed against you, how can you be so callous toward God as to not forgive your brother?

CHAPTER NINE

THE MORAL UNITY OF THE CHURCH
Ephesians 5:1-17

1 Be ye therefore followers of God, as dear children;
2 And walk in love, as Christ also hath loved us, and hath given himself for us an offering and a sacrifice to God for a sweetsmelling savour. (Eph. 5:1-2).

THIS SECTION (EPH. 5:1-16) IS ABOUT the Lord's moral standards. Verses 1 and 2 both look back at the previous chapter and look forward to what we are about to be told. After everything he has said about laying aside anger and bitterness and lying and the other things mentioned in the previous chapter, it is imperative that we commit ourselves to following God. To follow God means to walk in love, because God is love (1 Jn. 4:8, 16). The greatest illustration of God's love is the sacrifice that Jesus Christ made for us on the cross.

At the same time, a commitment to follow God would help Christians to successfully face the environment and conditions in which they find themselves. The Ephesians were in a city that was a cesspool of iniquity. The major religious worship of the city included many priestesses who were temple prostitutes. Today we find ourselves in similar environments. We may not have temple prostitutes, but temptations abound; pornography in books, internet, movies magazines, and TV; strip bars, prostitution, and cultural acceptance of fornication and living together. The necessity is: we must choose to avoid it, by the strength and help of God.

Let it Not be Once Named

3 But fornication, and all uncleanness, or covetousness, let it not be once named among you, as becometh saints;
4 Neither filthiness, nor foolish talking, nor jesting, which are not convenient: but rather giving of thanks.
5 For this ye know, that no whoremonger, nor unclean person, nor covetous man, who is an idolater, hath any inheritance in the kingdom of Christ and of God.
6 Let no man deceive you with vain words: for because of these things cometh the wrath of God upon the children of disobedience.
7 Be not ye therefore partakers with them. (Eph. 5:3-7).

There are three sets of triplets in these verses and they are all connected. The connections help us understand them:

3-Fornication	Uncleanness	Covetousness
4-Filthiness	Foolish talking	Jesting
5-Whoremonger	Unclean person	Covetous man

Let's get a few definitions so that we can correctly place the behaviors that are indicated by these verses. According to the *Word Study*, fornication is sexual conduct between unmarried persons and can be a general term for any sexual behavior outside the will of God. [107] The Greek word for fornication is *porneia*. If we couple that with the word for writing, *grapho*, from which we also get our word graphic, we come up with *porneia-grapho*. This is where the word *pornography* comes from; so, the word pornography means *graphic fornication.* The word *uncleanness* means not morally clean. It is the opposite of holiness (1 Thess. 4:7). *Covetousness* is to desire something, especially something God does not want you to have. To be covetous is to be an idolater (see Eph. 5:5; Col. 3:5), because you want something outside the will of God more than you want to love and obey God.

When we connect the other words with these defined words we understand how they are used here. Fornication (v. 3) is connected with "filthiness" (v. 4) and "whoremonger" (v. 5). All these are basically the same sin. The word filthiness describes a condition that seems worse than "unclean." It is a particularly dirty condition and activity before God. A whoremonger is another term for fornication. Fornication is the sin; whoremonger is an adjective describing the person who commits the sin. A whoremonger is a man and implies that the woman participating in the sin is a whore or *whorish* woman. A whorish woman is not always a woman who commits sexual sin *for pay.* The Book of Proverbs speaks of the "whorish" woman (Prov. 6:26). Although Ezekiel 16:30-32 is speaking of spiritual fornication, unfaithfulness to God, it describes a type of woman who uses her body with men who are not her husband and she does not take pay. Webster defines whorish as "lewd; unchaste; addicted to unlawful sexual pleasures." [108] We have many such women today and there is no lack of men (whoremongers) to take advantage of them.

The term *all uncleanness* (v. 3) is the same type of sin; morally unclean, worse than mere fornication (Gal. 5:19). It is connected with foolish talking (v. 4) and the unclean person (v. 5). It is easy to see how the term *unclean* can be connected with an *unclean person,* but what is the connection with *foolish talking*? If you take foolish talking out of the context, you can tie yourself in a knot trying to avoid saying frivolous statements. Keep it in the context. Foolish talking is *unclean talking.* It is to say unclean dirty things. "Wise men lay up knowledge: but the mouth of the foolish is near destruction" (Pr 10:14). "The tongue of the wise useth knowledge aright: but the mouth of fools poureth out foolishness: (Pr 15:2). Since the mouth speaks out of the heart (Mt. 12:34), "the thought of foolishness is sin" (Pr 24:9).

Finally, we come to the word *covetousness* (v. 3). In the context, this applies to sexual lust, although the word is not generally limited to that. The context of fornication and whoremongers indicates that here it is focusing on sexual lust. The other words connected with it are jesting (v. 4) and covetous man (v. 5). Once again we can easily see the connection of the sin of covetousness with a covetous man who commits the sin. What about *jesting?* It is telling a joke, but, if we are to keep it in context, the joke telling is connected with people who are filled with sexual lust. Therefore, it must be a joke that expresses sexual lust. It is what we call a *dirty joke.* Some people seem to find this hard to understand or believe. *Dirty jokes are sin*.

This type of behavior is exceedingly dangerous. God gives us several warnings about it in this passage. No whoremonger, unclean person, or covetous man who practices this behavior "hath any inheritance in the kingdom of Christ and of God" (v. 5). Do you really want to fellowship with this type of person in their actions? "Let no man deceive you with vain words: for because of these things cometh the wrath of God upon the children of disobedience" (v. 6). God is angry with the unsaved because of this kind of behavior. "Be not ye therefore partakers with them" (v. 7).

1 Thessalonians 4:3-5 commands, "For this is the will of God, even your sanctification, that ye should abstain from fornication: that every one of you should know how to possess his vessel in sanctification and honour; not in the lust of concupiscence, even as the Gentiles which know not God." The "vessel" is the body. We are commanded to know how to keep our bodies sanctified. That is, we are to control our bodies so that our physical actions are holy righteous actions.

Sexual Sin is Unwise and Dangerous

1 Corinthians 6 provides us with more reasons why we need to "flee fornication" (1 Cor. 6:18). It says:

> 14 Now the body is not for fornication, but for the Lord; and the Lord for the body.
> 15 And God hath both raised up the Lord, and will also raise up us by his own power.
> 15 Know ye not that your bodies are the members of Christ? shall I then take the members of Christ, and make them the members of an harlot? God forbid.
> 16 What? know ye not that he which is joined to an harlot is one body? for two, saith he, shall be one flesh.
> 17 But he that is joined unto the Lord is one spirit.
> 18 Flee fornication. Every sin that a man doeth is without the body; but he that committeth fornication sinneth against his own body.
> 19 What know ye not that your body is the temple of the Holy Ghost which is in you, which ye have of God, and ye are not your own?
> 20 For ye are bought with a price: therefore glorify God in your body, and in your spirit, which are God's. (1 Cor. 6:14-20)

God is the creator of the human body and, therefore, He is the creator of your body. The Psalmist said, "I will praise thee; for I am fearfully and wonderfully made: marvellous are thy works" (Ps. 139:14). The creator made your body for Himself. He did not make this fearful, wonderful, and marvelous body so it could be wasted on fornication (I Cor. 6:14). The Lord gave your body life and one day He will raise it from the dead and provide it with eternal life (1 Cor. 6:15). We owe the life of our bodies to the Lord.

So, why else is fornication so unwise and dangerous? It should be obvious to a Christian that anything God forbids is not a good thing. Certainly, for a Christian, that should be enough. However, God makes some things very clear, and there are reasons for God forbidding sexual activity outside marriage. In summary, consider the following thoughts.

First, Your "bodies are the members of Christ" (1 Cor. 6:15). A member of your body is anything that protrudes from the trunk of your body; arms. legs, head, etc. It is with these members that you perform actions and work. Our bodies are Christ's members in this world. It is through our bodies that Christ does His work. They are His instruments by which He accomplishes His plan. He can perform miracles without them, but His normal work is done through our bodies. Shall we "take the members of Christ, and make them the members of an harlot (whore)? God forbid (1 Cor. 6:15)" Shall we take instruments that are meant for the good, salvation, and happiness of others and turn them into instruments to accomplish the work of the flesh and the devil and promote evil in the world?

Second, When God brought Eve to Adam, he said of Adam and his wife that "they shall be one flesh" (Gen. 1:24). In 1Corinthians 6:16, we learn that the "one flesh" relationship is a sexual relationship. The Christian is joined to the Lord spiritually (1 Cor. 6:17) and His body is a member of Christ. Shall he or she take that body and join it sexually to a strange woman or man contrary to the will of God?

Third, there is a great danger in fornication, because "he that committeth fornication sinneth against his own body" (1 Cor. 6:18). The result of fornication can be venereal disease (sexually transmitted infections – STI's): gonorrhea, syphilis, herpes, genital warts, human papillomavirus, pelvic pain, sterility, AIDS, and more. Therefore, "flee fornication."

More than 30 different bacteria, viruses, and parasites can cause STIs. Bacterial STIs include chlamydia, gonorrhea, and syphilis among others. Viral STIs include genital herpes, HIV/AIDS, and genital warts among others. Parasitic STIs include trichomoniasis among others. While usually spread by sex, some STIs can also be spread by non-sexual contact with contaminated blood and tissues, breastfeeding, or during childbirth. STI diagnostic tests are easily available in the developed world, but this is often not the case in the developing world. [109]

Fourth, "your body is the temple of the Holy Ghost which is in you, which ye have of God, and ye are not your own ... For ye are bought with a price: therefore glorify God in your body, and in your spirit, which are God's" (1 Cor. 6:19-20). The Holy Spirit lives in saved people. He abides with us always, no matter where we go or what we do. He sees everything we do and hears everything we say and think. Your body is His dwelling place; it is His temple. Should we make His temple an instrument of uncleanness? The temple of the Holy Spirit should be holy and pure.

Ffifth, we cannot claim ownership of our bodies. The blood that Jesus Christ shed on the cross purchased our spiritual redemption and bought our physical redemption (Eph. 1:14). He bought our bodies as His possession. They are His. We do not have His permission to engage in fornication, adultery, or any other sexual sin.

Sixth, sexual sin corrupts your mind. This is especially true if you are into pornography. In God's eyes it constitutes evil imaginations (Gen. 6:5). God has said to think on things that are pure, lovely, of good report, virtuous, and worthy of praise (Phil. 4:8).

Clearly this behavior, speech, and lust is contrary to the will of God. Since "as he thinketh in his heart, so is he" (Prov. 23:7) and "out of the heart proceed ... fornications" (Mt. 15:19), this type of sin begins in the mind. God instructs us that "though we walk in the flesh, we do not war after the flesh: (For the weapons of our warfare are not carnal, but mighty through God to the pulling down of strong holds;) Casting down imaginations, and every high thing that exalteth itself against the knowledge of God, and bringing into captivity every thought to the obedience of Christ" (2 Cor. 10:3-5).

Seventh, sex was created for marriage. " Therefore shall a man leave his father and his mother, and shall cleave unto his wife: and they shall be one flesh" (Gen. 2:24). As noted above, the one flesh relationship refers to sexual intercourse. There are three elements that make a marriage: 1) a public breaking of the parent child relationship, 2) a public commitment to the new spouse, and 3) the sexual relationship. This (and this alone) creates a new family. Since sex is the final element, it was spoken of correctly in the past as "consummating the marriage." God expects a man to remain faithful to his wife sexually.

> 15 Drink waters out of thine own cistern, and running waters out of thine own well.
> 16 Let thy fountains be dispersed abroad, and rivers of waters in the streets.
> 17 Let them be only thine own, and not strangers' with thee.
> 18 Let thy fountain be blessed: and rejoice with the wife of thy youth.
> 19 Let her be as the loving hind and pleasant roe; let her breasts satisfy thee at all times; and be thou ravished always with her love.
> 20 And why wilt thou, my son, be ravished with a strange woman, and embrace the bosom of a stranger? (Prov. 5:15-20)

The cistern is one's wife and the fountains of verse 16 are children. Men are exhorted to "rejoice" with their wives and no other.

Eighth, sexual sin deadens your feelings. "But she that liveth in pleasure is dead while she liveth" (1 Tim. 5:6).

Ninth, sexual sin is exceedingly destructive. It can destroy your relationship with your spouse and lead to divorce. It can tear your family apart. It can corrupt your children. It can destroy your ministry. It can so misdirect you that you miss the will of God for your life.

Finally, sexual sin is self-centered and unloving. God's clear instruction on how to handle this type of thing includes the exhortation to walk in love. Fornication does not love others; it uses them for self-centered pleasure. Also, you are not to simply love others, you are also to love God. You are to love God "with all thy heart, and with all thy soul, and with all thy mind, and with all thy strength" (Mark 12:30). To love God means to keep His commandments (1 Jn. 5:3). That means to accept His will and do it.

In Ephesians 5:1-7, God gives us the following instructions regarding fornication:

1. "Let it not be once named among you" (v. 3).
2. Give thanks, instead of dirty talk and jokes (v. 4).
3. "Let no man deceive you" (v. 6).
4. Do not be a partaker with others in these actions and attitudes (v. 7).

Facing All the Issues

In the modern world of the twenty-first century, we have to face issues related to fornication that our fathers and grandfathers have not had to deal with extensively. These issues are not new, but they are increasingly a part of our culture. We are as bad as the old pagan Greek culture was in Paul's day, perhaps worse. We are facing issues like homosexuality, homosexual marriage, cross-dressing, transgenderism, pedophilia, beastiality, and incest. Even polygamy is now raising its ugly head. Much could be written on these subjects, but we will deal with them briefly.

We live in a day when even some "Christians" look at these things through the lens of the world's attitudes. They are ignorant of God's attitudes and Biblical truth on these matters. It's sad to say, but it's true. We will not be looking at the world's so-called "tolerant" attitudes here. The world is tolerant of many sins, but intolerant of the teachings in the Bible or anyone who declares what the Bible says. We are interested in God's attitudes and God's truth, not the world's.

Homosexuality and Homosexual Marriage

The Bible is very clear in both testaments on the subject of homosexuality. If homosexuality is wrong, then homosexual marriage is automatically wrong. I will list a few pertinent verses and make comment on them.

"Thou shalt not lie with mankind, as with womankind: it is abomination" (Lev. 18:22). No one could make a clearer statement. Homosexuality is an abomination, which means something that is extremely hated or detested. [110] God hates homosexual behavior so much that he made it punishable by execution under the Mosaic Law (Lev. 20:13).

In the New Testament, homosexuality is spoken of in Romans 1.

> **26** For this cause God gave them up unto vile affections: for even their women did change the natural use into that which is against nature:
> **27** And likewise also the men, leaving the natural use of the woman, burned in their lust one toward another; men with men working that which is unseemly, and receiving in themselves that recompence of their error which was meet. (Rom. 1:26-27)

The rebellion of man described in previous verses of Romans 1 causes God to take away His restraint on their indulgence in sin, and they go on to their destruction. The indulgence described in Romans 1 is in "vile affections." These activities are described as men leaving the natural use of women, lusting for one another, engaging in indecent behavior with one another, and even the women were involved with one another in actions which are against nature. This is a description of both gay and lesbian fornication. God considers it "vile" and "unseemly." Unseemly means indecent. [111] The term *indecent* means "unbecoming; unfit to be seen or heard; offensive to modesty and delicacy."[112]

Homosexuality was one of the reasons for the destruction of Sodom and Gomorrah in Genesis 19. Angels came to Sodom to deliver Lot and his family out of the city before its destruction (Gen. 18-19). A group of men gathered about Lot's door and demanded he send out the angels, who appeared as men, so that the men of the city could "know" them. The term *know* is Biblical idiom for sexual intercourse (Gen. 4:1). The Book of Jude comments, "Even as Sodom and Gomorrha, and the cities about them in like manner, giving themselves over to fornication, and going after strange flesh, are set forth for an example, suffering the vengeance of eternal fire" (Jude 1:7). Homosexual behavior is sin and brings down the judgment of God on those involved.

Two people of the same sex may say they are married and the government may agree, but in God's eyes they are not (see the definition of marriage above). They are not gay (a word meaning happy). Rather, as indicated before, they are filled with "vile affections." Homosexuality tears down the very foundations of an orderly society, which is built on marriage (between a man and a woman) and the family. It corrupts good morals and fills the soul with uncleanness. When homosexuality is accepted by the government, as it now is in the U. S. A., or by society in general then this saying is fulfilled in them and in their society:

> **28 And even as they did not like to retain God in their knowledge, God gave them over to a reprobate mind, to do those things which are not convenient;**
> **29 Being filled with all unrighteousness, fornication, wickedness, covetousness, maliciousness; full of envy, murder, debate, deceit, malignity; whisperers,**
> **30 Backbiters, haters of God, despiteful, proud, boasters, inventors of evil things, disobedient to parents,**
> **31 Without understanding, covenantbreakers, without natural affection, implacable, unmerciful:**
> **32 Who knowing the judgment of God, that they which commit such things are worthy of death, not only do the same, but have pleasure in them that do them. (Rom. 1:28-32).**

A reprobate mind is a mind that is thoroughly hardened against God to the point that God rejects it. How can such a mind draw true and right judgment concerning God's moral law? Few periods in history show this more than the current time in the U. S.

1 Corinthians 6:9-10 says, "Know ye not that the unrighteous shall not inherit the kingdom of God? Be not deceived: neither fornicators, nor idolaters, nor adulterers, nor effeminate, nor **abusers of themselves with mankind,** Nor thieves, nor covetous, nor drunkards, nor revilers, nor extortioners, shall inherit the kingdom of God." The phrase "abusers of themselves with mankind" comes from one Greek word, *arsenokoitēs*, which specifically means homosexuals. This word is included in a list of sinful practices, thereby identifying it as sin.

1 Corinthians 6 goes on in verse 11, " And such were some of you: but ye are washed, but ye are sanctified, but ye

are justified in the name of the Lord Jesus, and by the Spirit of our God." Notice the past tense. Some of the Corinthians *were* effeminate and homosexual. However, now that they have come to Christ, they are washed clean, sanctified, justified, and made brand new creatures (1 Cor. 5:17) by the blood and Spirit of Jesus Christ. Jesus Christ can grant recovery and transformation to a practicing homosexual, so that he or she is now operating and thinking in accordance with the nature God gave them.

Transgenderism

Transgenderism is sometimes called transsexualism or Gender Dysphoria or Gender identity disorder. It is described by one web site as "a feeling that your biological/genetic/physiological gender does not match the gender you identify with and/or perceive yourself to be. Transsexuals/transgenders often describe themselves as feeling 'trapped' in a body that does not match their true gender." [113] This is recognized by some unsaved people as a psychological disorder. In the past it would have been seen as a failure to face reality or as a failure to accept oneself. Some, who claim to have a gender identity different from their physical characteristics, have gone to an extreme and have had extensive surgery and hormone therapy that changed the appearance of their body from one sex to another.

I remind the reader, we are interested in truth. We are not interested in soothing feelings or being careful not to offend anyone. We are definitely not interested in coddling the feelings of any individual, whether they have a sincere belief or a failure to face reality. We are interested in bringing people to Biblical truth and thereby helping them to have sound minds and stable emotions.

In 1 Corinthians 6:9-10, the word E*ffeminate* is used. It is defined as a man who has "the qualities of the female sex; soft or delicate to an unmanly degree; tender; womanish." [114] This exactly describes a man or boy who feels that he is a woman inside. This word also is included in the list of sinful practices. I am forced to the conclusion that transgenderism is a mental and emotional confusion and a failure to face reality. It is also a failure to accept oneself, to love oneself. They need spiritual, mental, and emotional help from the Bible and the Spirit of God.

God created human beings to be male and female. God not only made the sexes, He also made the genetic material that makes up the human creature. Maleness and femaleness is genetically determined in the chromosomes of the developing child in the womb. A Chromosome, which is in our cells, is a DNA molecule that has all or part of the genetic material of an organism. The chromosomes of a human male and female have distinctive characteristics. The human male has a mismatched pair of one Y and one X chromosome. A human female has two X chromosomes. Maleness and femaleness is determined on a microscopic physical level. You are what your body is in that regard. What you think you are is irrelevant to the reality of what you are. You cannot change your maleness or femaleness, not even with surgery. Nothing can change DNA in this regard. God made our gender.

> 13 For thou hast possessed my reins: thou hast covered me in my mother's womb.
> 14 I will praise thee; for I am fearfully and wonderfully made: marvellous are thy works; and that my soul knoweth right well.
> 15 My substance was not hid from thee, when I was made in secret, and curiously wrought in the lowest parts of the earth.
> 16 Thine eyes did see my substance, yet being unperfect; and in thy book all my members were

written, which in continuance were fashioned, when as yet there was none of them.
17 ¶How precious also are thy thoughts unto me, O God! how great is the sum of them!
18 If I should count them, they are more in number than the sand: when I awake, I am still with thee. (Psalms 139:14-18)

God made us. He was present and watched us as we grew in the womb. He recorded all our members (arms, legs, etc.). He thought about us and His thoughts were wonderful. To reject your gender is to also reject the will and thoughts of God toward you. To reject your gender is to tell God that you were not wonderfully made. What we became in the womb effects our "reins." A person's reins are his "inward parts; the heart, or seat of the affections and passions." [115] The only healthy attitude is for each of us to accept who and what we are; the wonderful persons God made us.

The hope given to the homosexual in 1 Corinthians 6 is also given to the effeminate. Jesus Christ can straighten out the thinking and feelings of the transgender individual and grant them contentment with what God has made them by nature.

President Obama agreed with transgender thinking and tried to force schools to allow boys, who say they identify as a girl, to go into the girl's locker rooms and showers and vice-a-versa for girls who identify as boys. [116] This is nothing short of insane. Those who agree with this are clearly out of touch with reality.

A person who believes he is Napoleon has often been used as an example of a person with a psychosis. Is this not true also of someone who thinks he is a woman when in reality he is a man? Paul McHugh has been the University Distinguished Service Professor of Psychiatry at Johns Hopkins Medical School for forty years, twenty-six of which were also spent as Psychiatrist in Chief of Johns Hopkins Hospital. He has this to say about transgenderism.   Please read this paragraph all the way to its final conclusion at the end.

> A rare issue of a few men—both homosexual and heterosexual men, including some who sought sex-change surgery because they were erotically aroused by the thought or image of themselves as women—has spread to include women as well as men. Even young boys and girls have begun to present themselves as of the opposite sex. Over the last ten or fifteen years, this phenomenon has increased in prevalence, seemingly exponentially. Now, almost everyone has heard of or met such a person … The champions of this meme, encouraged by their alliance with the broader LGBT movement, claim that whether you are a man or a woman, a boy or a girl, is more of a disposition or feeling about yourself than a fact of nature. And, much like any other feeling, it can change at any time, and for all sorts of reasons … At Johns Hopkins, after pioneering sex-change surgery, we demonstrated that the practice brought no important benefits. As a result, we stopped offering that form of treatment in the 1970s …I have not met or examined Jenner, but his behavior resembles that of some of the transgender males we have studied over the years. These men wanted to display themselves in sexy ways, wearing provocative female garb. More often than not, while claiming to be a woman in a man's body, they declared themselves to be "lesbians" (attracted to other women) … First, though, let us address the basic assumption of the contemporary parade: the idea that exchange of one's sex is possible … Transgendered men do not become women, nor do transgendered women become men. All (including Bruce Jenner) become feminized men or masculinized women, counterfeits

or impersonators of the sex with which they "identify." In that lies their problematic future.

The idea that one's sex is a feeling, not a fact, has permeated our culture and is leaving casualties in its wake. Gender dysphoria should be treated with psychotherapy, not surgery. [117]

Transsexualism and homosexuality are not biological issues. They are mental, emotional, and spiritual perversions. They twist nature. Maleness or femaleness is determined by the person's DNA. "Human cells contain 23 pairs of chromosomes for a total of 46. There are 22 pairs of autosomes and one pair of sex chromosomes. The sex chromosomes are the X chromosome and the Y chromosome. These chromosomes determine gender." [118] No amount of twisted thinking or surgery will change the DNA. Therefore, sex change or sex reassignment is not possible. It is insanity. A transsexual born as a male who "marries" a male has sinned and is not married in God's sight. A homosexual who "marries" a same sex partner has sinned and is not married in God's sight.

I understand that evangelist Lester Roloff, a well-known evangelist and pastor in the mid to late twentieth century, once said that America is an insane asylum run by the inmates. Lester Roloff died in 1982. Today, things are much worse than they were then. His words are no longer adequate to describe the situation.

Cross-Dressing

Cross-dressing is a behavior that is seen more often these days. It was even exalted and made humorous (along with homosexuality) in Walt Disney's live action *Beauty and the Beast* movie. Wikipedia defined cross-dressing this way.

> **Cross-dressing** is the act of wearing items of clothing and other accoutrements commonly associated with the opposite sex within a particular society. Cross-

dressing has been used for purposes of disguise, comfort, and self-discovery in modern times and throughout history.

Almost every human society throughout history has had expected norms for each gender relating to style, color, or type of clothing they are expected to wear, and likewise most societies have had a set of guidelines, views or even laws defining what type of clothing is appropriate for each gender. [119]

God's will on this is found in Deuteronomy 22:6, "The woman shall not wear that which pertaineth unto a man, neither shall a man put on a woman's garment: for all that do so are abomination unto the LORD thy God." This is a much misapplied verse. In some Christian circles the only thing preached from this is that women should not wear pants, because pants are men's clothing. This is an unfortunate misapplication of the verse, although many of my fellow preachers would condemn me for saying so. Clothing is a cultural matter. The type of clothing worn in any society by men and women changes with time and is different between cultures. In Moses' day, men and women wore the same general *types* of garments. They both wore robes, tunics, girdles, and sandals. Women had certain distinctive types of clothing, such as veils, but otherwise their garments were different only in *detail and decoration*. Everyone knew what was man's clothing and what was women's clothing.

There was a time in Western society that women did not wear pants. That time is no more. Today men and women both wear pants and, for the most part, women's pants are different than a man's. They are different in cut and detail. For that matter, men and women both wear shirts, too (a woman's shirt is called a blouse). Women's shirts are generally different too. They button on the opposite side from a man's. Women and men also wear belts and shoes. These are the same *type* of garment for each sex, but they differ in *detail*. We should read and follow Romans 14. Many of us vary in our conviction on the *pants* issue and the Scripture says don't judge and don't try to make others conform to your conviction. Everyone "to his own master he standeth or falleth ... let every man be fully persuaded in his own mind ... why dost thou judge thy brother?" (Rom. 14:4-10).

Deuteronomy 22:5 is expressly God's condemnation of the modern practice of one sex wearing the clothing of and appearing as the opposite sex. To God it is once again a practice that He hates and detests. In almost every item of clothing, there is a distinction between men and women's clothing. Biblically speaking women are to appear as women and men are to appear as men. God made the distinctions between the sexes and they should not be blurred or erased. Those distinctions in dress and other differences are to be maintained. In his commentary David Guzik said:

> Some have taken this command to be the "proof-text" against women wearing pants and some Christian groups command that women wear only dresses. Yet, this is not a command against women wearing a garment that in some ways might be common between men and women; it is a command against dressing in a manner which deliberately blurs the lines between the sexes.
>
> The dramatic rise in cross-dressing, transvestitism, androgynous behavior, and "gender-bender" behavior in our culture is a shocking trampling of this command, and will reap a bitter harvest in more perversion and more gender confusion in our culture. This command to observe the distinction between the sexes is so important, those who fail to observe it are called **an abomination to the LORD**. This was not only because cross-dressing was a feature of pagan, idolatrous worship in the ancient world, but also because of the terrible cultural price that is paid

when it is pretended that there is no difference between men and women. [120]

Pedophilia

This refers to sex with a child. The Bible may not explicitly mention pedophilia, but there are biblical principles which apply. A survey of sex in the Bible, both its teachings and its examples, shows that God expects sex to be an activity that is restricted to adults. This is especially shown by the fact that sexual activity is restricted to marriage. One passage of Scripture that has some bearing on this issue is Ezekiel 16:7-8, where God described the timing of his marriage to Israel. He described it in terms of a man and woman.

> 7 I have caused thee to multiply as the bud of the field, and thou hast increased and waxen great, and thou art come to excellent ornaments: thy breasts are fashioned, and thine hair is grown, whereas thou wast naked and bare.
> 8 Now when I passed by thee, and looked upon thee, behold, thy time was the time of love; and I spread my skirt over thee, and covered thy nakedness: yea, I sware unto thee, and entered into a covenant with thee, saith the Lord GOD, and thou becamest mine. (Ezek. 16:7-8)

The passage doesn't give an age for marriage, but clearly describes a woman who has completed puberty and is sexually mature, physically and emotionally, ready for marriage. Children do not qualify.

Pedophilia harms children. It harms them emotional and mentally. Many times, it harms them physically. Some children who are engaged sexually in some way by an adult never recover from the harm. Jesus warned people who would do this kind of thing, "It were better for him that a millstone were hanged about his neck, and he cast into the sea, than that he should offend one of these little ones" (Lk. 17:2).

Beastiality

We will toss sex with animals into the sin trash heap with a reference to one command from the Old Testament, Leviticus 18:23, "Neither shalt thou lie with any beast to defile thyself therewith: neither shall any woman stand before a beast to lie down thereto: it is confusion."

Incest

Incest is sex between closely related people. This is another very clear issue. Sex is to remain only between married individuals. Leviticus 18:6-18 gives a list of people with whom sexual activity is forbidden by the Lord God Almighty (v. 6). This list includes father, mother, step mother, your full sister or half-sister, grand-daughter, aunt, uncle, daughter-in-law, sister-in-law, step daughter, or any other that is near kin.

Polygamy

Finally, we come to the issue of having more than one spouse. This is actually one of the more difficult issues, because the Old Testament presents several examples of godly men who had multiple wives. These include Jacob, David, Solomon (who had 700 wives and 300 concubines), and others.

However, there are several facts that indicate polygamy is not God's intended norm. The first is in Deuteronomy 17:17. God commanded the kings of Israel to not multiply wives (they disobeyed). There was a reason for this command. The king was not to have multiple wives for fear they would turn his heart away from the Lord. A wife has a very strong influence on her man.

The first woman was created in Genesis 2 from one of Adam's ribs (Gen. 2:18-25). God had given Adam the job of naming the animals. God said, "It is not good that the man should be alone; I will make him an help meet for him." God said He made Adam a "help meet," singular. God determined to give Adam one wife, not many. This certainly indicates that one wife is enough to meet the needs of lonliness. A man does not need many wives.

Finally, we will learn later in Ephesians 5 that marriage is a picture of Christ and the church. There, the church is called Christ's body (Eph. 1:22-23; 5:30). According to chapters 2 and 3 there is only one body. It makes sense then, that only a marriage with one husband and one wife is a proper picture of the relationship between Christ and the church.

Additional Instructions

8 For ye were sometimes darkness, but now are ye light in the Lord: walk as children of light:
9 (For the fruit of the Spirit is in all goodness and righteousness and truth;)
10 Proving what is acceptable unto the Lord.
11 And have no fellowship with the unfruitful works of darkness, but rather reprove them. (Eph. 5:8-11)

These verses continue the instruction begun in the previous verses:
1. "Walk as children of the light" (v. 8).
2. Prove what is acceptable to the Lord (v. 10).
3. "Have no fellowship with the unfruitful works of darkness (v. 11).

"For ye were sometimes darkness, but now are ye light in the Lord: walk as children of light." It is absolutely

The Book of Ephesians 241

essential that we know our identity! We must know who we are. We are not who we were. We were "darkness." We were sinners walking in darkness and death; the very behavior just described in verses 1-7. However, now we are new creatures. We have been born into the family of God. God is our Father and Christ is our Lord. We are children of God and God is constantly with us. The Spirit of God dwells in us and will never leave us. We are *SAINTS*. I know we don't feel like saints a lot of the time and we don't act like saints sometimes, but we are still *saints*. We are children of light in the Lord.

We are more than children of the light, we are the light of the world. Jesus is the true light of the world (Jn. 1:4, 9; 8:12; 9:5). Christians are lights in the world also. "Ye are the light of the world. A city that is set on an hill cannot be hid" (Mt. 5:14). Just as the moon shines in the night by reflecting the light of the sun, we shine as light in the darkness of this world by reflected SON light. The light of the Son of God in us shines through us into a dark world. "Let your light so shine before men, that they may see your good works, and glorify your Father which is in heaven" (Mt. 5:16).

"The fruit of the Spirit is in all goodness and righteousness and truth" (v. 9). In contrast to the wicked behavior described in the first part of this chapter, the Spirit of God produces the "fruit of the Spirit" listed in Galatians 5:22-23 in us: love, joy, peace, longsuffering, gentleness, goodness, faith, meekness, temperance. That fruit exists in goodness and righteousness and truth. These things are what should characterize our lives.

"Walk as children of the light: ... proving what is acceptable unto the Lord" (v. 10). The word "prove" means *to test and to approve*. In our walk as children of the light, we are constantly putting God's truth, wisdom, direction, principles, advice, and commands to the test. We do that by obedience. Before we obey, we believe God's wisdom is best, but in obedience we find by experience that His wisdom and ideas are better than ours. They are better for our own life. They work out better in our family relationships. They are better in all ways. However, sometimes we find that obedience gives no immediate good results (or it seems that way) or the results seem bad or we have problems and trouble. Even then, we learn that His ways are better, because they make the way we live our lives *acceptable to Him*. Ultimately, we don't obey God, because we have good results. We obey Him, *because we love Him and want to please Him*.

"And have no fellowship with the unfruitful works of darkness, but rather reprove them." Fellowship carries the idea of sharing. So, fellowship with the unfruitful works of darkness means to share in those works. We can share in sinful works by thought, word, attitude, or deed. We can think about them and get pleasure from the imaginations or we can secretly approve of some action taken by another. We can actually agree with actions taken by others, even though the actions are outside the will of God.

Our true job is to reprove the works of darkness. To reprove involves revealing blame and fault for sin. In addition to reprove, the KJV translates the Greek word as rebuke, fault, convince, and convict. Be careful, however, that you do not set about to reprove the world with a condescending arrogant attitude. "I would never smoke. It's a sin!" "Wow! Are you ever a sinner to do that!" "What a liar you are!" These may be somewhat exaggerated examples, but if you approach someone with an arrogant, holier than thou attitude, you will drive them away from the gospel. Remember that you used to be darkness. It is only by God's grace that you are different now. It is far better to approach people (on an individual level, preaching requires a different approach) with a soft humility and give them a clear witness of the gospel. One way to do that is with a personal testimony. Tell them what God has done for you like Paul did in Acts 26: what I was before I was saved (Acts 26:1-11); How the Lord saved me (Acts 26:12-18); what the Lord has done for me since I was saved (Acts 26:19-21); and include a clear presentation the gospel and how to be saved (Acts 26:22-23).

> **12 For it is a shame even to speak of those things which are done of them in secret.**
> **13 But all things that are reproved are made manifest by the light: for whatsoever doth make manifest is light.**
> **14 Wherefore he saith, Awake thou that sleepest, and arise from the dead, and Christ shall give thee light. (Eph. 5:12-14)**

"For it is a shame even to speak of those things which are done of them in secret." We must not partake of the sins people do and we ought not to sit around talking about them. The Lord is not saying that these things can never be mentioned, sometimes it may be necessary. However, as we have already noted, the mouth speaks out of the treasure of the heart and someone who enjoys talking of these things has the wrong treasure in his heart. His treasure is rusty. Not only that, but his thoughts are not entirely subject to Christ; "bringing into captivity every thought to the obedience of Christ" (2 Cor. 10:5).

"But all things that are reproved are made manifest by the light: for whatsoever doth make manifest is light." The fact that we are light in the world means that we will do more than just show what the will of God is (see above). It also means we will reprove the world by the way we live and by the words we speak. The Light is within us and is the Lord Jesus Christ. We cannot separate ourselves from it and, it will have its effect.

"Wherefore he saith, Awake thou that sleepest, and arise from the dead, and Christ shall give thee light." This "wake up call" is the natural follow up to the previous verse. He is speaking to Christians here not the unsaved. Look, you are saved and you are light in the world. The world is filled with darkness and you are tempted to partake of it. But, it's a sin to partake and a shame to talk about it. You are light in the world and you ought to be reproving the darkness. Wake up! Get yourself separated from the darkness and stand up for Christ in the world! Show by your life and words that Christ is real and different from the world. When you do this you will also find the light of Christ shining in your soul. "Restore unto me the joy of thy salvation; and uphold me with thy free spirit" (Ps. 51:12).

> **15 See then that ye walk circumspectly, not as fools, but as wise,**
> **16 Redeeming the time, because the days are evil.**
> **17 Wherefore be ye not unwise, but understanding what the will of the Lord is.**
> **(Eph. 5:15-17).**

"See then that ye walk circumspectly, not as fools, but as wise." Another response we should have to all that the Lord has shown us in verses one through fourteen is to be wise and walk circumspectly. The Greek word for *circumspectly* is translated two other ways : *diligently* and *perfect*. It means "Cautious; prudent; watchful on all sides; examining carefully all the circumstances that may affect a determination, or a measure to be adopted." [121] That is why it is connected with wisdom, walk "as wise." "Be sober, be vigilant; because your adversary the devil, as a roaring lion, walketh about, seeking whom he may devour: whom resist stedfast in the faith" (1 Pet. 5:8-9). "He that handleth a matter wisely shall find good: and whoso trusteth in the LORD, happy is he" (Prov. 16:20). We all want to be happy. Here is the secret to happiness. Be circumspect in all matters in your life and handle them with wisdom.

How do you get wisdom? Wisdom involves "sound judgment and good sense." [122] Remember, "happy is the man that findeth wisdom, and the man that getteth understanding" (Prov. 3:13). "Wisdom is the principal thing; therefore get wisdom: and with all thy getting get understanding" (Prov. 4:7). Wisdom is riches beyond compare. Wisdom fills your life with good things. "For wisdom is better than rubies; and all the things that may be desired are not to be compared to it" (Prov. 8:11). "So teach us to number our days, that we may apply our hearts unto wisdom" (Ps. 90:12).

You need wisdom and, if you want it, wisdom results from both an *attitude* and an *activity*. "The fear of the LORD is the beginning of wisdom: a good understanding have all they that do his commandments: his praise endureth for ever" (Ps. 111:10; see Prov. 9:10). This is the necessary *attitude*. Wisdom begins with the fear of the Lord as does knowledge (Prov. 1:7). The fear of the Lord leads us to depart from evil (Prov. 3:7). That is the essence of wisdom, obedience to God's will. There is a fountain that flows with wisdom and is open to those who seek it. Diligent searching and seeking is the *activity* that fills us with all three of the great virtues of the Book of Proverbs: wisdom, understanding, and knowledge. Seeking wisdom begins with prayer (Prov. 2:3). Then you have to come to the fountain of all wisdom: "For the LORD giveth wisdom: out of his mouth cometh knowledge and understanding. He layeth up sound wisdom for the righteous: he is a buckler to them that walk uprightly" (Prov. 2:6-7). Wisdom is found in the words of God's mouth (Mt. 4:4). Those words are in the Bible, the Words of God. You must "incline thine ear unto wisdom, and apply thine heart to understanding" (Prov. 2:2) and "if thou seekest her as silver, and searchest for her as for hid treasures; then shalt thou understand the fear of the LORD, and find the knowledge of God" (Prov. 2:4-5). We must incline our ears, apply our hearts, seek as for silver, and search as for hid treasures out of the Book of God, the Bible. That is where we will find all the wisdom we need.

"Redeeming the time, because the days are evil" (v. 5:16) is a participial phrase describing the previous command to walk circumspectly. Walking in wisdom requires that we use our time wisely. To do that, we must understand "what the will of the Lord is" (v. 5:17). To repeat, the only way you will ever understand the will of the Lord and use your time wisely or do anything else wisely is to study His words in His book! You have to get into the Bible.

The next verse in Ephesians five (v. 18) gives us the ultimate key to living an obedient Christian life, the filling of the Holy Spirit. We will look at that in the next chapter.

CHAPTER TEN

THE FILLING OF THE SPIRIT FOR THE CHURCH
Ephesians 5:18

And be not drunk with wine, wherein is excess; but be filled with the Spirit; Speaking to yourselves in psalms and hymns and spiritual songs, singing and making melody in your heart to the Lord; Giving thanks always for all things unto God and the Father in the name of our Lord Jesus Christ (Eph. 5:18).

YEARS AGO, SHORTLY AFTER I WAS SAVED, I was a member of the youth group in my local church. There were a couple of us in that group, who were called to preach. Sometimes we had an opportunity to preach in the youth meetings. Sometimes we had free discussions. During such a discussion, one of the girls said (the best I can remember), "We are always told what we should do, but we're never told how." Over the years, I have remembered those words as one of the most significant statements I have ever heard. How true it is! There is, of course, no other way to do what is right except with the help of the Holy Spirit.

However, explanations of the work of the Holy Spirit in our lives sometimes tend to be anything but practical. Theological definitions and declarations often leave few clues as to how we can appropriate the power of the Holy Spirit in our lives. At the same time, practical applications may avail little, when there are foundational truths we must know first.

Having just given a long list of do's and do not's starting in Ephesians 4:1, where Paul says to walk worthy of our vocation, he tells us how to do it in Ephesians 5:18. Although, he is not finished with his exhortations and commands, he interjects one verse with the key to it all, "be filled with the Spirit." What follows this command is a series of further commands and statements that show how being filled with the Holy Spirit will thoroughly change our lives.

All of the practical instructions Paul has given in chapters four and five are built upon the solid and firm foundation of a relationship with God through the Lord Jesus Christ. He has chosen and predestinated us (1:4-5), He has given us grace (1:6-8), He has made us accepted in Christ, the Beloved One (1:6), He has sealed us (1:13), and He has given us the earnest of the Spirit (1:14). Even with all these blessings, we need something more. We need to be filled with the Holy Spirit.

What Spirit Filling is NOT

There are a number of misconceptions about being filled with the Spirit. These misconceptions are frequently based on the experience of famous Christians, rather than the Scriptures. For example, I heard the testimony of Dr. Jack Hyles a number of years ago. His testimony was about his long time seeking and begging God until he had a wonderful tremendous spiritual experience. I do not question his experience, but experience, anyone's experience, is not our authority. What we need to know is the Word of God on the matter. The Scriptures are the final authority and it is to them we must look, not to experience.

The key to being filled with the Spirit is not in tarrying and waiting. The experience of the first group of Christians in Jerusalem in Acts 2 could mistakenly be understood as the norm for believers. Jesus promised that the Holy Spirit would come to them.

> **4** And, being assembled together with them, commanded them that they should not depart from Jerusalem, but wait for the promise of the Father, which, saith he, ye have heard of me.
> **5** For John truly baptized with water; but ye shall be baptized with the Holy Ghost not many days hence. (Acts 1:4-5)

When the Holy Spirit came a few days latter, "they were all filled with the Holy Ghost" (Acts 2:4). Yes, they were told to wait and, yes, they spent the time in prayer. But, why did they have to wait? As we have noted before, Acts 2 was the birthday of the church, because they were not only filled with the Spirit, they were also baptized by the Spirit into the body of Christ. In His sovereign will, God had chosen the day of Pentecost to be that birthday. When Jesus promised the Spirit in Acts 1, He had been with them for forty days (Acts 1:3). Pentecost was fifty days after Passover (Lev. 23), therefore it was still several days until Pentecost. They simply waited those days until God's appointed day. There was nothing special about the waiting.

The key to being Spirit filled is not in pleading and begging. We are never commanded to pray for the filing of the Spirit, although we may. We are to pray for things that come to us through the Spirit's ministry in our lives, such as strength (see Eph. 1). That strength comes by the filling of the Spirit. But, if we do pray for the filling, God is ready to respond. Note the words of Jesus Christ.

> **If ye then, being evil, know how to give good gifts unto your children: how much more shall your heavenly Father give the Holy Spirit to them that ask him? (Luke 11:13)**

Do you want to ask the Lord for the filling of the Spirit? Go right ahead. Jesus made it clear that God is eager and ready to give it. However, the thing that may be more important is to pray for your own willingness to yield to God's will.

The filling of the Spirit is often given spontaneously as God's response to a new need, without anyone asking for it. When Paul and Barnabas left Antioch on the first missionary journey, they first preached to the Roman deputy Sergius Paulus on Cyprus, they were opposed by the sorcerer, Elymas. Paul was immediately filled with the Spirit and spoke thus to Elymas.

> **9** Then Saul, (who also is called Paul,) *filled with the Holy Ghost,* set his eyes on him,
> **10** And said, O full of all subtilty and all mischief, thou child of the devil, thou enemy of all righteousness, wilt thou not cease to pervert the right ways of the Lord?
> **11** And now, behold, the hand of the Lord is upon thee, and thou shalt be blind, not seeing the sun for a season. And immediately there fell on him a mist and a darkness; and he went about seeking some to lead him by the hand.
> **12** Then the deputy, when he saw what was done, believed, being astonished at the doctrine of the Lord. (Acts 13:9-12)

We can and should ask God for anything we need. In fact, we are encouraged to do so (Phil. 4:1-5). However, the filling of the Spirit does not require days and days of pleading and begging God to get some special experience of being filled. Remember, "Ask, and it shall be given you; seek, and ye shall find; knock, and it shall be opened unto you (Matt. 7:7) "And whatsoever ye shall ask in my name, that will I do, that the Father may be glorified in the Son. If ye shall ask any thing in my name, I will do it" (John 14:13-14).

The filling of the Holy Spirit does not necessarily come with a special emotional spiritual experience. The purpose of the filling of the Spirit is enablement to live a holy life of obedience to God, to have the fruit of the Spirit (Gal. 5:22-23), and to have effective service and good works for His glory (John 15:1-8). There is no consistent momentous emotional experience connected with Spirit filling in the New Testament. The Bible says the fruit of the Spirit includes love and joy, but that is experienced often in the daily Spirit filled walk of a Christian.

The filling of the Spirit is not sudden spiritual maturity or perfection. To be filled with the Spirit means enablement to live an obedient Christian life and to serve Him, but we still must go through the spiritual growth process. "As newborn babes, desire the sincere milk of the word, that ye may grow thereby" (1 Peter 2:2). "But grow in grace, and in the knowledge of our Lord and Saviour Jesus Christ. To him be glory both now and for ever. Amen" (2 Peter 3:18).

The filling of the Spirit is not the initial receiving of the Spirit upon salvation through faith. As we have seen, the Holy Spirit does several things when one receives Christ (John 1:12). He gives the new birth (John 3:1-5; Titus 3:5). He baptizes the believer into the body of Christ (1 Cor. 12:13). He seals the believer (Eph. 1:13-14). He also comes to dwell in the believer forever (John 14:16; Rom. 8:9). None of these is the same as being filled with the Spirit.

Do Not be Drunk with Wine

Ephesians 5:18 starts out with a clear command not to be drunk with wine. In order to understand what Spirit filling is and how to get it, we must start with this. Drunkenness is advised against and condemned throughout Scripture (Prov. 20:1; 21:17; 23:29-31; Is. 5:22; 28:1-7; Joel 1:5) and strong drink is also warned against (Is. 5:11, 22; Is. 28:7; Is. 56:12).

Alcohol is precisely the same thing in the wine that it is in the brandy after it is distilled; in the cider or the beer that it is in the whisky or the rum; and why is it right to become intoxicated on it in one form rather than in another? Since therefore there is danger of intoxication in the use of wine, as well as in the use of ardent spirits, why should we not abstain from one as well as the other? [123]

Why shouldn't we be drunk with wine (or strong drink)? Because in doing so there is "excess." The Greek word for "excess", *asotia*, is used three times in the New Testament, here and Titus 1:6 and 1 Peter 4:4. In both of the latter two verses, the word is translated *riot*. Titus 1:6 connects it with *unruly*. According to Vine, the word means, "prodigality, profligacy… 'lasciviousness, outrageous conduct, wanton violence.'" [124] Even if a person does not generally live an outrageous lifestyle, being drunk can cause him to act in such a way. John Gill, in his commentary, says:

> It hurts the mind, memory, and judgment; deprives of reason, and sets a man below a beast; it brings diseases on the body, and wastes the estate; it unfits for business and duty; it opens a door for every sin, and exposes to shame and danger; and therefore should be carefully avoided, and especially by professors of religion. [125]

Rather be Filled with the Spirit

So, what does being drunk have to do with being filled with the Spirit? Why does Paul contrast the two? Being drunk affects and influences a person. The Scriptures make this clear.

> **29 ¶Who hath woe? who hath sorrow? who hath contentions? who hath babbling? who hath wounds without cause? who hath redness of eyes?**

30 They that tarry long at the wine; they that go to seek mixed wine.
31 Look not thou upon the wine when it is red, when it giveth his colour in the cup, when it moveth itself aright.
32 At the last it biteth like a serpent, and stingeth like an adder.
33 Thine eyes shall behold strange women, and thine heart shall utter perverse things.
34 Yea, thou shalt be as he that lieth down in the midst of the sea, or as he that lieth upon the top of a mast.
35 They have stricken me, shalt thou say, and I was not sick; they have beaten me, and I felt it not: when shall I awake? I will seek it yet again.
(Proverbs 23:29-35).

The basic concept seems to be one of influence and control. Being drunk causes a person to say things they normally wouldn't, it causes a person to think differently, it causes a change in behavior, it causes sorrow, and it can be addictive. It influences and changes your behavior, thinking, and feelings. Being filled with the Spirit has similar results. It causes us to speak, think, and act differently. It causes a change in emotion except, instead of sorrow, it gives joy (Acts 13:52). In each case, the cause is something other than you. In one case it is alcohol; in the other case, it is the Spirit of God. The key words are *control and influence.* Who controls you? Is it alcohol? Is it the Spirit? Or, is it simply *self*? Control and influence are the issues.

The filling of the Spirit is not optional. It is not automatic, but, rather, Eph. 5:18 is a command to be obeyed. This shows that it is not optional. If God demands it, we must obey. In fact, the filling of the Spirit is absolutely necessary if we are to live the Christian life. "This I say then, Walk in the Spirit, and ye shall not fulfil the lust of the flesh. For the flesh lusteth against the Spirit, and the Spirit against the flesh: and these are contrary the one to the other: so that ye cannot do the things that ye would (Gal. 5:16-17). To live in holiness and obedience, we must "walk in the Spirit," making a Spirit filled life an absolute necessity. However, being filled with the Spirit is not automatic. We are born again by the Spirit, sealed by the Spirit, baptized by the Spirit, and indwelt by the Spirit immediately and automatically when we believe the gospel. But, this is not true of being filled with the Spirit. There are conditions. John Walvoord, in his book *The Holy Spirit*, says:

> While all men are commanded to obey the Gospel and believe in Christ unto salvation, no one is ever exhorted to be born again by any effort of the flesh, or exhorted to be indwelt, or sealed, or baptized by the Spirit. These ministries of the Spirit come at once upon saving faith in Christ. They pertain to salvation, not to the spiritual life of the Christian. Christians are, however, commanded to be filled with the Spirit. [126]

The filling of the Spirit may also be repeated. The filling of the Spirit is mentioned several times in the Book of Acts. Peter was filled with the Holy Spirit on the day of Pentecost (Acts 2:4) and again in Acts 4:8 and again in Acts 4:31. Paul was filled with the Spirit in Acts 9:17 and again in Acts 13:9. The filling of the Spirit is an experience that relates to all of life and service for the Lord. As such the experience is a repeated experience. If we have lost our Spirit filling, we will need it again. When new challenges confront us, we may need a filling of the Spirit for that need (Acts 4:23-31).

The Conditions for Being Filled with the Spirit

The conditions necessary to be filled with the Spirit are to be yielded to God and live in moment by moment dependence on Him. John Walvoord says this about being yielded to God.

> Every historic instance of the filling of the Spirit illustrates the principle that only Christians yielded to God are filled ... It is, of course, impossible for any Christian to be filled with the Spirit simply by willing it. The Scriptural conditions for this fullness are revealed. It is the responsibility of the Christian to meet these conditions of yieldedness. The fullness of the Spirit will inevitably result ... No Christian can be said to be in the will of God unless he is filled with the Spirit. It is a universal responsibility as well as a privilege, extending equally to all Christians, but never addressed to the unsaved. [127]

God has made us free to yield and obey, thereby providing all that is necessary to be filled with the Spirit. We went over this briefly in chapter 7, under the heading "One Baptism." I will summarize these foundational truths found in Romans 5, 6, 7, 8, and 12 here.

As explained in Romans 5, we are all descendants of Adam. As such we have inherited death and we have inherited a sinful nature (Rom. 5:12). Romans 5 ends with these words, "That as sin hath reigned unto death, even so might grace reign through righteousness unto eternal life by Jesus Christ our Lord (Rom. 5:21-22). Up to that point in Romans, we learned that the entire world has gone wrong (Rom. 1), both Jews and Gentiles are in a state of sinful defeat (Rom. 2), the entire world is in the depths of depravity (Rom. 3), and man can be righteous only through faith in Jesus Christ (Rom. 4). To this end, Jesus Christ paid for our sins by His death on the cross and He did this in view of the fact that we are condemned through sin inherited from Adam (Rom. 5). Chapter five closes with the ray of hope in verses 21-22. As sin has reigned in our past, God's grace can reign in our future!

Romans 6 opens with an assurance that living a righteous life is a possibility and hints at the reason why, "What shall we say then? Shall we continue in sin, that grace may abound? God forbid. How shall we, that are dead to sin, live any longer therein?" (Rom. 6:1, 2). Romans 6 goes on to explain things that happened to us when we received Christ. First, we were baptized *into* His death (verse 3). This can only be the baptism of the Spirit, because no water on earth can put us *into* His death. Verse 4 tells us that just as He rose from the dead we can now live in newness of life. How is this so? First, it is because we were born again. Second, it is because we died in Him when He died and he who is dead is *free from sin* (Rom. 6:6-7). The control of the flesh is broken! It is now possible to live for Christ. In view of this, we are commanded to do three things in verses 11-13, 1) recon ourselves to be dead to sin and alive to God, 2) do not let sin reign in our mortal bodies, and 3) yield to God, not to sin. The whole thing begins with considering ourselves to be dead and free from sin. We have to know that we are capable, by the grace of God, of living an obedient life. We may look at ourselves and think there is no way it can be true. When God says we are dead to sin and alive to God, it may seem foreign to our actual experience, but we must believe it because God says it. It is true whether we feel it or not. It is true, whether we believe it or not. We must accept this. Romans six gives us that basis for walking in the Spirit.

Romans 7 describes the conflict that continues to go on within us, because our flesh still desires sin. Our personal strength in not enough. Then Romans 8 declares that obedience depends on the fact that Jesus Christ lives within us and that the righteousness of the law can be fulfilled within us through Him. We can be obedient by His strength (Phil. 4:13).

The yielded life begins with an initial dedication spoken of in Romans 12:1-2. The first step is dedicating myself to the will to God. This is a point of dedication to which every Christian needs to come. It is described in Romans 12:1, "I beseech you therefore, brethren, by the mercies of God, that ye present your bodies a living sacrifice, holy, acceptable unto God, which is your reasonable service." Each of us must come to a point of decision. Will you live your whole life, the rest of your life, completely to the will of God? Shall His will be more important than your own? Will Christ be more important than your husband or your wife or any friend and what they want? Paul said, "For me to live is Christ..." (Phil. 1:21).

Charles Ryrie, in *Balancing the Christian Life,* says there are two aspects to walking in the Spirit; initial dedication (Rom. 12:1-2) and daily yielding and trust.

> Yieldedness includes both the initial, crises, complete act of dedication ... and a daily walk in dependence on the power of the Spirit .. the Christian walk can be done successfully only by constant dependence on the Holy Spirit's control over one's life. To be Spirit-filled, then, is to be Spirit controlled. And to be thus controlled requires the yieldedness of a dedicated life and of a daily dependence on the power of the Spirit. [128]

The next verse in Romans 12:2 says, "And be not conformed to this world: but be ye transformed by the renewing of your mind, that ye may prove what is that good, and acceptable, and perfect, will of God." This speaks of a process following the initial dedication of verse one. To be continually conformed to the will of God requires a continuous yielding to God. Before, the will was a slave to the flesh, now it is free. It is free to yield to God. We are also free from Satan. God has delivered us from the power of darkness and put us into the Kingdom of His dear Son (Col. 1:13), where we are free to live a life of victory over sinful flesh and the attacks of the devil. It is not necessary to yield to sin. We can yield to God.

Walking in the Spirit

"Walk in the Spirit, and ye shall not fulfil the lust of the flesh" (Gal. 5:16). Being filled with the Spirit is necessary to walk in the Spirit. To walk in the Spirit means to follow the lead of the Spirit by the enabling power of the Spirit (Gal. 5:18). Paul expresses it elsewhere as "walk after the Spirit" (Rom. 8:1), "through the Spirit do mortify the deeds of the body" (Rom. 8:14), "led by the Spirit of God" (Rom. 8:14), "to be spiritually minded is life and peace" (Rom. 8:6), and "work out your own salvation with fear and trembling. For it is God which worketh in you both to will and to do of his good pleasure" (Phil. 2:12-13).

What does it mean to be led by the Spirit? Does it mean the Spirit regularly whispers in our ears to go right or left? Not at all. I do not mean that God never actively works in our hearts, but that the guidance of the Spirit is always in accord with the Word of God and, if we want the Spirit's guidance, we must seek it there.

Walking in the Spirit is a life of battle. Gal. 5:16-17 makes it clear that there is a conflict going on inside of us. The flesh, our sinful human nature, desires to be free from the will of God and to do things contrary to the will of God. A list of those things the flesh lusts for is found in Galatians 5:19-21. This flesh is in every Christian; it is a part of us. Yet, there is a part of each of us that always wants to do the will of God. We know that our spirit has been born again (John 3:6) and the Holy Spirit dwells in us. So, part us desires to do the will of God and part of us desires to commit sin. This is the battle that must be won by the power of the Spirit who lives in us. This battle will never end until this life is over. The battle will not end, but we can still walk in daily obedience.

Walking in the Spirit is a life of faith, depending on God. The filling of the Spirit may depend on yielding to God, but it also requires trusting God. As said above, the benefits listed in Colossians 1:9-13, quoted above, come to us through prayer. Prayer is always based on trust in God. Ask God for what you need (James 1:5-6). The Christian life is a life of dependence on the Spirit of God in all aspects and circumstances of life. We trust God's commands and promises (2 Pet. 1:4-5).

Walking in the Spirit is a life of strength and power. In Colossian 1:11, Paul prayed that they would be strengthened with all might. This "might" is described in the prayer of Ephesians 1:19-20 and 3:16 as the power He exhibited when He raised Jesus from the dead and made Him sit at His own right hand. This is the Spirit's power that is working in us (Eph. 3:20) and strengthening us (Eph. 3:16). In his book, The Pursuit of Holiness, Jerry Bridges said this about strength.

> This is the first implication we should grasp of being 'alive to God.' We are united with the One who is at work in us to strengthen us with His mighty power. We have all known the awful sense of hopelessness caused by sin's power...But we are alive to God, united to Him who will strengthen us. By reckoning on this fact-counting it to be true-we will experience the strength we need to fight that temptation.[129]

It is the strength of the Holy Spirit that enables us to overcome the flesh and temptation. When we battle with only our own strength we experience the defeat Paul described, "For the good that I would I do not: but the evil which I would not, that I do. Now if I do that I would not, it is no more I that do it, but sin that dwelleth in me" (Romans 7:19-20). Yet, with Christ's strength, we can obey Him. "I can do all things through Christ which strengtheneth me" (Phil. 4:13). With the filling of the Spirit comes God's strength and enablement. When we are defeated and we cry out to God for help, His answer is the filling of the Spirit. In that power, we are more than conquerors.

Walking in the Spirit involves the mind as a major place of battle and transformation. Romans 12:1-2 says you must be "transformed by the renewing of your mind." The devil fights for possession of the mind also. Therefore, the renewing of the mind involves a battle of its own.

> **3** For though we walk in the flesh, we do not war after the flesh:
> **4** (For the weapons of our warfare are not carnal, but mighty through God to the pulling down of strong holds;)
> **5** Casting down imaginations, and every high thing that exalteth itself against the knowledge of God, and bringing into captivity every thought to the obedience of Christ;
> **6** And having in a readiness to revenge all disobedience, when your obedience is fulfilled. (2 Cor. 10:3-6)

God expects obedience in our thinking as well as our acting. We need to bring "into captivity every thought to the obedience of Christ." As stated before, it is so important that Proverbs indicated *we are what we think.* "For as he thinketh in his heart, so is he" (Prov. 23:7). Peace comes to him whose mind is stayed on Christ (Is. 26:3). In fact, we are to love God with all our minds (Mt. 22:37). Since loving Christ means keeping His commandments (John 14:21), then loving God with all the mind means to obey Him and trust Him with all our thoughts. Paul outlined the thoughts we are to think in Philippians 4:8.

> **Finally, brethren, whatsoever things are true, whatsoever things are honest, whatsoever things are just, whatsoever things are pure, whatsoever things are lovely, whatsoever things are of good report; if there be any virtue, and if there be any praise, think on these things. (Phil. 4:8)**

Walking in the Spirit is a life of responsibility. Some have thought of the Spirit-filled life as a life that Christ lives through us without our effort. "Stop trying and start trusting." This is not the picture given in the Scriptures. It is God who works in us to will and to do, but it is our responsibility to work out our own salvation in practical everyday living (Phil. 2:12-13). The deeds of the flesh are put to death through the Spirit, but it is we who put them to death (Rom. 8:13). God is the only one who saves people (John 1:12), but it is we who do the preaching, witnessing, and giving out tracts (Rom. 10:14-15; 1 Cor. 1:15). Sometimes we think in terms of God giving us the victory over our sins. The truth is that He has already provided the victory and the tools to obtain it. We ought to seek not only victory, but more so obedience. We do that through the Spirit He has given us. See further the advice of Hebrews 12:1 and James 4:7. The only way we can do this is with the power of the Spirit, but it is we who do it.

> God's provision for us consists in delivering us from the reign of sin, uniting us with Christ, and giving us the indwelling Holy Spirit to reveal sin, to create a desire for holiness, and to strengthen us in our pursuit of holiness. Through the power of the Holy Spirit and according to the new nature He gives, we are to put to death the misdeeds of the body (Romans 8:13).
>
> Though it is the Spirit who enables us to put to death our corruptions, yet Paul says this is our action as well. The very same work is from one point of view the work of the Spirit, and from another the work of man ...
>
> It is clear from this passage (Rom. 8:13-author) that God puts responsibility for living a holy life squarely on us. [130]

After exhorting Christians not to be unequally yoked to unbelievers, Paul said, "Having therefore these promises, dearly beloved, *let us cleanse ourselves* from all filthiness of the flesh and spirit, perfecting holiness in the fear of God" (2 Cor 7:1). Notice the command to cleanse *ourselves*. That command is based on promises he gave us in 2 Corinthians 6. What are these promises? God promises that he will receive us and be our God and Father and we will be His children (2 Cor. 6:16-18). Furthermore, God promises to dwell in us and *walk in us.* God doesn't leave us alone in the effort to live right. He wants us to walk in holiness, but He has promised to walk in us at the same time, just as Philippians 2:12-13 says. Jerry Bridges further explains:

> During a certain period in my Christian life, I thought that any effort on my part to live a holy life was "of the flesh" and that "the flesh profits for nothing." I thought God would not bless any effort on my part to live the Christian life, just as He would not bless any effort on my part to become a Christian by good works. Just as I received Christ Jesus by faith, so I was to seek a holy life only by faith. Any effort on my part was just getting in God's way. I misapplied the statement, "Ye shall not need to fight in this battle: set yourselves, stand ye still, and see the salvation of the LORD" (2 Chron. 20:17-KJV substituted in quote), to mean that I was just to turn it over to the Lord and He would fight the sin in my life ... How foolish I was. I misconstrued dependence on the Holy Spirit to mean I was to make no effort, that I had no responsibility. [131]

While we "walk by faith" it must be balanced with the fact that God has made provision for us to live a holy life and the Holy Spirit dwells in us to provide all we need to do so. Dr. Martyn Lloyd-Jones says:

> The Holy Spirit is in us; He is working in us, and empowering us, giving us the ability ... This is the New Testament teaching - "Work out your own salvation with fear and trembling." We have to do so. But note the accompaniment - "Because it is God that

worketh in you, both to will and to do of His good pleasure"! The Holy Spirit is working in us "both to will and to do," It is because I am not left to myself, it is because I am not "absolutely hopeless," since the Spirit is in me, that I am exhorted to work out my own salvation with fear and trembling. [132]

I can do all things through Christ which strengtheneth me. (Phil. 4:13)

Walking in the Spirit involves changing ingrained habits. Colossians 3:8, 12 says to "put off all these" followed by a list and "put on therefore" followed by another list. We have built sinful habits over the years. For example, some who have been newly born again may have a problem with anger. They have to learn to keep their anger in check and display kindness and meekness. Some have a problem with habitual filthy language, for example. They need to learn to speak words of truth, kindness, purity, and grace. This is a process that the Holy Spirit leads us through. He enables to us to make the changes.

The Basics of Walking in the Spirit

There are basic elements through which the power of God flows into our lives. These are activities which have been present in the lives of believers from the earliest days of the church. They are all outlined in Acts 2:41-42, 47.

41 Then they that gladly received his word were baptized: and the same day there were added unto them about three thousand souls.
42 And they continued stedfastly in the apostles' doctrine and fellowship, and in breaking of bread, and in prayers.
47 Praising God, and having favour with all the people. And the Lord added to the church daily such as should be saved. (Acts 2:41-42, 47)

We have already noted that being filled and walking in the Spirit requires a dedicated and yielded heart, soul, and mind. It requires daily submission to Christ and daily dependence on Him. The necessary basic elements through which the power of the Spirit flows into us listed in Acts 2 are the Word of God ("the Apostle's doctrine"), prayer, fellowship, and witnessing ("the Lord added to the church daily such as should be saved"). All these elements are necessary for the corporate life of the church and for the life of the individual. They can be pictured as illustrated below.

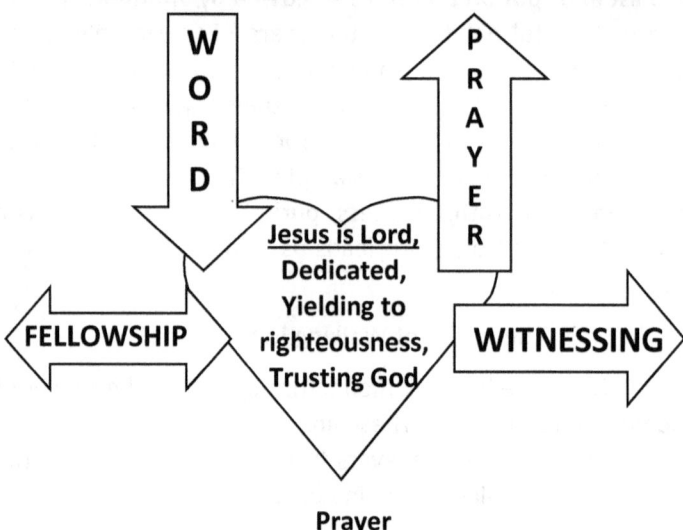

Prayer

Praying has been mentioned several times in this commentary, including this chapter. The reason for this is the major importance it has. Prayer and the Word are the ways we communicate with God. Prayer brings the power of God into our hearts and lives. By it, we experience the filling of the Spirit. Do you need strength? Ask God for it. Do you need wisdom? Ask God for it. Do you need guidance? Ask God for it. Do you need help in trouble? Ask God for it. Are you wrestling with a bad habit? Ask God for strength and help. Do you have need of anything? Ask God for it. Do you need knowledge of God's will or grace to deal with others or fruitfulness or, even, help to yield to God? Pray for these things (Col. 1:10-12). In every instance God's answer involves the enablement or filling of the Spirit for the yielded Christian. God will answer.

> The more praying there is in the world the better the world will be, the mightier the forces against evil everywhere. Prayer, in one phase of its operation, is a disinfectant and a preventative. It purifies the air; it destroys the contagion of evil ... It is no voice crying unheard and unheeded in the silence. It is a voice which goes into God's ear, and it lives as long as God's ear is open to holy pleas, as long as God's heart is alive to holy things. God shapes the world by prayer ... It is true that the mightiest successes that come to God's cause are created and carried by prayer ... Everything then, as now, was possible to the men and women who knew how to pray. Prayer, indeed opened a limitless storehouse, and God's hand withheld nothing ... More prayer and better is the secret of the whole matter ... Man's access in prayer to God opens everything, and makes his impoverishment his wealth ... Prayer can do anything that God can do ... Prayer and a holy life are one. They mutually act and react. The absence of the one is the absence of the other ... We are in danger of substituting churchly work and a ceaseless round of showy activities for prayer and holy living. A holy life does not live in the closet, but it cannot live without the closet. [133]

> Trust in him at all times; ye people, pour out your heart before him: God is a refuge for us. Selah. (Ps. 62:8)

Fellowship with Other Believers

Fellowship is another necessary activity that lets the power of the Holy Spirit flow into us. Fellowship means "Companionship; society; consort; mutual association of persons on equal and friendly terms; familiar intercourse" and "partnership; joint interest." Fellowship is based on the love each of us has for our brothers and sisters in Christ (1 John 3:11-19). Fellowship is what we do when we provoke and exhort one another (Heb. 10:24-25; 1 Pet. 1:22), prefer one another in honor (Rom. 12:10), receive one another (Rom. 15:7), admonish one another (Rom. 15:14), greet one another (1 Cor. 16:20), serve one another (Gal. 5:13), esteem one another better than ourselves (Phil 2:1-4), forbear one another (Eph. 4:2), forgive one another (Eph. 4:32), teach one another (Col. 3:16), love one another (1 Thess. 4:9; 1 Pet. 1:22), comfort one another (1 Thess. 4:18; 5:11), edify one another (1 Thess. 5:11), consider one another (Heb. 10:24), and serve with one another in the gospel (Phil. 1:3-5). Fellowship happens when we minister grace to one another by edifying words (Eph. 4:19). Fellowship occurs when we minister our gifts to one another, are kindly affectionate toward one another, give, and show mercy (Rom. 12:4-16). Fellowship is what God instructed us to do in Galatians 6:1, "Brethren, if a man be overtaken in a fault, ye which are spiritual, restore such an one." The interaction between believers in fellowship is used by the Holy Spirit to fill believers and motivate them and help them walk closer to God.

Witnessing

Witnessing is an activity whereby we proclaim the gospel of Jesus Christian to an unsaved world. The gospel is the "power of God" (Rom. 1:16) to save sinners who believe. It is also a method by which we confess our faith in the gospel to the world. When Jesus commanded the apostles to go and teach the gospel to all nations (Mt. 28:18-20), he began by saying, "All power is given unto me in heaven and in earth." He ended the command by promising, "lo, I am with you alway, even unto the end of the world." By making these statements, He promised His power and His presence when we proclaim the gospel. Since He told the apostles to teach their converts to do all things he had commanded, both the command and the promises are for us as well as for them. Proclaiming the gospel involves more than talking to unsaved people. It also involves fellowship with the Lord Jesus Christ and partnering with Him in the work that is dearest to His heart.

Acts 4:1-31 relates how the lame man at the temple was healed. Peter and John were called to answer to the council for the healing. The Jewish leaders did not want this movement to go any further. "Then Peter, filled with the Holy Ghost, said unto them ... Neither is there salvation in any other: for there is none other name under heaven given among men, whereby we must be saved" (Acts 4:8-12). Boldness was given to Peter to proclaim the gospel by the filling of the Holy Spirit. They were commanded by the council not to speak or teach in Jesus name. When they reported to the church, the congregation prayed for boldness to speak. "And when they had prayed, the place was shaken where they were assembled together; and they were all filled with the Holy Ghost, and they spake the word of God with boldness" (Acts 4:31). They did not pray for the filling of the Spirit. They prayed for boldness to speak the Word. God's answer was the filling of the Spirit.

The Word of God

Walking in the Spirit is a life of being filled by the Word of God. I have left this to the last, because it is the most powerful activity that helps us obey the command to be filled with the Spirit. Every truth we have examined in this commentary is from the Scriptures. An intake of the Word of God into our hearts has a direct effect on being filled with the Spirit. When Paul gave God's command to be filled with the Spirit in Ephesians 5:18, it was followed in Ephesians 5:19 - 6:9 by a list of actions, all of which depend on and result from being filled with the Spirit. If you look in Colossians 3:16 through 4:1, you will find an almost exact duplicate of this list:

Ephesians	Verse	Colossians	Verse
Spiritual songs	5:19	Spiritual songs	3:16
Give thanks	5:20	Give thanks	3:17
Submit to one another	5:21		
Wives submit	5:22	Wives Submit	3:18
Husbands love	5:25	Husbands love	3:19
Children obey	6:1	Children obey	3:20
Fathers provoke not	6:4	Fathers provoke not	3:21
Servants obey	6:5	Servants obey	3:22
Masters	6:9	Masters	4:1

There is almost no difference in the lists. This is not just the same writer making two similar lists in two different letters. At the beginning of these lists is a very significant difference. Eph. 6:18 says, "be filled with the Spirit." Col. 3:16 says to *be filled with the Word of God*, "Let the word of Christ dwell in you richly in all wisdom..." The same thing results from being filled with the Word in all wisdom as results from being filled with the Spirit. To be filled with the Word in all *wisdom* requires a humble, believing heart yielded to God. It requires a heart that is seeking God's wisdom for living. As we are filled with the wisdom of the word, we will be filled with the Spirit.

Final Thoughts

So, then, the baptism of the Spirit (Rom. 6) provides the freedom to live a holy obedient life and the filling of the Spirit provides the power and the help. This is a firm steady reality that allows us to face the contingencies and issues of life successfully with dependence on God. Knowing that we are dead to sin and alive to God and that we are free to live our lives to the will of God, we can yield ourselves to God and righteousness in every thought, decision, and action. Seeking Him in prayer and faith, consistently fellowshipping with other believers, and being filled with the wisdom of God's word, we are strengthened with might by the Holy Spirit, we are filled by the Spirit.

CHAPTER ELEVEN

THE MUSIC OF THE CHURCH
Ephesians 5:19-20

**19 Speaking to yourselves in psalms and hymns and spiritual songs, singing and making melody in your heart to the Lord;
20 Giving thanks always for all things unto God and the Father in the name of our Lord Jesus Christ; (Eph. 5:19-20)**

THESE VERSES THAT ACCOMPANY THE COMMAND to be filled with the Spirit, reveal some profound truths about Christian music. There is a great deal of argument over what constitutes Christian music. So-called Contemporary Christian Music has nearly entirely been captured by the rock and roll music forms of the 1950s, 60s, 70s, and 80s. It has both its supporters and its detractors among Christians. As we draw near to the 2020s, there is not nearly as much fight as there was 30 or 40 years ago. Churches, including fundamental churches, seem to have given up and accepted most forms of CCM. Nevertheless, the Bible has something to say about this matter of Christian music. Ephesians 5:19-20 is among the most important places in the Bible about music. Music in the heart is an outcome of being filled with the Spirit.

Christian Music

Emotions run high when it comes to opinions about music. In most cases, opinions are based on what type of music a person *prefers.* In the final analysis, the only thing that should matter for a Christian is what the Bible says. In Ephesians 5:19-20, we have a definitive statement on music. A similar statement is found in Colossians 3:16, "teaching and admonishing one another in psalms and hymns and spiritual songs, singing with grace in your hearts to the Lord." Paul is plainly recommending three types of music that can be called "Christian music": Psalms, hymns, and spiritual songs. In the last chapter, we talked about the necessity to yield ourselves to the will of God. This statement listing the three categories of Christian music is not any person's *opinion.* It is a statement of the *will of God* and every believer needs to submit his musical opinions to it.

Psalms: There is no mystery what a psalm is. Psalms have been sung by the Hebrews since the days of Moses and the Kings (1 Chron. 16:9). According to tradition, Moses composed Psalms 90-100. Singing of psalms is mentioned three times in the Old Testament and six times in the New Testament. Ps. 95:2 connects the singing of Psalms with giving thanks. Psalm 105:2 couples singing psalms with speaking praise to God for His wonderful works.

Hymns: Hymns are sung in praise to God. Missionary Eddie Mills commented on hymns.

> Revelation_5:9 And they sung a new song, saying, Thou art worthy to take the book, and to open the seals thereof: for thou wast slain, and hast redeemed us to God by thy blood out of every kindred, and tongue, and people, and nation;
>
> TRUTH: Hymns are no longer the standard in some churches? Why are they being dropped?
>
> I truly believe that Hymns can be as convicting as old fashion preaching.
>
> Consider the themes of the following songs:

The Fellowship of the Mystery

1. Onward Christians Soldiers -- What's the theme?
2. Victory in Jesus -- What's the theme?
3. Amazing Grace -- What's the theme?
4. How Great Thou Art? -- What's the theme?
5. What a Friend we have in Jesus -- What's the theme?
6. Holy, Holy, Holy -- What's the theme?
7. Be thou my Vision -- What's the theme?
8. At Calvary -- What's the theme?
9. Take my Life and Let it Be -- What's the theme?
10. It is Well with My Soul -- What's the theme?

You see these songs PREACH and this is why many churches refuse to sing them.

FYI: You do not sing "praise" songs, you sing Psalms and Hymns and spiritual songs with Praise. Praises are found in the words that you sing as they glorify the Saviour. [134]

A hymn declares how great God is. [135] It is a song that focuses on God, not people. Many modern Christian songs are centered on personal experience. The hymns are different. They may speak of personal experience, but they center on who God is and what He is doing in that experience or in the world. We have a rich heritage of great hymns. Looking through a hymn book will tell you that hymns are strong in praise and doctrinal teaching. Being such, the lyrics must be true according to the Scriptures.

> All hail the power of Jesus' name!
> Let angels prostrate fall.
> Bring forth the royal diadem,
> and crown him Lord of all.
> Bring forth the royal diadem,
> and crown him Lord of all!
> O seed of Israel's chosen race
> now ransomed from the fall,

hail him who saves you by his grace,
and crown him Lord of all.
Hail him who saves you by his grace,
and crown him Lord of all! [136]

Spiritual songs: in Greek a *song* is an *Ode* and can be any kind of song, such as a ballad, historical song, or a harvest song. [137] Music in the Old Testament was sometimes a part of a celebration (e,g, 1 Sam. 18:6). Paul qualifies a Christian song as a "spiritual" song. The opposite of "spiritual" is carnal (Rom. 8:6-7; 1Cor.3:1). If "carnal" means the things that come from the flesh, then "spiritual" means the things that come from the Spirit of God. The term "spiritual" refers to that which has its origin in God and is in agreement with God's truth.

Spiritual songs are also centered on God but can be more bent toward the benefits God gives to human beings. Nevertheless, they are also songs of praise. It is often hard to tell whether a piece of music is a hymn or a spiritual song. It really matters little. A song, to be spiritual at all, must focus on what is spiritual. So, the real questions are: 1) are the lyrics spiritual, 2) are the lyrics Scriptural, and 3) are the lyrics true? The answer to these questions must be "yes," if it is to qualify as spiritual. Jesus, who has the name above all names (Phil. 2:9), should be preeminent if it is truly "spiritual" music (Col. 1:18). The singing should be about Him, about what He has done, and it must not be shy about naming Him.

Many songs which pretend to be "Christian" contain untrue lyrics, even classic songs. In the "Battle Hymn of the Republic," written by Julia Ward Howe, for example, there are several untruths. "Mine eyes have seen the glory of the coming of the Lord:" no she did not. The Lord hasn't come the second time and she certainly wasn't there when He came as a baby. "God has sounded forth the trumpet that shall never call retreat and is sifting out all human hearts before the judgment seat:" this is a blatant unscriptural falsehood. The Judgment Seat of Christ will not take place until after the Rapture. He is not sifting hearts before His Judgment Seat *now*. "In the beauty of the lilies Christ was born across the sea." No, He was not. He was born in a stable, with animals and the smell of dung. "As he died to make men holy" is a half truth. He died to save men from their sins. This particular song is full of error. It was written to encourage northern young men to go to war and kill southern young men in the Civil War. It has no place in our hymn books. We need to be honest and discerning and careful when it comes to music.

Musical Accompaniment

An emphasis is made in Ephesians 5:19 on the lyrics of a song. However, most songs are accompanied by musical instruments. This aspect of music was mentioned often in the Old Testament.

All songs and instrumental music or accompaniment are not equal. Some may say that instrumental music is neutral and any style can be used to accompany Christian music. Saying this fails to take into account the fact that instrumental music has a language of its own. All one has to do to discover this is to listen to a variety of music. For example, there are compositions that are called "marches." Very often when listening to a march one can see in his mind a company of soldiers on parade and can feel like marching himself. I have heard classical music that can gear you up for action or make you feel you are walking down a path in a pleasant flower and tree garden. Music speaks to the emotions, mind, and spirit. It definitely carries a message of its own.

General revelation, the creation, gives us some information about music. In an article entitled *An Introduction to the Elements of Music*, Espie Estrella (a songwriter and lyricist) lists and briefly explains ten elements of music: beat and meter, dynamics, melody, harmony, pitch, rhythm, tempo, texture, and timbre. [138] The first thing to notice is that beat, meter, and tempo are part of the rhythm [139] Also, notice that dynamics, pitch, and timbre have to do with the quality and volume of the sound. Finally, the texture has to do with building the composition. This leaves three elements that actually *produce* the sound: Rhythm, harmony, and melody.

From studying the nature of music, then, we learn that music consists of three primary foundational parts: rhythm, harmony, and melody. Without these, none of the rest would exist. *Rhythm* is formally defined as "the aspect of music comprising all the elements (such as accent, meter, and tempo) that relate to forward movement ... a characteristic rhythmic pattern (such as Rumba or waltz pattern- author)."[140] As said before, rhythm includes the beat and speed (tempo) of the music. Rhythm exists is all music, but it does not always involve drums. [141]

Harmony is "the simultaneous combination of tones, especially when blended into chords pleasing to the ear; chordal structure." [142] Harmony is the blend of the instruments or the blend of the voices.

Finally, *melody* is "the succession of single tones in musical compositions." [143] It generally follows the flow of the lyrics.

A whole piece of music will have all three of these parts. Classical music strives for a balance between them. Much modern music tends to emphasize the rhythm above the other two, creating an imbalance. This is the basic nature of rock music. The effect of this imbalance is not always pleasant. In fact, most contemporary Christian music is based on Rock and Roll or similar forms. Often, the rhythm is so strong that it pushes the harmony and melody to secondary status. Many times melody is pushed out altogether.

How does music affect a human being? As we have seen a human consists of body, soul, and spirit. The soul of man has the capacities of mind, emotions, and will.

It should seem obvious that the rhythm of music has a particular affect on the body. For instance, dancing is based on the rhythm. I heard a preacher, who had been a dance band drummer in his unsaved days, tell a story about a performance his band did one night. The guests were enjoying themselves dancing. At one point all the performers except the drummer (the preacher) took a break. The drummer continued to bang away at the drums, during which all the dancers continued to dance with nothing playing but drums. That taught him something of the physical effect of rhythm.

The harmony is a combination of sounds that can soothe or excite the emotions. It *can have a great effect on the soul.* Harmony is the vertical line of simultaneous notes on the musical staff. In a balanced composition it follows the melody.

There is one part of music that God has created and designed to specifically connect with the spiritual nature of mankind: "speaking to yourselves in psalms and hymns and spiritual songs, singing and **making melody** in your heart to the Lord" (Col. 3:16). The melody is the chief theme of a composition. The psalms, hymns, and spiritual songs are based on *melody* in particular. It is the *melody* that is "to the Lord." Some famous musicians have recognized the importance of melody.

> Melody is the essence of music. (Wolfgang Amadeus Mozart) [144]

> Three things belong to composing, first of all melody; then again melody; then finally, for the third time, melody. (Salomon Jadassohn-German pianist and composer. [145]

> Melody is the main thing; harmony is useful only to charm the ear. (Joseph Haydn-Austrian classical composer) [146]

> True godly music will be composed of three elements - all in perfect balance with each other. They are: melody, harmony, and rhythm ... Rock "music" has no melody only fragments of melody endlessly repeated. Since there is no true melody, there is no real harmony. There is only rhythm. And rhythm in and of itself is not music. (Leonard J. Seidel, concert pianist and twenty-five year Christian music scholar, Face the Music – Contemporary Music On Trial, pp. 46-51) [147]

There are many arguments that have been made for and against Contemporary Christian Music (CCM). One of the great weaknesses of today's Christian music is that melody is deemphasized in favor of rhythm. Whereas, melody should be the central part of a piece of Christian music, it is the least important part in much CCM. That is because there is a tendency to follow the norms, forms, and standards of rock music rather than traditional Christian music. Music speaks. Music tells a story. The music of the instruments backs up the message of the lyrics or interferes with it. Even when the lyrics are glorifying to God, the musical background can weaken or destroy the power of the words, if they over-emphasize rhythm and de-emphasize melody.

Lyrics are central in Biblical Christian music. It is the lyrics whereby we speak to ourselves, teach and exhort one another, and give thanks in the music. A failure of contemporary Christian music is its lack of emphasis on lyrics in favor of the accompaniment. This has been done by making the beat of the rhythm so prominent it is hard to hear anything else. Another way it is done is by making the instrumental portion of the music or just the beat so loud that it drowns out the lyrics, making them hard to understand. Sometimes, it is done by creating discordance between the accompaniment and the lyrics. I once heard a CCM song that had beautiful lyrics that could lift your heart to heaven, but the accompaniment was so full of low dark minor chords arranged in such a fashion as to bring the heart down to the ground-or hell-I couldn't tell which. In other words, the musical accompaniment should support and enhance the message of the lyrics.

The Purpose of Christian Music

What is the purpose of Christian music? In our hearts, we should be "singing and making melody ... ***giving thanks always*** for all things unto God and the Father in the name of our Lord Jesus Christ" (Eph. 5:19-20). "Let the word of Christ dwell in you richly in all wisdom; ***teaching and admonishing*** one another in psalms and hymns and spiritual songs, singing with grace in your hearts ***to the Lord***" (Col. 3:16).

First it is "to the Lord," not for entertainment to an audience. It is for praise and thanksgiving. Notice:

> I will be glad and rejoice in thee: I will **sing praise** to thy name, O thou most High. (Psalm 9:2)
> Be thou exalted, LORD, in thine own strength: so will we **sing** and **praise** thy power. (Psalm 21:13)
> The LORD is my strength and my shield; my heart trusted in him, and I am helped: therefore my heart greatly rejoiceth; and with my **song** will I **praise** him. (Psalm 28:7)
> **Praise** the LORD with **harp: sing** unto him with the **psaltery** and an **instrument of ten strings. Sing** unto him a **new song;** play skilfully with a loud noise. (Psalm 33:2-3)
> And he hath put a new **song** in my mouth, **even praise unto our God**: many shall see it, and fear, and shall trust in the LORD. (Ps. 40:3)

The second purpose of Christian music is "teaching and admonishing one another." We know what it means to teach. According to Webster, *admonish* means "warn or notify of a fault; to reprove with mildness ... counsel against wrong practices; to caution or advise." [148] Music can be a good way to do that. For example, one song says, "Trust and obey, for there's no other way, to be happy in Jesus." This is an admonishment. This capacity of music to teach and admonish is one of the reasons why the lyrics must be scriptural and true. Anything less is not a psalm, a hymn, or a spiritual song.

Let's look at one more example of inaccurate lyrics. The lyrics in the contemporary song, *Here I am to Worship*, have a number of good things to commend them, but some very wrong lyrics as well. At one point it has a repeating line that says, "I'll never know how much it cost to see my sin." However, the Bible says, "For now we see through a glass, darkly; but then face to face: now I know in part; but then shall I know even as also I am known" (1 Cor. 13:12). How well does God know you? That is how we will know. To say that we will never know how much it cost is to contradict Scripture. The second error is the object of the knowing. It says that I will not know "how much it cost to *see my sin* upon that cross." The Bible does not say that Jesus *saw* my sin on the cross. He had to *carry my sins* in His body on the cross. "Who his own self bare our sins in his own body on the tree, that we, being dead to sins, should live unto righteousness: by whose stripes ye were healed" (1 Peter 2:24). That is the Biblical statement. This is exceptionally important. We wouldn't want a preacher to teach people errors from the pulpit, would we? Of course, we wouldn't. Why should we think it is acceptable for singers to sing falsehoods to people, especially to our youth? Michael Card said this about Contemporary Christian Music.

The lyrics of a good number of the songs don't betray anything specifically Christian —they may have some moral message, **but not a lot of the big songs are identifiably Christian**. . . 'What happens to the message when we start getting the music to as many people as possible?' There is an essential part of the gospel that's not ever going to sell. **The gospel is good news, but it is also bad news:** 'You are a sinner, and you are hopeless.' How is a multimillion-dollar record company going to take that? That's a part of the message, too, **and if that's taken out—and it frequently is in Christian music—** it ceases to be the gospel. *(Michael Card-Can't Buy Me Love, Christianity Today, May 20, 1996, p. 25)*

Because of these things, the lyrics of Christian music should be crystal clear. The lyrics contain the message which accomplishes the purpose of the music. If the lyrics are uncertain, the message will not be delivered. If the accompaniment makes the lyrics hard to be understood, the message will not be delivered. If the accompaniment music does not say the same thing as the lyrics, the message will be obscured. "I will sing with the spirit, and I will sing with the understanding also" (1 Cor. 14:15).

Finally, Christian music is NOT for evangelism. It may have some positive affect in that regard, but evangelism is not the intended purpose of Christian music. Christian music is to praise and worship God and to edify believers. In the Bible we learn "it pleased God by the foolishness of preaching to save them that believe" (1 Cor. 1:21). Preaching is the method of evangelism. The content of the preaching is the gospel (1 Cor. 1:18).

In today's world, many "Christian" musicians seem to think in terms of "fans," "Grammy Awards," "Dove Awards," applause, "performing," being "critically acclaimed," the "music *industry*" (not ministry), and being an "artist." These things all smack of entertainment and making money, as if it's all about the musicians (John 12:42-43!). This desire for the praise of men is not new.

> There exists a vast mass of love songs of the poets, written in a fashion **entirely foreign to the profession and name of Christians. They are the songs of men ruled by passion, and a great number of musicians, corrupters of youth, make them the concern of their art and their industry; in proportion as they flourish through praise of their skill,** so do they offend good and serious-minded men by the depraved taste of their work. I blush and grieve to think that once I was of their number. But while I cannot change the past, nor undo what is done, I have mended my ways. **Therefore, I have labored on songs which have been written in praise of our Lord, Jesus Christ."**
> Giovanni Pierluigi da Palestrina (c. 1525-1594) [149]

Music is one of the most important and most influential aspects of the Christian church and the Spirit-filled walk. By it, we worship and praise God. We fellowship with one another through music, as we teach and admonish one another and praise God together. Maintaining the spiritual nature of music and its focus on the Lord Jesus Christ is paramount.

Christian music isn't for entertainment or fame. It is for worship and ministry to believers. God's singers are not entertainers. They are supposed to be God's servants.

Music is not about what kind of music you and I like. Jesus said that if you are to be His disciple, you must take up your cross daily and deny yourself (Luke 9:23). Sometimes denying yourself is about laying aside what you like in favor of what He likes.

CHAPTER TWELVE

MARRIAGE: A PICTURE OF THE CHURCH
Ephesians 5:21-33

21 Submitting yourselves one to another in the fear of God.
22 Wives, submit yourselves unto your own husbands, as unto the Lord.
23 For the husband is the head of the wife, even as Christ is the head of the church: and he is the saviour of the body.
24 Therefore as the church is subject unto Christ, so let the wives be to their own husbands in every thing.
25 Husbands, love your wives, even as Christ also loved the church, and gave himself for it;
26 That he might sanctify and cleanse it with the washing of water by the word,
27 That he might present it to himself a glorious church, not having spot, or wrinkle, or any such thing; but that it should be holy and without blemish.
28 So ought men to love their wives as their own bodies. He that loveth his wife loveth himself.
29 For no man ever yet hated his own flesh; but nourisheth and cherisheth it, even as the Lord the church:
30 For we are members of his body, of his flesh, and of his bones.
31 For this cause shall a man leave his father and mother, and shall be joined unto his wife, and they two shall be one flesh.
32 This is a great mystery: but I speak concerning Christ and

the church.

33 Nevertheless let every one of you in particular so love his wife even as himself; and the wife see that she reverence her husband. (Eph. 5:22-24).

FROM HERE TO THE END OF THE CHAPTER, Paul lays out several foundational principles about marriage. The first section is about the submission of the wife. Next there is a firmly taught commandment that the husband love his wife. There are a few words about the unity of the relationship and, finally, one more bit of advice for the wife.

Submit to One Another

This passage begins with an admonishment to submit to "one another in the fear of God." There are several areas of submission specifically mentioned in Ephesians five and six: wife submitting to husband (Eph. 5:22), children submitting to parents (Eph. 6:1), and servants submitting to masters (Eph. 6:5). There are other submission relationships in the Christian life, as well. We are to submit to government powers (1 Pet. 2:13), submission to leaders and laborers (1 Cor. 16:10-16), the younger should submit to the elder (1 Pet. 5:5), and submission to God (James 4:7). In fact, 1 Peter 5:5 also says, "Yea, all of you be subject one to another, and be clothed with humility: for God resisteth the proud, and giveth grace to the humble." Submission can involve obedience, but our general submission to one another is connected with humility. We do not push and shove against one another seeking advantage for ourselves. Submission to one another is seeking to exalt others as in Philippians 2:3-4, "Let nothing be done through strife or vainglory; but in lowliness of mind let each esteem other better than themselves. Look not every man on his own things, but every man also on the things of others." This has been described as "submitting to the needs of others."

Submission to one another is to be done "in the fear of Lord." The primary motive for submission is the fear of God. There is a misunderstanding of the meaning of the fear of the Lord on the part of some. Some say it means a reverential awe, respect, and honor for God. Is this Biblically correct?

Webster says that the term *fear* involves a feeling associated with the "expectation of evil or the apprehension of impending danger." [150] The Greek word is *phobos*. Thayer defines it as "fear, dread, terror." [151] Although the Word Study has one definition that agrees with the meaning of holy awe and reverence, the word has come into the English language as *phobia*. A phobia is a psychological term for an *anxiety disorder,* that is, fear. It is applied to many things such as, arachnophobia (fear of spiders), acrophobia (fear of heights), ophidiophobia (fear of snakes), agoraphobia (fear of leaving home), and many others. [152] The Scriptures seem to back up this understanding of the Greek word and our general understanding of the English word as "dread" and "terror." Consider the following places in Scripture:

"And he took a yoke of oxen, and hewed them in pieces, and sent them throughout all the coasts of Israel by the hands of messengers, saying, Whosoever cometh not forth after Saul and after Samuel, so shall it be done unto his oxen. And the **fear of the LORD** fell on the people, and they came out with one consent" (1 Sam. 11:7). This is the first use of the phrase "fear of the Lord" and it definitely includes real fear.

"And the **fear of the LORD** fell upon all the kingdoms of the lands that were round about Judah, so that they made no war against Jehoshaphat" (1 Chron. 17:10). This is clearly fear in the classic sense. They did not attack Jehoshaphat because they were *afraid* to attack him.

"But the former governors that had been before me were chargeable unto the people, and had taken of them bread and wine, beside forty shekels of silver; yea, even their servants bare rule over the people: but so did not I, because of the fear of God" (Neh. 5:15). Nehemiah did not make the same mistakes the former governors made because he feared God.

These verses establish the fact that the phrase, "the fear of God," includes the presence of real fear. Having come to that point, let's look at a definitive Bible verse that establishes the presence of feelings beyond pure fear. "God is greatly **to be feared in the assembly** of the saints, and to be had **in reverence of all them** that are about him" (Ps. 89:7). This is a Hebrew parallelism, where in poetry a concept is stated twice. Reverence is connected with the fear of God. Reverence is defined by Webster to be, "Fear mingled with respect and esteem." [153] In fact, a related emotion, awe, is defined as, "Fear mingled with admiration or reverence." [154] In reality, *reverence* includes an element of real fear and Psalm 89:7 couples the fear of God with reverence. In a believer's heart, the fear of God includes the emotions of fear, respect, esteem, and admiration intertwined. We fear God because we reverence Him and stand in awe of Him.

If we are truly in awe of God, then we know He is someone to fear. He will chastise His people (Heb. 12:4-8), and He will judge the unsaved (John 5:22-30) and nations that run away from Him (Ps. 9:17). God is worthy of fear. Some might point out that 1 John 4:18 says, "There is no fear in love; but perfect love casteth out fear: because fear hath torment. He that feareth is not made perfect in love." This is true, however, those who fear the Lord also know the love of the Lord. The love between a child and a parent gives the child security and peace, but they fear the parent's reaction to disobedience. The fear of the Lord results in confidence.

The fear of God is an attitude toward God with good results. In fact, "in the fear of the LORD is strong confidence (Prov. 14:26). "The fear of the LORD is the beginning of wisdom: a good understanding have all they that do his commandments" (Ps. 111:10) and the "fear of the LORD is the beginning of knowledge" (Prov. 1:7). "The fear of the LORD is to hate evil" (Prov. 8:13). "The fear of the LORD is clean, enduring for ever: the judgments of the LORD are true and righteous altogether" (Ps. 19:9). "The fear of the LORD prolongeth days" (Prov. 10:27). "The fear of the LORD is a fountain of life, to depart from the snares of death" (Prov. 14:27). "The fear of the LORD tendeth to life: and he that hath it shall abide satisfied; he shall not be visited with evil" (Prov. 19:23). "By humility and the fear of the LORD are riches, and honour, and life" (Prov. 22:4). Riches are not always money. Sometimes they are health, family, peace, and emotional satisfaction. "Better is little with the fear of the LORD than great treasure and trouble therewith" (Prov. 15:16).

How does one get the fear of the Lord? Once again, let the Lord Himself answer from His Word.

1 My son, if thou wilt receive my words, and hide my commandments with thee;
2 So that thou incline thine ear unto wisdom, and apply thine heart to understanding;
3 Yea, if thou criest after knowledge, and liftest up thy voice for understanding;
4 If thou seekest her as silver, and searchest for her as for hid treasures;
5 Then shalt thou understand the fear of the LORD, and find the knowledge of God.
6 For the LORD giveth wisdom: out of his mouth cometh knowledge and understanding.
7 He layeth up sound wisdom for the righteous: he is a buckler to them that walk uprightly.
8 He keepeth the paths of judgment, and preserveth the way of his saints. (Prov. 2:1-8).

You do not gain the fear of God by directly seeking it, but through Biblical knowledge, understanding, and wisdom.

You learn the fear of the Lord by whole heartedly seeking for wisdom. You cry out for it in prayer and search for it, as for hid treasures, with strong effort and much time in the study of God's Word. True wisdom comes from the words of His mouth. "Open thou mine eyes, that I may behold wondrous things out of thy law" (Ps. 119:18).

"Wives, submit yourselves unto your own husbands"

The Biblical words quoted above are among the most maligned and hated words in the whole Bible. The very idea of submitting to a man runs contrary to the (fallen) human nature of a woman. Also, the idea is repugnant to modern society and modern women (at least, to hear the news media tell about it). How could God require such a thing?

The answer lies in God's chosen order and God's purposes for wives. There is also a certain attitude we must maintain. It would be well to discuss the attitude first. The hatred some have for the idea of submission to a husband reveals an attitude that 1) disagrees with the Bible and 2) rebels against submission to the Bible. It also reveals an inner presence of pride, because it is pride which rebels against a subordinate role. This attitude fails to accept the fact that the Bible is God's Word, not just a human book. It fails to recognize the fact that God is right and any disagreement on our part is always absolutely wrong.

This rebellious attitude may be expected from an unsaved person, but it is absolutely inexcusable coming from a Christian. The attitude of a Christian toward all that the Bible says should be the same attitude exhibited by the Lord Jesus as He faced the coming crucifixion, "Father ... not my will, but thine, be done" (Lk. 22:42). If the Lord Jesus could submit to God when He was being led to suffer the scourging and the crucifixion, then we can certainly submit to our God given roles in life. Trust God, even if you don't understand why.

God's wants all mankind to live their lives in orderly and peaceful relationships. Even the Trinity operates with an order of authority. God the Father is over all. The Lord Jesus Christ, the Son, submitted to God the Father during His life on earth. When the Lord Jesus went back to heaven, he and the Father sent the Holy Spirit to continue Christ's work on earth. Of the Spirit, Jesus said "when the Comforter is come, whom I will send unto you from the Father, even the Spirit of truth, which proceedeth from the Father, he shall testify of me" (John 15:26). Even the Spirit is submissive to the Father and the Son. Likewise, there is an order God has designed for the family. "But I would have you know, that the head of every man is Christ; and the head of the woman is the man; and the head of Christ is God" (1 Cor. 11:3). 1 Corinthians 11 certainly has the family in view. Take careful notice that the Bible includes God the Father and Christ in the family arrangement. The wife may look to the husband for leadership in the family, but the husband is responsible to God for leading his family in a holy and godly manner and direction. The wife is to submit to her husband "as unto the Lord" (Eph. 5:22).

Therefore, the husband is the leader of the family and the wife is to follow. "For after this manner in the old time the holy women also, who trusted in God, adorned themselves, being in subjection unto their own husbands: even as Sara obeyed Abraham, calling him lord: whose daughters ye are, as long as ye do well, and are not afraid with any amazement" (1 Pet. 3:5-6). 1900 years after Abraham, this was still the standard. This is not a standard based on the culture of the time. It is a timeless standard of our loving God.

The family is a team. Every team needs a team leader. In God's plan, that leader is the husband. The team follows the team leader. This does not mean she is a dog to be led with a leash or a horse to be controlled with a bridle. It does not mean she is a mindless creature who must be led about by an all wise husband. Nor is she to withhold her advice until he asks for it. The truth is just the opposite. She is an equal partner with him on the same team. She is his chief adviser and confidant. Very often, he comes to decisions based on her wisdom.

God has designed a special marital purpose for the female of the human race. "And the LORD God said, It is not good that the man should be alone; I will make him an help meet for him" (Gen. 1:18). Two purposes are revealed here. First, she was created so the man does not have to be alone. Loneliness is a problem for both men and women. They are created to provide a relationship which would take away that loneliness. I used to work in an office with quite a number of others around. I had interaction with some of them and it certainly was not a lonely place to work as long as people were friendly. While I was there, a friend and I started our current ministry. The day came when I left the bustling office and became full-time in the global Bible translation ministry. Now my office is at home. Only one other person is there, my wife. Am I lonely? I am not the slightest bit lonely, because my wife is there, and she is enough.

The second purpose is that the wife is to be a *help meet*. What in the world is a "help meet?" The English word *meet* means "fit; suitable; proper; qualified; convenient; adapted, as to a use or purpose." [155] She is a helper fit for him. God adapted Eve's nature (as a woman) to be exactly what Adam's male nature needed. We are not talking here about physical needs alone, but, rather, a wide range of aspects that include mental, spiritual, and emotional areas of life. She is a helper that is suitable for him. God made man as a creature who needs what she can provide. She is an invaluable and necessary companion.

A woman can add a great deal to a man. The passage about godly womanhood in Proverbs 31:10-31 lists some of those benefits. There, she is a very diligent and intelligent person who works very hard for the success of her family. She makes sure her family is well supplied with necessities.

She makes sure they are well clothed. She has a practical sense about her that enables her to consider real estate, and buy it (v. 16) and to run a business (v. 24). She is a wise woman (v. 26) which makes her the first and best advisor for her husband (v. 26). However, when she advises him, it is with kindness and respect (v. 26; see Eph. 5:32) and she does not nag (Prov. 19:13). Because of her character and activities, her husband has a prominent place among the judges and leaders of the land (v. 23). "Her children arise up, and call her blessed; her husband also, and he praiseth her" (Prov. 31:28). "House and riches are the inheritance of fathers: and a prudent wife is from the LORD" (Prov. 19:14). "Whoso findeth a wife findeth a good thing, and obtaineth favour of the LORD" (Prov. 18:22).

Husbands, Love Your Wives

> *25 Husbands, love your wives, even as Christ also loved the church, and gave himself for it;*
> *26 That he might sanctify and cleanse it with the washing of water by the word,*
> *27 That he might present it to himself a glorious church, not having spot, or wrinkle, or any such thing; but that it should be holy and without blemish.*
> *28 So ought men to love their wives as their own bodies. He that loveth his wife loveth himself.*
> *29 For no man ever yet hated his own flesh; but nourisheth and cherisheth it, even as the Lord the church:*
> *30 For we are members of his body, of his flesh, and of his bones.* (Eph. 5:25-30).

One theme runs through this whole passage regarding the husband's responsibility. He is to *love* his wife. He is to love her like Christ loved the church when He gave His life for it. He is to love his wife like he loves his own body.

Of course, he is to be her leader. But what does that mean? It is God's will for the husband to lead. It is not a God given job for a man to *force* his wife into submission. That is *her* decision to make. It is *her* job. Do you remember what Jesus said about leadership?

> **42 But Jesus called them to him, and saith unto them, Ye know that they which are accounted to rule over the Gentiles exercise lordship over them; and their great ones exercise authority upon them.**
> **43 But so shall it not be among you: but whosoever will be great among you, shall be your minister:**
> **44 And whosoever of you will be the chiefest, shall be servant of all.**
> **45 For even the Son of man came not to be ministered unto, but to minister, and to give his life a ransom for many. (Mark 10:42-45).**

Jesus taught the concept of *servant-leadership*. The greatest leader is the one who has the good of the people most in the center of his heart and effort. The Lord Jesus used Himself as an example of the servant-leader. It is evident in the gospels that he is a leader, but it is a benevolent leadership based in love. This context is the same as in Ephesians 5:25, "Husbands, love your wives, even as Christ also loved the church, and gave himself for it." Men are to love their wives the same way the Lord loves the church. The Lord came as a servant (Phil. 2:7). So, the principle of servant-leadership applies to marriage also. The husband's whole focus is on the good and welfare of His wife. What does this mean in a practical sense?

First, the husband's love for his wife is to be self-sacrificial. His love is to be "as Christ also loved the church, and gave himself for it." The Lord Jesus sacrificed Himself completely for the church. Can a woman's husband do any less? Sometimes he will have to give up what is best for him to do what is good and right for her. A husband should be glad to do this. Look at 1 Corinthians 13. A husband is extremely patient with her (suffers long) and is kind. He does not put himself above her (vaunteth not) and he does not let his pride be hurt (not puffed up). He does not seek his own good above hers. He does not think badly of her and is not easily angered (provoked). He bears everything. He believes and trusts her in everything.

The husband seeks to provide spiritual leadership for his wife and family. The Lord Jesus is our Shepherd who leads us into green pastures (Ps. 23). In the same way, the husband and father in a family should lead his wife and children into opportunities for spiritual growth. He should lead them to church. He should pray with them and teach them the Scriptures. He should live an example of the Christian life before them.

The husband seeks to help his wife become all she can be in the will of God (vv. 26-27). Since the Lord's goal for the church is to make it holy, without spot or wrinkle, a husband should strive to make it possible for his wife to be all God wants her to be. That includes her character, of course, but it also includes the use of her gifts and talents. The husband should want her gifts developed and used for the glory of God. Sometimes that may take encouragement or teaching. Sometimes it may take urging her to go forward. Sometimes he may simply need to get out of her way and let her do what is in her heart. It is clear, that is what the Proverbs 31 husband did.

The husband needs to create an atmosphere in which the wife has freedom to express her opinions and advice; and the husband must listen. The ability to express her opinion is necessary for the husband to fulfill 1 Peter 3:17, "Likewise, ye husbands, dwell with them according to knowledge." The husband must know his wife. Where will he get this knowledge of her, if he does not listen to her or let her freely express her opinions? We have already mentioned the fact that Proverbs 31 speaks of a woman's wisdom. A man is a fool if he does not seek and listen to his wife's wisdom. This is especially true if his wife is smarter or wiser than he is.

A corollary to listening to your wife is that a husband must talk with his wife. Wives need to talk. It satisfies their need for companionship and, whether he knows it or not, it also satisfies a husband's need for companionship. It is part of the solution for that troublesome problem of loneliness. The command of God in 1 Peter 3:7, "dwell with them according to knowledge," is that you must treat her in the way you have learned that she needs to be treated. Just general observation will show you that nearly any woman loves to talk. They love to have the give and take of conversation. It seems, their preferred conversation companion is their husbands.

Some men complain that their wives will not try to understand their feelings, even when they try to communicate them. I wonder if they let their wives share their feelings and try to understand. If you and your wife have a habit of open, kind, and considerate conversation, you both will be listened to and understood. Wise up. Talk to your wives. Do not ignore them.

A husband must give honor to his wife (1 Pet. 3:7). The word honor means to value, [156] respect, and esteem. [157] You value her very highly; you esteem her to be of more value than great wealth. You highly respect her. You consider yourself to be very rich just by virtue of having this woman as your wife. How can you express this honor? You may express it with your words; words that minister grace to her. You may compliment her; you may say good and sweet things to her. Being considerate of her is a great help. To notice positive things about her is another way to honor her. Be sure to treat her well in public.

Husbands must nourish their wives. Ephesians 5:28-29 tells husbands to love their wives like they love their own bodies. We tend to nourish our flesh, so we ought to nourish our wives. We give our bodies the things we think it needs. We should do no less for our wives; give them what they need. We tend to be sensitive to any thing our bodies want; relief from pain, hunger, etc. We should be just as sensitive to our wives and their needs and desires

Husbands must cherish their wives. Just like we nourish our bodies, we also cherish them (Eph. 5:29). Webster says *cherish* means, "To treat with tenderness and affection; to give warmth, ease or comfort to." [158] A wife needs tenderness. A husband must often give her kind and concerned attention. Kindness requires a soft sensitivity to her feelings. Affection is a feeling that is mid-way between thought and passion. Wives generally love this kind of attention from their husbands. Sometimes they like affection that comes without expectation of intimacy, simply as an expression of love. What if a husband doesn't *feel* affectionate? I once heard David Jeremiah give advice I thought was very good. His advice was that if you do not feel love, do the acts of love anyway. [159]

"He that loveth his wife loveth himself" (v. 5:28). I once heard a story about a wife who would get into kitchen cabinets and leave the doors open when she was finished. It irritated her husband, who could never get her to close the cabinet doors. So, one day, he decided he would close them and take on the job of being the "cabinet closer." He thought it was a small price to pay for a happy wife. Anything a man can do to truly love his wife in deed and in truth (1 John 3:18) will be to his own benefit. The more true love that can be poured on a wife the happier she will be and that will give the husband peace and happiness.

Do you want your wife to submit? Then love her with all your might. Remember, Christ did not wait for us to love Him before He died for us. No, He loved us first and gave Himself for us. We love Him, *because* He first loved us (1 John 4:19).

Unity of the Husband and Wife

30 For we are members of his body, of his flesh, and of his bones.
31 For this cause shall a man leave his father and mother, and shall be joined unto his wife, and they two shall be one flesh.
32 This is a great mystery: but I speak concerning Christ and the church.
33 Nevertheless let every one of you in particular so love his wife even as himself; and the wife see that she reverence her husband.(Eph. 5:30-32).

Verse thirty-one is taken from Genesis 2:24. The meaning of this "one flesh" statement is revealed in 1 Corinthians 6:15-16, "Shall I then take the members of Christ, and make them the members of an harlot? God forbid. What? know ye not that he which is joined to an harlot is one body? for two, saith he, shall be one flesh." A casual reading of these verses makes it clear that the one flesh relationship is a sexual relationship. That's why we used to refer to consummating the marriage on the first night. Marriage may have a ceremony, but it is not complete until it is consummated sexually. That's one reason sex is not something to be done casually or haphazardly. God did not make sex just to be a pleasant experience. It is intended to create a bond between a man and woman that cannot be easily broken. It is a relationship that creates a new family unit that did not exist before. The verses in 1 Corinthians indicate that such a bond can be (at least partially) initiated by casual fornication, as well. However, many flippant relationships can deaden this response to intimacy. Nevertheless, a sexual relationship coupled with leaving your parents and making a public commitment to your new spouse will create a seal that binds two people together into a single unit (Gen. 2:23-25).

Notice please, that the Scriptures are consistent from Genesis to Revelation that a marital relationship can only exist between a man and a woman. One does not need Greek or Hebrew to see this. However, even Greek grammar backs it up. The Greek word for wife, *gine*, is a feminine noun and the Greek word for husband, *aner*, is a masculine noun. The gender of a noun in Greek is important when it comes to persons. If it is feminine then the actual object is feminine and likewise for the male. The exception is that sometimes the masculine is used for general terms meaning mankind, including both sexes. The wife is female and the husband is male. This is the consistent testimony of Scripture, whether it is in English or Greek or Hebrew.

The Necessity of Respect

32 This is a great mystery: but I speak concerning Christ and the church.
33 Nevertheless let every one of you in particular so love his wife even as himself; and the wife see that she reverence her husband. (Eph. 5:32-33).

"Me? Reverence that man? Not on your life!" This seems to be the attitude of some wives. Some may even point out that the term *reverend* is used only once in God's Word and refers to God's name (Ps. 111:9). However, *reverence* is used several times and relates to both God and men. Among the definitions given by Webster, we find this, "Fear mingled with respect and esteem; veneration ... to regard with fear mingled with respect and affection." [160] One aspect of this emotion, listed twice here, is *respect*. Webster defines *respect* as "to esteem as possessed of real worth." [161] Respect is probably the single most important thing a husband needs from his wife. He needs to be held in high regard and affection. He needs her to consider him to be worthy of high regard. He wants her to look up to him and to approve of him. Having this encourages him, strengthens him, and makes him feel he and his wife are a team. It may actually make the difference as to whether he personally feels worth or not. If she takes away her reverence, she may take away his self-worth as well, create real depression, and set him on a downward spiral.

The wife is commanded to reverence her husband. In fact, the command is put in strong terms: "and the wife *see that* she reverence her husband." Some say you must *earn* respect. That is not what the Bible says here. She is to respect him whether he earns it or not. No man is without faults, but men usually have good qualities as well. A wife should know and focus on those good qualities. Do you want your husband to excel? Then view him and treat him like a winner. Do you want your husband to deeply love you? Then submit to him and respect him. It will help him to be successful and to love you more deeply.

A Picture of the Body of Christ

This is a great mystery: but I speak concerning Christ and the church (Eph. 5:32)

There is a great deal more in Ephesians 5:22-33 than advice on marriage. The Book of Ephesians is about the church, Christ's body. We have looked at the spiritual nature of the church, the spiritual structure of the church, and some of the practical operation of the church. In this passage, we view Christ's relationship with the church. God designed marriage to illustrate this relationship. Marriage creates a picture that can help both the saved and the unsaved to understand the relationship between Christ and His body, the Church.

"*Wives, submit yourselves unto your own husbands, as unto the Lord*" (v. 22). The wife is to submit "as unto the Lord." So, first, being a Christian is a life of submission to the

Lord. Jesus said, "If ye love me, keep my commandments ... He that hath my commandments, and keepeth them, he it is that loveth me ... If a man love me, he will keep my words" (John 14:15, 23). A Christian must be fully committed to this principle. The commitment to follow God in obedience in all areas of life has a definite starting point (Rom. 12:1-2). This commitment may come simultaneous with salvation or it may come later. The wife is a picture of the submission of the church.

There is only one Head of the church. "Christ is the head of the church: and he is the saviour of the body" (v. 23). The "body" in this verse refers to the church, which is His body. The statement that He is the Savior of the body is a reference to His death, burial, and resurrection (see Ephesians 2). Christ is said to be the head of the body in Ephesians 1:22-23 and Colossians 1:18. Furthermore, He is the *only* head of the body. There are no others. The marriage relationship ably illustrates this in the fact that the husband has been placed by God as the head of the family.

This explains one of the most important reasons God assigns a subordinate role to the wife and a leadership role to the husband. The husband is a picture of Christ and the wife is a picture of the church. Their relationship, based on love and reverence, is a picture of the relationship between Christ and the church. This brings to light just how important it is that husband and wife accept their God given roles.

"Christ also loved the church, and gave himself for it" (v. 25). This verse and the two following it describe God's goals for the church. His immediate goal is that the church be washed and made clean by the Word of God (v. 26). His ultimate goal is that there will be nothing wrong anywhere among all the believers in the church; that it be holy without spot, wrinkle, or blemish. God is at work among us now to accomplish this, but it will be ultimately finished at the Judgment Seat of Christ (1 Cor. 3:11-15; 2 Cor. 5:10-11). Marriage pictures these things in that it is the responsibility

of the husband to minister the Word to his wife and children and to lead them into righteousness.

God's goal to iron out all the wrinkles in the Church, should encourage believers to settle their problems with other believers now. Problems between Christians often take place. Even as it happens in an earthly family, it happens among Christians. Jesus taught us to reconcile with one another when these problems arise (Mt. 5:23-25; 18:15-17). What do you think will happen if we do not reconcile? The problem will likely show up as a wrinkle in the Church. If you do not solve these problems on earth, you will likely face them again at the Judgement Seat of Christ.

"For we are members of his body, of his flesh, and of his bones" (v. 30). We have extensively discussed the fact that every believer is in Christ no matter where he is or what church he attends. If a person believes the gospel and has trusted Christ as his savior, he is in Christ. However, what is this about being members of His flesh and His bones? When Jesus died on the cross, he gave His body for us. The bread we eat at communion commemorates His body, which was broken for us (1 Cor. 11:23-26; 10:16). After Jesus rose from the dead, He appeared to the disciples and said, "Behold my hands and my feet, that it is I myself: handle me, and see; for a spirit hath not flesh and bones, as ye see me have" (Luke 24:39). The text says that the church is *of* His flesh and *of* His bones. It is true that the church was created out His flesh and bones that He gave for us on the cross. It is because of this that we are in Christ and one with Him.

However, the flesh and bones speak of the unity of Christ and the church. The church is considered to be the Bride of Christ. Just as a man and woman become one flesh, the church is one flesh with Christ in a spiritual sense; we are "members of His flesh and bones." "For I am jealous over you with godly jealousy: for I have espoused you to one husband, that I may present you as a chaste virgin to Christ" (2 Cor. 11:2; cf. John 3:29; Rev. 22:17). Who is the bride of Christ? Is it just the Corinthian church? If it was just the Corinthians, it is irrelevant for the rest of us. No, this revelation was given to them, but the benefits are not restricted to them. Are all believers in Christ? Of course, they are. Is Christ divided? Of course, He is not. I remind you that we are *one* in Christ (John 17:11, 21-23) and that there are no divisions in Christ. "There is neither Jew nor Greek, there is neither bond nor free, there is neither male nor female: for ye are all one in Christ Jesus" (Gal. 3:28). There are some who believe that the Bride of Christ is restricted to one certain denomination. On the contrary, if Galatians 3:28 is true and there are no distinctions among believers in Christ, then there are no Baptists, Presbyterians, Episcopalians, Anglicans, Pentecostals, or any other denomination **in Him.** ***All believers*** are in Him and in Him there are neither denominations nor any other kind of division. *Everyone, who is in Christ, is in the Bride of Christ.*

CHAPTER THIRTEEN

MORE RELATIONSHIPS OF THE CHURCH
Ephesians 6:1-9

1 Children, obey your parents in the Lord: for this is right.
2 Honour thy father and mother; (which is the first commandment with promise;)
3 That it may be well with thee, and thou mayest live long on the earth.
4 And, ye fathers, provoke not your children to wrath: but bring them up in the nurture and admonition of the Lord.
5 Servants, be obedient to them that are your masters according to the flesh, with fear and trembling, in singleness of your heart, as unto Christ;
6 Not with eyeservice, as menpleasers; but as the servants of Christ, doing the will of God from the heart;
7 With good will doing service, as to the Lord, and not to men:
8 Knowing that whatsoever good thing any man doeth, the same shall he receive of the Lord, whether he be bond or free.
9 And, ye masters, do the same things unto them, forbearing threatening: knowing that your Master also is in heaven; neither is there respect of persons with him.
(Eph. 6:1-9)

THIS SECTION DEALS WITH FOUR CLASSES OF PEOPLE: children, fathers, servants and masters. The purpose is to advise children on how to submit to and honor their parents, fathers on how to raise their children, servants on how to be a good servant, and masters on how to treat servants. There have been whole volumes written on these relationships (if we apply the principles of master-servant to employer-employee). It's interesting to think that when Paul begins to advise these specific relationships he does not write a whole book on the subjects. His advice is given in just a few words, nine verses, that point out important key principles. He has a way of addressing the most important aspects of a topic (under the inspiration of the Holy Spirit). However, what is given on a particular subject in one spot in the Bible is not necessarily the total teaching on that subject. The Bible has more to say on these things elsewhere and we will look at some of them.

The Responsibility of Children (Eph. 6:1-3)

The key job of a child is to obey and learn. It certainly is an extensive process. The Scripture says, "Foolishness is bound in the heart of a child" (Prov. 22:15a). The response to this is a verse that has become very familiar, "Train up a child in the way he should go: and when he is old, he will not depart from it" (Prov. 22:6). Why is it so important that a child learns to obey? There are several reasons.

The first reason children should obey is because it is right (v. 1). It is right to obey, because God wants children to obey. The command comes from God and that is all that is needed to make us know it is right. On the other hand, God has reasons for His commands. They are not only right, but they are wise. To get some idea of God's reasons, all we need to do is look at the good obedience brings. For one thing, obedience does much toward the stability and peace of the family. It stops a lot of conflicts and arguments.

Obedience teaches them submission. Obedience to parents teaches children to keep rules of various institutions, such as school. It helps prepare him to be involved in organized associations and activities with others. It helps them to develop and exhibit manners along with gentlemanly or lady-like behavior. Learning obedience at home teaches the child to obey the law of the land. This helps to produce stability and peace in the country where the family lives. It also keeps them out of jail. Finally, learning to obey at home helps a child's heart to be humble enough to listen to God and obey Him. Learning obedience has a generally positive effect on all the child's relationships throughout life.

Obedience is a way to honor your mother and father (v. 2). The term *honor* means many things, but the definition that applies to children and parents is "esteem due or paid to worth; high estimation." [162] John Wesley expressed it this way, "Honour - That is, love, reverence, obey, assist, in all things." [163] The statement in verses two and three is taken from the Ten Commandments, Deuteronomy 5:16. To honor one's father and mother certainly includes willing, humble obedience, but it does not end there. The King James Version translates the Greek word as "honor" in all, but one place. In that verse, the word is translated "value" (Mt. 27:9). To honor your parents is also to value them highly in respect and love and to treat them so.

Obedience and honor carry a promise of life (v. 3). The original promise was made to the Jews living in Palestine and applied to their dwelling in that land ("that thy days may be long upon the land which the LORD thy God giveth thee"- Ex. 20:12). Paul, under the inspiration of the Holy Spirit, reapplies and expands it to "the earth," in order to make it apply to the church dispensation. A shorter life is sometimes a chastisement to God's people who are disobedient (Rom. 8:13; 1 Cor. 11:30). Conversely a longer life can be a reward. "The fear of the LORD prolongeth days: but the years of the wicked shall be shortened" (Prov. 10:27). These statements are general statements only. God has a plan for each of us individually. His plan for some may be a short life, but not because of sin in their lives. It is just His plan. "For I know the thoughts that I think toward you, saith the LORD, thoughts of peace, and not of evil, to give you an expected end" (Jer. 29:11).

The Responsibility of Fathers (Eph. 6:4)

There is only one verse directed toward fathers, but what a verse! There are three topics of instruction given in that one verse: do not provoke, do nurture, and do admonish. Each of these topics has a lot of information hidden within them. Fathers, rather than mothers, are singled out here regarding their child rearing responsibilities. Being the head of the family carries a lot of accountability. The old saying, "The buck stops here," seems to apply. The Father is responsible for directing his entire family toward God. The Mother has immense influence and is as involved as the Father, but the Father must take the lead and has the most responsibility and liability to God. It must be noted that the nurture and admonition mentioned in the verse are "of the Lord." It is the kind of training God gives us. Although God is dead serious about the training he gives us, He also balances it with love, mercy, and kindness. The standards we give our children and the content of all our teaching should be founded on Biblical truth and principles. Fathers and mothers will have to spend a considerable amount of time studying the Bible.

Mark this well. The Bible gives God's instructions on child rearing. You cannot count on instructions from the world in general or from psychologists or so-called experts to give you the truth about how to rear children. If you insist on going to them to learn, you *must* compare what they say to the instructions of the Word of God. God made children and God knows what methods will be successful in discipline and training. Do not be deceived by those professing to have the answers, when they are destitute of the wisdom of God themselves. God is the only trustworthy source of wisdom in this matter.

A father must not provoke his children to great anger. Keep this in perspective. There will be times when your child gets angry just because you ask him to do something and he doesn't want to do it. The fault is in him in those cases. It is called rebellion and requires training and discipline. What Paul is teaching in Ephesians 6 has to do with situations in which the father acts unreasonably. These are cases where the cause of the anger does not lie in the heart of the child, but the provocation comes from the father.

Colossians 3:21 puts it this way, "Fathers, provoke not your children to anger, lest they be discouraged." What kinds of things could provoke a child to wrath toward his parents? First, I am reminded of the necessity for a child to be obedient and then I think about the commands of God, which we are to obey. The Scriptures describe God's commands this way: "his commandments are not grievous" (1 John 5:3). A commandment that is grievous is one that is heavy, oppressive, burdensome, or hard to be carried out. It is severely difficult and even unreasonable. If God does not do that to us, then we should not do it to our children. Anger is the natural result when unreasonable or even impossible orders and expectations are given to a child. There are times when children are growing up that we may find ourselves expecting more than is reasonable for their age. They may take it well at first and later rebel and it will cause them to be discouraged. They may feel there is no way they could ever please you. If they do please you, let them know.

Another action that will stir up wrath in your children is *grievous words*, "A soft answer turneth away wrath: but **grievous words stir up anger**" (Prov. 15:1). This is true with children as well as adults. Words matter, especially to young children who believe what you say. Hurt feelings can last a life time. If you tell a child, "You can't do anything right," he may believe you and it will create a lack of self-confidence that may last the rest of his life and greatly damage his life. There are many things a parent can say that will damage a child emotionally. These things are rarely, if ever, necessary to say. There is also, no excuse, for calling a child hurtful and grievous names or harshly balling him out, especially with cussing. This is not at all to say that a child should not be rebuked. But, that is very different from a harsh balling out. Even adults do not care for this.

Another way fathers can stir up anger in a child is to be an angry man. "A wrathful man stirreth up strife: but he that is slow to anger appeaseth strife" (Prov. 15:18) and "An angry man stirreth up strife, and a furious man aboundeth in transgression" (Prov. 29:22). An angry person easily spouts off grievous words. An angry man easily makes a lot of mistakes, especially with his words. He also provides a poor example. If a child, watching his father, sees a man who often loses his temper, the child will be inclined toward the same behavior. Learn to control your temper. Temperance, self-control, is a fruit of the Spirit (Gal. 5:22-23). "He that is slow to anger is better than the mighty; and he that ruleth his spirit than he that taketh a city" (prov. 16:32).

It's a good idea for a father to think about what should get him excited and what should not. "The discretion of a man deferreth his anger; and it is his glory to pass over a transgression" (Prov. 19:11). Children, at best, are foolish creatures whose job is to learn, obey and grow. A father should learn to tell the difference between a foolish or silly action and a deliberately hurtful action. Sometimes a child may do a careless accidental act that causes another child to fall and cry. He should be instructed and made to apologize. At other times a child may angrily knock another child down with hurtful intentions. In that case, he should be swiftly and clearly reprimanded and punished.

A father must rear his children in the nurture of the Lord. Nurture is a noun and according to Webster means,

"That which promotes growth; education; instruction." [164] The King James translates the word several ways: chastening, instruction, learn, and teach. So, basically, it covers the training of a child through teaching and discipline.

Training and instructing a child may seem to be a straightforward thing, but it is not. You have to modify teaching methods based on the child's age and ability to understand. You cannot even have a family devotion that is very meaningful to the child in the first year or so. In fact, family devotions are not the only way. They are good and should not be neglected, however, there must also be a lot of informal teaching. The Lord gave the Israelites the plan in Deuteronomy 6:5-7, "And these words, which I command thee this day, shall be in thine heart: and thou shalt teach them diligently unto thy children, and shalt talk of them when thou sittest in thine house, and when thou walkest by the way, and when thou liest down, and when thou risest up." When the circumstances of life bring up an issue, tell your children what God's Word says about that issue. You may be in a restaurant, at school, at home, or some other place, but let the Bible be a part of your conversation with your children constantly. This will let them know that the Bible is important to you; it will let them know the Bible is relevant to all the issues of their lives; and it will let them know that the Bible contains real wisdom and has the answers for life's problems.

It is inevitable that children will make wrong decisions and do wrong things. When they do, they must be corrected. At least, three things are important for them to learn in this regard. One is humility. They must admit they have done wrong. Second, there is reconciliation with others. If they wronged someone else, they must apologize to that person and, if needed correct what they did. Third, they must learn that they have offended God and they must confess to Him.

Finally, when a child's error warrants it, there needs to be chastisement. I think most parents agree with this. What they do not agree about is what kind of punishment a child should get. There may be several types of chastisement used with a child. Time outs can be used for minor infractions. However, for rebellion or serious disobedience and deliberate harm, a parent is justified in using corporal punishment or "spanking." This should be done moderately in proportion to the seriousness of the wrong done.

The "politically correct" worst thing to do is spank a child. This is an activity unacceptable to many in the world, but the world is not our standard. Politically correct standards created by men who have rejected God and His truth, are not our guidelines, either. God's written Word is our authority in this matter. So, what does God say about spanking? "Foolishness is bound in the heart of a child; but the rod of correction shall drive it far from him" (Prov. 22:15). "The rod and reproof give wisdom: but a child left to himself bringeth his mother to shame" (Prov. 29:15). "Thou shalt beat him with the rod, and shalt deliver his soul from hell" (Prov. 23:14). "Chasten thy son while there is hope, and let not thy soul spare for his crying" (Prov. 19:18).

Corporeal punishment for a child is legitimate whether anyone likes it or not. The above verses do not express the opinion of men. They express the opinion of our almighty creator. One further shock that may hit society in the face is the use of the term *beat*. "Withhold not correction from the child: for if thou beatest him with the rod, he shall not die" (Prov. 23:13). The "beating" referred to is called that only because it is several strikes one after another by some sort of "rod." This could be fulfilled by a flat paddle on the abundantly padded behind. It could be a "switch" flicked along the legs. Something that wil get their attention and connect pain with disobedience. It is not intended to inflict serious or long-term damage.

Notice, "he shall not die." I would caution today's parents that the best way to do this may be with a paddle. It leaves a short-term redness on the behind, but it does not leave marks. In the current day, leaving any mark on a child creates the danger that the authorities will question the parent's fitness and remove the child from the home. Parents should still use corporeal punishment, but cautiously, and they should not do it while angry.

Corporeal punishment has great results in the life and heart of the child. Proverbs 23:13, quoted above, says that spanking corrects the child. When a child has done wrong, correction is the goal of discipline. In fact, the hope is that discipline will so direct his life that it will lead him to heaven (Prov. 23:14). Some might say, "How can you whip your child? Do you hate him?" The real truth is just the opposite. If corporeal punishment will help turn a child from hell, it's a good thing. "He that spareth his rod hateth his son: but he that loveth him chasteneth him betimes" (Prov. 13:24). You actually hate your child if you refuse to spank him. If you love your child and want his life to be successful, you must spank him when it is warranted. The word "betimes" means *early*. You cannot wait. You must start early. Either the parents or the child will become the authority in the family. Parents must establish themselves as the authority and they must start early in the child's life.

A father must raise his children in the admonition of the Lord. The word admonition indicates a type of training that is only verbal. It involves warning and urging, motivating, encouraging them to do the right thing. When they have failed, it is rebuke and instruction on how to correct their behavior. All this verbal instruction must be based on the truths and principles of the Word of God.

Instructions to Servants (Eph. 6:5-8)

The servant spoken here is from the Greek word *doulos*. In these verses it means a bondman or slave. It also is used of ministers as servants of those to whom they minister (2 Cor. 4:5) and as a servant of Christ (Col. 4:12). Jesus was a servant, but not a slave (Phil. 2:7). Nevertheless, slavery is in view here in Ephesians 6. Slavery was a large institution in the Roman Empire. In *Manners and Customs of Bible Lands,* Fred Wright says this:

> *Character and extent of slavery.* In the first century human life was indeed cheap, for it has been estimated that a half of the total population of the empire, or about sixty million people, were slaves. Some wealthy Romans possessed as many as twenty thousand slaves. Slave owners became very brutal, and the slaves themselves were without hope and many of them very corrupt. [165]

Wikipedia expands on this:

> **Slavery in ancient Rome** played an important role in society and the economy. Besides manual labor, slaves performed many domestic services, and might be employed at highly skilled jobs and professions. Accountants and physicians were often slaves. Greek slaves in particular might be highly educated. Unskilled slaves, or those sentenced to slavery as punishment, worked on farms, in mines, and at mills. Their living conditions were brutal, and their lives short. Slaves were considered property under Roman law and had no legal personhood. Unlike Roman citizens, they could be subjected to corporal punishment, sexual exploitation (prostitutes were often slaves), torture, and summary execution. The testimony of a slave could not be accepted in a court of law unless the slave was tortured—a practice based on the belief that slaves in a position to be privy to their masters' affairs would be too virtuously loyal to reveal damaging evidence unless coerced.

Over time, however, slaves gained increased legal protection, including the right to file complaints against their masters. Attitudes changed in part because of the influence among the educated elite of the Stoics, whose egalitarian views of humanity extended to slaves. Roman slaves could hold property which, despite of the fact that it belonged to their masters, they were allowed to use as if it were their own. Skilled or educated slaves were allowed to earn their own money, and might hope to save enough to buy their freedom. [166]

Due to the great potential of brutality and abuse, not to mention that a slave could be forced into many sinful practices or be corrupt all on his own, Biblical guidance was needed. Slavery was a fact of life and needed to be handled according to God's will. Today slavery is illegal in all countries, but there are still estimated to be around twelve to thirty million slaves worldwide. [167] The principles here are still valid for them and can be applied to our servant hood in the sense of employer-employee relationships.

The key statement in these verses is "as the servants of Christ, doing the will of God from the heart" (v. 6). The servant is first the servant of Christ. We are to do service "as unto Christ" (v. 5). We are not to be "men pleasers" (v. 6). It is to be "as to the Lord, and not to men" (v. 7). The great value in any kind of service was (and is) the glory of God.

Servants are to be obedient "in singleness of heart." They are to be determined in their heart to do what the master commands, "as unto Christ." Failure to serve the master (or employer) with all your might is to risk bringing dishonor to the Lord. "Let as many servants as are under the yoke count their own masters worthy of all honour, that the name of God and his doctrine be not blasphemed" (1 Tim. 6:1).

Service is not to be done with eye service, as men pleasers," but as "doing the will of God from the heart." A servant doesn't just do the minimum required to make it look good on the surface, so that it is acceptable to his boss. The servant's goal is that the job would be pleasing to God. The story is told that one day Dawson Trotman of the Navigators had some men working on fixing up a building. They worked on the front door and made it look fantastic. However, they took little effort on the back door. When he asked why the back door didn't look as good as the front. They told him, "It's the back door. No one will see it." His reply was, "When you're doing a job for the Lord, the back door looks as good as the front door!"

A servant does his job with "good will." The attitude you have when doing a job is important, because the job is "to the Lord." On any job there are people who may not treat you right. I'm not sure I have ever been on any job that didn't have its share of complainers. It is not becoming for a Christian to join the complainers. God has you on that job and you are doing the job to please Him and to glorify Him. Keep a positive attitude and a kind attitude. I have noticed that many times employee complaints are a result of misunderstanding the intentions of the supervisors. There is place on the job for proper communication. Sometimes complaints are legitimate. In those cases, you should communicate to supervisors. If there is not a solution, you may want to leave the job. If you leave, do it with a good attitude. I heard about one person who was laid off after several years on the job. He actually came back to the manager and thanked him for the privilege of working there for those years. If you stay, stay with a good attitude for the Lord's sake.

The Lord will reward you for your service: "Knowing that whatsoever good thing any man doeth, the same shall he receive of the Lord, whether he be bond or free" (v. 8). We should keep this in mind. I can think of several jobs I've had where it would have helped had I kept this in mind. The Lord will reward you. That reward will probably be given at the

Judgment Seat of Christ or it may be in this life, but it will come.

Masters (Eph. 6:9)

The commands given to masters are about how to treat their servants. They are not told to free their servants. However, they are told certain major things that would make the lives of the servants better. In Colossians 4:1, Paul says this: "Masters, give unto your servants that which is just and equal; knowing that ye also have a Master in heaven."

Masters are to "do the same things unto" their servants. They were to have the same heart and spirit toward their servants, that the servants are to have toward them. They are to exercise their rights and responsibilities as to the Lord and not to men. After all, every master has a master in Heaven, the Lord Jesus Christ, who is the Lords of lords. They are to act as the servants of Christ, doing His will from their hearts. This would require good, just, equal, and loving treatment toward their servants. They also know that if they do right, the Lord will reward them.

Masters are to forebear threatening. This would end cruelty of both actions and words toward slaves. Under this standard, slaves would be treated with kindness, mercy, purity, and justice. At the very least, these standards would change the fundamental nature of slavery.

Masters are to give that which is just and equal to their servants. In our current day, this would take care of any concern about paying women less than men for the same job. Masters or employers are to give what is equal. Justice would make an accusation of wrong doing against a servant to be of no effect without proof. Masters or employers are to give that which is just (righteous) to their servants. The Old Testament law required at least two or three witnesses whose testimony agreed (2 Cor. 13:1; Heb. 10:28).

CHAPTER FOURTEEN

THE WARFARE OF THE CHURCH
Ephesians 6:10-24

10 Finally, my brethren, be strong in the Lord, and in the power of his might.
11 Put on the whole armour of God, that ye may be able to stand against the wiles of the devil.
12 For we wrestle not against flesh and blood, but against principalities, against powers, against the rulers of the darkness of this world, against spiritual wickedness in high places.
13 Wherefore take unto you the whole armour of God, that ye may be able to withstand in the evil day, and having done all, to stand.
14 Stand therefore, having your loins girt about with truth, and having on the breastplate of righteousness;
15 And your feet shod with the preparation of the gospel of peace;
16 Above all, taking the shield of faith, wherewith ye shall be able to quench all the fiery darts of the wicked.
17 And take the helmet of salvation, and the sword of the Spirit, which is the word of God:
18 Praying always with all prayer and supplication in the Spirit, and watching thereunto with all perseverance and supplication for all saints;
19 ¶And for me, that utterance may be given unto me, that I may open my mouth boldly, to make known the mystery of the gospel,
20 For which I am an ambassador in bonds: that therein I may speak boldly, as I ought to speak. (Eph. 6:10-20).

THE FINAL CHAPTER IN OUR STUDY of Ephesians is about the warfare of the church. The warfare depicted in this final chapter is a warfare with "principalities and powers" of the spiritual realm of darkness. This is Satan's realm. We will restrict our discussion to our fight against that realm, although the complete subject of the warfare of the church would include our conflict with the flesh and the world. We have already dealt with that conflict in detail. These three, the devil, the flesh, and the world are the three great enemies of Christians. At this point, we will concentrate on fighting demonic forces.

The Identity of Our Enemy (Eph. 6:10-12)

There are four specific titles given of our enemy in verse 12: principalities, powers, rulers of the darkness of this world, and spiritual wickedness in high places. As we discussed earlier in Ephesians three, the terms "principalities" and "powers" are used in fourteen places in the Scriptures. Sometimes the context shows their meaning to be earthly government powers, as in Titus 3:1. That is not the context here. In other places, such as Colossians 2:25, the meaning is Satan and his demonic forces. They are the rulers of the darkness of the world. Satan is called the god of this world (2 Cor. 4:4) and he is the one who works in the children of disobedience (Eph. 2:2). These beings are spiritual wickedness in high places. "High places" are explained in Eph. 3:10 as "heavenly places." There are three heavens and the atmosphere (the air) is the first heaven. Satan is called the Prince of the power of the air (Eph. 2:2). The Lord Jesus Christ spoiled the principalities and powers and triumphed over them at the Cross (Col. 2:15).

General Preparation for Warfare (Eph. 6:10)

When a person joins the military to become an airman, a sailor, a marine, or a soldier, the officers do not immediately load them down with weapons and sent them into battle. First, they must be prepared; they must be trained. When I went into the Army, the first thing I had to do was undergo eight weeks of basic training. This was a process of strengthening and elementary combat training. I have heard that the way you build a soldier is to persecute him and my own experience bears that out. The drill sergeants determine to strengthen you physically and emotionally. When I was in the Army, they strengthened me physically by a good diet and regimented exercise, marching, running, etc. Their plan to strengthen me emotionally seemed to be through the frequent and controlled use of yelling, insulting, and cussing. If you could not take the strengthening process, it broke you and you never saw combat (or should not have). I made it through and found a place in the Army Security Agency.

The preparation for spiritual combat is also a strengthening process. "Finally, my brethren, be strong in the Lord, and in the power of his might" (Eph. 6:10). Physical strength comes through proper nutrition and proper exercise. Spiritual strength is the same. The only proper nutrition is the Word of God. "Man shall not live by bread alone, but by every word that proceedeth out of the mouth of God" (Mt. 4:4). Jesus often prayed before He ate. Likewise, we should pray, before we consume God's Word. A good request to make is found in Psalm 119:18 "Open thou mine eyes, that I may behold wondrous things out of thy law." Regular time should be spent in the Bible reading, studying, memorizing, and meditating on it. Strength comes from the Holy Spirit working through His Word. The importance of this cannot be overestimated.

Spiritual exercise is godliness. 'For bodily exercise profiteth little: but godliness is profitable unto all things, having promise of the life that now is, and of that which is to come" (1 Tim. 4:8). The principle was restated and summarized by James, "But whoso looketh into the perfect law of liberty, and continueth therein, he being not a forgetful hearer, but a doer of the work, this man shall be blessed in his deed" (Jam. 1:25). Godly exercise happens when you learn the Word of God, apply it to some area of your life, and put it into practice. Another Scripture that brings this home is found in 1 Corinthians 7:1, "Having therefore these promises, dearly beloved, let us cleanse ourselves from all filthiness of the flesh and spirit, perfecting holiness in the fear of God." Spending time in the Scriptures and applying them to our lives, should be developed into a consistent habit. We must do this day after day in spite of demands on our time, emergencies, or other distractions.

As drill sergeants give a hard time to soldiers to prepare and harden them against the onslaught of war, so God takes us through experiences that are designed to prepare us for spiritual warfare. The Bible refers to these experiences as trials or temptations. James explained the value of these trials, "My brethren, count it all joy when ye fall into divers temptations; knowing this, that the trying of your faith worketh patience. But let patience have her perfect work, that ye may be perfect and entire, wanting nothing" (Jam. 1:2-4). The God given trials of life are designed to strengthen us, train us, and prepare us. They are meant to make us complete, so we have everything we need. God has promised he will go with us through the trial and will not let it go beyond our ability to endure (1 Cor. 10:13).

The Wiles of the Devil (Eph. 6:11)

So, the devil is going to unleash his arsenal against you. Sounds wonderful, huh? But, what are his weapons and strategies? When faced with Satanic opposition, Paul said, "Lest Satan should get an advantage of us: for we are not ignorant of his devices" (2 Cor. 2:11). Satan has specific strategies and those strategies are hard to see and they are changeable. In the Book of Job, we are introduced to a godly man. Satan was given permission to attack this godly man. The devil caused the death of all Job's cattle; he caused the death of all Job's children; he caused the death of most of Job's servants and ran off the rest; he caused job's wife to forsake him; and, finally, he took Job's health. However, the example of Job teaches us that Satan cannot touch a Christian without God's permission. In God's great wisdom, He sometimes gives Satan permission to engage us in battle. If we win, we do it by trusting in God alone, not our own wisdom or ability, and God teaches us from the victory. If we fail, we also learn from that

Satan's attacks are often characterized by deception. The Bible says Satan is a liar. Jesus said He is a murderer and a liar, "He was a murderer from the beginning, and abode not in the truth, because there is no truth in him. When he speaketh a lie, he speaketh of his own: for he is a liar, and the father of it." (John 8:44). His major endeavor in this age is to oppose the gospel. In doing so, deception is a major tool. "But if our gospel be hid, it is hid to them that are lost: In whom the god of this world hath blinded the minds of them which believe not, lest the light of the glorious gospel of Christ, who is the image of God, should shine unto them." (2 Cor. 4:3-4). He has his own Jesus, spirit (s), and gospel. "For if he that cometh preacheth another Jesus, whom we have not preached, or if ye receive another spirit, which ye have not received, or another gospel, which ye have not accepted, ye might well bear with him" (2 Cor. 11:4). You can bet he has his own counterfeit Bibles. He even transforms himself into an angel of light and employs his own ministers (and, no doubt, teachers and college professors). "For such are false apostles, deceitful workers, transforming themselves into the apostles of Christ. and no marvel; for Satan himself is transformed into an angel of light" (2 Cor. 11:13-14). We have been inundated with false religions and false philosophies and false advice. Jehovah's Witness, Mormonism, Dominionism, Roman Catholicism (teach salvation by faith plus works), political correctness, evolution, humanism, Nazism, socialism, and communism are just a few of the names that have their source in Satanic deception. Unfortunately, space does not permit a detailed examination of each of these.

Satanic attacks often center on our minds. 2 Corinthians 11:3 says, "But I fear, lest by any means, as the serpent beguiled Eve through his subtilty, so your minds should be corrupted from the simplicity that is in Christ." Satan and his devils are capable of putting thoughts and ideas in our minds. Sometimes they do this through other people. At other times, a thought may come into our minds out of the blue and we believe it is our own thought. So, we take the thought and develop it in our minds, but it leads to no good, or to confusion, or to deception. These thoughts can be a suspicious thought about a brother or sister in Christ. They may lead to anger and quarrels. They could lead to split churches, split families, or worse. Deceptive thoughts come through various media sources, books, magazines, movies, and so on. Deception comes through education and philosophy. "Beware lest any man spoil you through philosophy and vain deceit, after the tradition of men, after the rudiments of the world, and not after Christ" (Col. 2:8).

These are some of the reasons God gave instructed us to guard our thoughts (2 Cor. 10:4-5). First, we have to "cast down imaginations and every high thing that exalteth itself against the knowledge of God." Somehow, we must recognize thoughts that are not godly or not true and resist them ("Resist the devil, and he will flee from you"-James 4:7). Then we must bring every thought into obedience to Christ. How can we recognize ungodly thoughts? We may not be sure if they come from the devil or our own flesh. They are subtle and deceptive. The best way to guard against this is by knowing the Word of God so well that it forms a filter in your mind that all thoughts must pass through. That will help both in recognizing bad thoughts and resisting them.

Satan may actually hinder us by physical ailments. He did this to Job. It seems that some kind of physical or emotional ailment strikes on many Saturday nights or Sunday mornings. Why is it occasionally so hard to sleep on Saturday night? Resistance in such cases may be to go to church anyway in spite of being tired. This can be an especially hard one. Even Job did not know his sickness was from Satan.

Satan may appeal to us through the lust of the flesh, the pride of life, and the lust of the eyes (1 John 2:16). Paul was concerned about this for the Thessalonian Christians. "For this cause, when I could no longer forbear, I sent to know your faith, lest by some means the tempter have tempted you, and our labour be in vain" (1 Thess. 3:5). Devils know us better than we think. They know what will *distract us, tempt us, and spoil us*. One of the dangers here is that we will be *distracted* from living for God or serving God and cause us to reach for a goal that is outside God's will. There is a danger that we will seek for pleasure, power, accomplishment or anything that takes our time and attention from God's will. The devil would love it if we became selfish and self-seeking, rather than seeking for the glory of God. Everything we do must be kept in perspective. There are priorities to life. The very first of these is our devotion to God and commitment to His glory.

The devil may take advantage of our failures and mistakes: "Be ye angry, and sin not: let not the sun go down upon your wrath: **neither give place to the devil** (Eph. 4:26-27). In this example, the devil can take unresolved anger and turn it to trouble in the church or a relationship. I am struck by how many problems can be prevented or solved by everyone having a commitment to know God's will and do it.

Finally, the devil will do anything he can to hinder the gospel of the Lord Jesus Christ. It has been said that the devil cannot make you lose your salvation, so he settles for second best. He will try to make you lose your testimony or your effectiveness. Paul encountered this situation. "Wherefore we would have come unto you, even I Paul, once and again; but Satan hindered us" (1 Thess. 2:18).

Put on the Whole Armor of God (Eph. 6:13-20)

The armor is God's weaponry against Satan and his principalities and powers. Paul uses an analogy to the armor of the Roman soldier, so that we would all have a general picture of the pieces he describes. There are seven pieces of armor listed:

1. A girdle for the loins (v. 14),
2. A breastplate (v. 14),
3. Boots (v. 15),
4. A Shield (v. 16),
5. A helmet (v. 17),
6. A sword (v. 17), and
7. Leg guards (v. 18).

All of these pieces are defensive except for two. The sword is for offense and, in this case the leg guards are for offense and defense. The latter are interesting, because they are not specifically mentioned. What we are told in place of the leg guards is "Praying always with all prayer and supplication in the Spirit." Since prayer is inserted into the place of the leg guards, this soldier is fighting on his knees. Therefore, his lower legs are protected. His activity of prayer can be used to call upon the Lord for help, thereby used as a defensive tool. Prayer can also call upon the Lord to enter the battle and defeat the enemy, thereby becoming effective for offense. There is no back armor for this solder. He is not expected to turn and run in the face of the enemy. If he does, he gets wounded.

Loins Girt with Truth (Eph. 6:14)

In light of the fact that this is a very practical war, the armor is a very practical armor. That is, it is practical as opposed to positional. For example, we are righteous in our position before God, but our practical behavior may not be so righteous. In regard to truth, the Lord Jesus Christ is truth (Jn. 14:6) and the Word of God is truth (Jn. 17:17), but how does that apply in practice? Consider the function of the girdle. It is a belt around the waste to which the sword was attached. In Roman days it was called an *accintus.* The word *accintus* means "a soldier," but the litteral meaning is "girt as for battle." [168] We will find that the "Sword of the Spirit" is the Word of God. Therefore, this girdle represents knowledge of the truth of the word of God.

However, it is more than just a surface knowledge. *This soldier is a person who thoroughly knows what he believes and why.* He is well learned in Bible doctrine. He is a person who will stand strong for the truth when challenged. We sometimes think that if a person is called to the "ministry," he should go to Bible College and study "theology." When he does that, he will know the Bible better than the average Christian and be able to teach them. I believe every Christian should know the Bible as well as or better than any Bible college student. Someone once told me that the average Christian did not know the Bible as well as I did. I thought, "What a shame!" I have been to Bible College. I have studied the Bible for fifty years and more. I know the bible well enough to have an idea how ignorant I actually am. It is a terrible shame if any believer does not have a thorough knowledge of the Scriptures. They can know the Bible, and they do not have to go to Bible College to get the knowledge.

The Breastplate of Righteousness (Eph. 6:14)

This involves the practical application of the Scriptures. It is the *practice* of righteousness that is in view here. This is what the Book of Ephesians was talking about when it said to put off the old man and put on the new. Colossians says to put off the practices of the flesh and put on the characteristics of Christ (Col. 3:5-15). Peter said that we must be holy (1 Peter 1:15-16; 2 Peter 1:4-11). Paul said we must lay aside all filthiness of the flesh and perfect holiness (2 Cor. 7:1). Hebrews says. "Wherefore seeing we also are compassed about with so great a cloud of witnesses, let us lay aside every weight, and the sin which doth so easily beset us, and let us run with patience the race that is set before us, looking unto Jesus the author and finisher of our faith; who for the joy that was set before him endured the cross, despising the shame, and is set down at the right hand of the throne of God" (Hebrews 12:1-2).

This is the practical righteous living that is expected of a Christian. This does not come from just going to church three times per week. It comes from a daily diet of the word of God. We must spend time in the word of God daily with a view to applying its truths and principles to our lives. We don't just ask ourselves, What does this Bible passage say? We go deeper and delve into its secrets. We ask, what does this Bible passage mean? However, to stop there would be to stop too soon. We finally must ask, what does the passage mean to me? How does it apply to my life? How does it change me? What must I change in my behavior and thinking? If we live this way, we will not have anything in our lives the devil can grab hold of and use to damage us or the work of God.

In the *Bible Believer's Commentary*, William McDonald and Art Farstad, made this comment.

> The second piece is **the breastplate of righteousness**. Every believer is clothed with the righteousness of God (2 Cor. 5:21), but he must also manifest integrity and uprightness in his personal life. Someone has said, "When a man is clothed in practical righteousness, he is impregnable. Words are no defense against accusation, but a good life is." If our conscience is void of offense toward God and man, the devil has nothing to shoot at. David put on **the**

breastplate of righteousness in Psalm 7:3–5. The Lord Jesus wore it at all times (Isa. 59:17). [169]

Feet Shod with the Preparation of the Gospel (Eph. 6:15)

The Bible says, "How then shall they call on him in whom they have not believed? and how shall they believe in him of whom they have not heard? and how shall they hear without a preacher? And how shall they preach, except they be sent? as it is written, How beautiful are the feet of them that preach the gospel of peace, and bring glad tidings of good things" (Rom. 10:14-15). This does not have to do with knowing the gospel, Christ's death for our sins, burial, and resurrection of Christ. Every saved person should know the gospel. I do not believe foot covering has to do with living according to the gospel, because that is covered by the breastplate of righteousness. *The shoes have to do with being prepared to preach the gospel to the unsaved around you.* You may tell them you are saved, but can you tell them why? The Lord commands, "But sanctify the Lord God in your hearts: and be ready always to give an answer to every man that asketh you a reason of the hope that is in you with meekness and fear." Are you ready and prepared to lead someone from one verse to another showing them why they need to get saved and how to do it? If not, seek out a good soul-winner who can show you. When you learn from this person, memorize the verses you will use so that they are ready even if you do not have a Bible with you.

The Shield of Faith (Eph. 6:16)

The shield is intended to stop all the arrows of the enemy that come your way. It is faith, but not *doctrinal* faith. It is not a set of beliefs that you may find in a theology book. It is "faith in God" (Mark 11:22). It is utter confidence in God and in His Word. Harry Ironside shared an illustration of what this means.

Here is a preacher who stands up to preach the gospel to an audience, and says, "Well, I have an old sermon here. I have used it seventy-two times already; it is nearly worn out, but I think it will do for this audience. Yes, I think I will use it again. I remember years ago there were eighteen converted when I preached this sermon, and it is still good." The devil hears all that, and he says, "I will show you that you have come up against a greater foe than you realize." The meeting is a poor, wretched failure, and the preacher says, "I do not understand it. I have preached that sermon any number of times. I wonder what the trouble was." It was that the confidence of the preacher was in himself instead of in the living God. [170]

The Helmet of Salvation (Eph. 6:17)

The helmet of salvation refers to just what it says: salvation. If you are not saved in the first place, you have no hope of standing against the devil. But, there is something else. One problem many Christians have and a problem I had as a young Christian is doubt that they are really saved. The devil causes doubt. You cannot defeat him as long as you are not sure you are saved. The devil had me twisted in knots about this when I was young. He had me conditioned so that every time I felt a certain way, I would doubt my salvation. Finally, I read a booklet that convinced me feeling had nothing to do with it. The key is the Word of God. The Bible says "Believe on the Lord Jesus Christ and thou shalt be saved" (Acts 16:31). Do you believe? Do you believe He died for you on the cross? Do you believe He rose physically from the dead? If the answer is yes, you are saved no matter what you feel and no matter what else you think about it.

The helmet is meant to protect the soldier's head. Therefore, salvation also protects your mind. Many times, in this commentary, I have said that God expects obedience in our thoughts. Salvation makes us new creatures (1 Cor. 5:17). This means that our minds are also made new, and it leads to consistent renewal of our minds and transformation of ourselves (Rom. 12:1-2).

The Sword of the Spirit, Which is the Word of God (Eph. 6:17)

In thinking about these pieces of armor, it is striking how central the Bible, the Word of God, is to all of them. However, this mention of the Word is different. Here it is to be used as an offensive weapon. It is a stabbing, cutting weapon. The Book of Hebrews says, "For the word of God is quick, and powerful, and sharper than any twoedged sword, piercing even to the dividing asunder of soul and spirit, and of the joints and marrow, and is a discerner of the thoughts and intents of the heart" (Heb. 4:12). The word of God is capable of piercing and cutting the devil, as well. Be ready to use the Word; "Let the high praises of God be in their mouth, and a twoedged sword in their hand" (Ps. 149:6). Don't be shy about quoting the Bible. In this day and age, someone who quotes the Bible is often thought to be weird, but that is because of the deception of the devil, who we are fighting. Quote the Bible! "Cursed be he that doeth the work of the LORD deceitfully, and cursed be he that keepeth back his sword from blood" (Jer. 48:10). Our best example on the use of the Bible to defeat Satan is the Lord Jesus Christ. Look at the narrative in Matthew 4:1-11. Three times the devil tempted the Lord Jesus, and three times the Lord answered with, "it is written." Finally, "the devil leaveth him, and, behold, angels came and ministered unto him" (Mt. 4;11).

Adam Clarke says this in his commentary.

> The sword of which St. Paul speaks is, as he explains it, the word of God; that is, the revelation which God has given of himself, or what we call the Holy Scriptures. This is called the sword of the Spirit,

because it comes from the Holy Spirit, and receives its fulfillment in the soul through the operation of the Holy Spirit. An ability to quote this on proper occasions, and especially in times of temptation and trial, has a wonderful tendency to cut in pieces the snares of the adversary. In God's word a genuine Christian may have unlimited confidence, and to every purpose to which it is applicable it may be brought with the greatest effect. [171]

Praying with All Prayer in the Spirit (Eph. 6:18-20)

Prayer is generally not a mystery for Christians. There may be a lot we do not know about prayer, but we have a general idea of what it is about. There is an old saying that Satan fears when he sees the weakest Christian on his knees. Although prayer does not require being on your knees, prayer is powerful and effective. The Bible says, "The effectual fervent prayer of a righteous man availeth much" (Jam. 5:16). Prayer should be involved in every aspect of spiritual warfare. Prayer is needed for becoming strong in the Lord. Prayer is necessary to stand firm against the wiles of the Devil. As Matthew Henry said, "Prayer must buckle on all the other parts of our Christian armour." [172]

Prayer is said to be done "always." Albert Barnes said this in his notes on the Bible.

> It would be well for the soldier who goes forth to battle to pray - to pray for victory; or to pray that he may be prepared for death, should he fall. But soldiers do not often feel the necessity of this. To the Christian soldier, however, it is indispensable. Prayer crowns all lawful efforts with success and gives a victory when nothing else would. No matter how complete the armor; no matter how skilled we may be in the science of war; no matter how courageous we may be, we may be certain that without prayer

we shall be defeated. God alone can give the victory; and when the Christian soldier goes forth armed completely for the spiritual conflict, if he looks to God by prayer, he may be sure of a triumph. This prayer is not to be intermitted. It is to be always. In every temptation and spiritual conflict we are to pray. [173]

Matthew Henry rounds out Barnes comments.

We must join prayer with all these graces, for our defence against these spiritual enemies, imploring help and assistance of God, as the case requires: and we must pray always. Not as though we were to do nothing else but pray, for there are other duties of religion and of our respective stations in the world that are to be done in their place and season; but we should keep up constant times of prayer, and be constant to them. We must pray upon all occasions, and as often as our own and others' necessities call us to it. We must always keep up a disposition to prayer and should intermix ejaculatory prayers with other duties, and with common business. [174]

Prayer is to be with "all prayer and supplication." "All prayer" reminds me of the various kinds of prayer: public prayer, private prayer, prayer in church, family prayer, spontaneous prayer, unplanned and sudden prayer, scheduled prayer, etc. I think of the different aspects of prayer: confession, adoration, thanksgiving, and, as stated here, supplication.

Supplication means "Petition; earnest request." [175] "Be careful for nothing; but in every thing by prayer and supplication with thanksgiving let your requests be made known unto God" (Phil. 4:6). Supplication is the part of prayer promised an answer in Matthew 7:7-8, "Ask, and it shall be given you; seek, and ye shall find; knock, and it shall be opened unto you: For every one that asketh receiveth; and he that seeketh findeth; and to him that knocketh it shall be opened." James gives a warning in James 4:2-3, "ye have not, because ye ask not. Ye ask, and receive not, because ye ask amiss, that ye may consume it upon your lusts."

Prayer is to be with "watching." To watch means to be alert for danger. Jesus said, "And this know, that if the goodman of the house had known what hour the thief would come, *he would have watched*, and not have suffered his house to be broken through" (Luke 12:39). The problem with watching is that we do not know when our adversary will attack, so, we must watch always. Peter exhorted, "Be sober, be vigilant; because your adversary the devil, as a roaring lion, walketh about, seeking whom he may devour: Whom resist stedfast in the faith, knowing that the same afflictions are accomplished in your brethren that are in the world" (1 Pet. 5:8-9). The only way we can constantly watch is to "pray always." Be diligent to maintain regular prayer habits.

Prayer is to be with "all perseverance." Stick to the job. Don't give up. In Luke 18, Jesus told the parable of the unjust judge "to this end, that men ought always to pray, and not to faint" (Lk. 18:1). When the widow insisted on making her request repeatedly known to the judge, he finally granted her request, even though he neither cared for people nor feared God. Jesus concluded, "And shall not God avenge his own elect, which cry day and night unto him, though he bear long with them? I tell you that he will avenge them speedily" (Lk. 18:7-8).

Prayer is to be in the Spirit. That is, it is to be with the help of the Spirit. Prayer must be from our hearts in accordance with the Word and with the guidance and help of the Spirit of God.

Prayer is to be for "all saints." Our prayers should not be limited to our own church, friends, and family. Our prayers are to be wide spread for God's people everywhere. Paul was constantly praying for the churches. Many of his prayers were general prayers, like those in Colossians 1 and Ephesians 1 and Philippians 1, which were prayed for groups of Christians. Epaphras was an example of a prayer warrior. "Epaphras, who is one of you, a servant of Christ, saluteth you, always labouring fervently for you in prayers, that ye may stand perfect and complete in all the will of God" (Col. 4:12). We need many prayer warriors.

Prayer is also to be made for specific needs. An example of specific prayer is found in Ephesians 6:19-20. Paul requested prayer that God would enable him to speak the gospel boldly as he should. This is a good prayer to pray for us all. Paul, as an "ambassador in bonds," was on house arrest in Rome when he wrote Ephesians (see Acts 28). Regardless, he still wanted to be ready to preach the gospel. All he needed was boldness and opportunity.

Final Conclusions (Eph. 6:21-24)

21 But that ye also may know my affairs, and how I do, Tychicus, a beloved brother and faithful minister in the Lord, shall make known to you all things:
22 Whom I have sent unto you for the same purpose, that ye might know our affairs, and that he might comfort your hearts.
23 Peace be to the brethren, and love with faith, from God the Father and the Lord Jesus Christ.
24 Grace be with all them that love our Lord Jesus Christ in sincerity. Amen. (Eph. 6:21-24)

Paul, from prison in Rome (Acts 28), sent a fellow-laborer, Tychicus, to Ephesus with news of how things were with him. Regarding Tychicus, William Farstad gives further information.

> Paul was sending **Tychicus** from Rome to Ephesus to let the saints know how he was getting along. He commends **Tychicus** as **a beloved brother and faithful minister** (servant) **in the Lord**. There are only

five references to this man in the NT. He was one of the party that traveled with Paul from Greece to Asia (Acts 20:4). He was the apostle's messenger to the Christians at Colosse (Col. 4:7); to Ephesus (cf. 6:21 with 2 Tim. 4:12) and possibly to Titus in Crete (Titus 3:12). His twofold mission at this time was to inform the saints concerning Paul's welfare in prison, and also to encourage their **hearts**, allaying any unnecessary fears. [176]

Regarding the lack of personal greetings in the remainder of the epistle, Harry Ironside has this to say.

And then in verses 23, 24 we have the closing words. You will observe there are no personal salutations in Ephesians. The reason probably was that the Epistle to the Ephesians was a circular letter, intended not only for the saints in Ephesus, but sent around a circle of assemblies until it reached Laodicea. Paul, writing to the Colossians, said, "Read the epistle from Laodicea." Some think of this as a lost letter, but it is undoubtedly this letter to the Ephesians, and on account of its general character there are no personal salutations for individuals in the Ephesian church. [177]

Among the greatest blessings any church could hope for are "peace" and "love." It is these two elements, along with truth, that will hold any church together through all the attacks of Satan and all the confusion of false teachers. Love will also allow open communication around the Word of God. And that will lead to peace. And peace will help usher in unity. All of this is from the grace of God.

Grace be with all them that love our Lord Jesus Christ in sincerity. Amen.

About the Author

Dr. Steve Combs is an ordained minister. He spent his early years in Kentucky, Virginia, and finally Ohio. He was not raised in a Christian home. He had some Christian influence from his grandmother, but that had little effect on him. Due to discussions with a Baptist preacher and a Sunday School teacher, who visited his home, he began to read the Bible. The Word of God had its effect. He came under strong conviction of his sins. A friend invited him to a nearby church during revival meetings. As a result, he received Christ as his Savior.

Since then there have been major transformations to his life. God called him to preach and enabled a backward shy individual suffering from an inferiority complex to stand before crowds and confidently proclaim the Word of God. God gave him a business background as a CPA. God put him in several ministry positions. He has served as a Bible Institute teacher, a youth pastor, and a senior pastor. He holds a Doctor of Theology from Covington Theological Seminary.

Currently Steve Combs is Assistant Director and a Global Translation Advisor for Bearing Precious Seed Global/ Global Bible Translators, www.bpsglobal.com. BPS Global starts and assists Bible translation projects around the world.

He is married and has four married children.

Notes

[1] MacDonald, William and Farstad, Art. "Believers Bible Commentary." Libronix Digital Library System. System 1.0c. Oak Harbor, WA: Libronix Corporation, copyright 2000-2001. CD-ROM.

[2] Padfield, David. "The Biblical City of Ephesus." 2015. Bible Land History Exploring the Lands of the Bible with David Padfield. Web. 24 February 2015

[3] Webster, Noah. "Webster's Dictionary of American English." 1828 edition. E-Sword. Rick Meyers. Version 10.2.1. Franklin, Tn.: 2013. Downloaded computer software.

[4] Thayer, Joseph. "Thayer's Greek Definitions." E-Sword. Rick Meyers. Version 10.2.1. Franklin, Tn.: E-Sword, 2000. Downloaded computer software.

[5] Vine, W.E. "Vine's Complete Expository Dictionary of New Testament Words." E-Sword. Rick Meyers. Version 10.2.1. Franklin, Tn.: 2013. Downloaded computer software.

[6] GBOLOU, Yao Mawouli. "Re: Translation Seminar in Togo?" Message to Steve Combs and Steve Zeinner. 10 October 2014. Email.

[7] Easton, M. G. "Easton's Bible Dictionary." Gill, John. "John Gill's Exposition of the Entire Bible." E-Sword. Rick Meyers. Version 10.2.1. Franklin, Tn.: 2013. Downloaded computer software.

[8] Gill, John. "John Gill's Exposition of the Entire Bible." E-Sword. Rick Meyers. Version 10.2.1. Franklin, Tn.: 2013. Downloaded computer software.

[9] Vine's NT

[10] Gill

[11] Webster

[12] Smith, William. "Smith's Bible Dictionary." 1863. E-Sword. Rick Meyers. Version 10.2.1. Franklin, Tn.: 2013. Downloaded computer

[13] Walvoord, John F. The Holy Spirit. Grand Rapids: Zondervan, 2008. Amazon.com. Kindle download. 18 Oct. 2014

[14] Williams, Dr. H. D. An email sent to the author Apr. 5, 2007.

[15] Thayer

[16] MacDonald, William and Farstad, Art. "Believers Bible Commentary." Libronix Digital Library System. System 1.0c. Oak Harbor, WA: Libronix Corporation, copyright 2000-2001. CD-ROM.

[17] Erickson, Millard J. Christian Theology 2nd Edition. (Grand Rapids: Baker Academic, 2005) 929.

[18] VOR. "1689 London Baptist Confession." Vor.org. 1996. Web. 28 March 2016.

[19] Calvin, John. Institutes of the Christian Religion, Book 3 Ch. 21. 1559. E-Sword. Rick Meyers. Version 10.2.1. Franklin, Tn.: 2013. Downloaded computer software.
Erickson, 929

[21] 1689 Baptist Confession.http://creeds.net/baptists/1689/kerkham/1689.htm#Ch02. Nov. 2017.

[22] Thayer

[23] Thayer

[24] Thayer

[25] ⍰ Pappas, John. Bible Greek Basic Grammar of the New Testament. John Pappas: http://biblegreekvpod.com/File/Bible_Greek_vpod.pdf. 2008. Web Book, 65.

[26] Thayer

[27] Thayer

[28] Webster

[29] VOR. 1689 Baptist Confession

[30] (C.H. Spurgeon, New Park Street Pulpit, Vol. 4, 1858, p. 337. Cited. David Cloud. The Calvinism Debate. Port Huron, Michigan: Way of Life Literature. 2006. Web. January 2019.

[31] Jones, Steve. Calvinism Critiqued by a Former Calvinist. Auburn University. Open House Church Articles. Web. June 11, 2015.

[32] Thayer

[33] Webster

[34] Webster

[35] **Easton's Bibl Dictionary**. 1897. E-Sword. Rick Meyers. Version 10.2.1. Franklin, Tn.: 2013. Downloaded computer software.

[36] Vine's NT

[37] Strong's

[38] Thayer

[39] Abbott-Smith, G. *A Manual Greek Lexicon of the New Testament*, 3rd Ed. New York: Charles Scribner's Sons, 1936. Print.

[40] Barnes, Albert. *Albert Barnes' Notes on the Bible*. E-Sword. 1847. Rick Meyers. Version 10.2.1. Franklin, Tn.: 2013. Downloaded computer software.

[41] Ironside, H. A. *Galatians Ephesians*. Neptune, New Jersey: Loizeaux Brothers, 1981. Print.

[42] Barnes

[43] Jamieson, Faussett, and Brown. "Jamieson, Faussett, and Brown Commentary." 1871. *E-Sword*. Rick Meyers. Version 10.2.1. Franklin, Tn.: 2013. Downloaded computer software.

[44] Wesley, John. "John Wesley's Notes on the Bible." 1755-1766. *E-Sword*. Rick Meyers. Version 10.2.1. Franklin, Tn.: 2013. Downloaded computer software.

[45] Scofield, Clarence I. "Old Scofield Reference Bible." 1917. *E-Sword*. Rick Meyers. Version 10.2.1. Franklin, Tn.: 2013.

Downloaded computer software.

[46] Hindson, Edward and Kroll, Woodrow. "The K. J. V. Bible Commentary." Libronix Digital Library System. System 1.0c. Oak Harbor, WA: Libronix Corporation, copyright 2000-2001. CD-ROM.

[47] MacDonald and Farstad

[48] Pollard, Joyce. "The Dispensation of the Fullness of Times." Rightly Dividing the Word of Truth. Com. 2015. Web. March 2016.

[49] Elliott, Dr. Paul. "What is the Dispensation of the Fullness of Times in Ephesians 1:10?" Teaching the Word .com. 1998-2016. Web. March 2016.

[50] Barnes

[51] Abbott-Smith

[52] Abbott-Smith

[53] Barnes

[54] VOR, 1689 Confession

[55] Ante-Nicene Fathers. Vol. 1. *E-Sword*. Rick Meyers. Version 10.2.1. Franklin, Tn.: 2013. Downloaded computer software.

[56] Ante-Nicene Fathers Vol. 1

[57] Ante-Nicene Fathers Vol. 1

[58] Ante-Nicene Fathers Vol. 1

[59] Ante-Nicene Fathers. Vol. 3. *E-Sword*. Rick Meyers. Version 10.2.1. Franklin, Tn.: 2013. Downloaded computer software.

[60] Ante-Nicene Fathers Vol. 5. *E-Sword*. Rick Meyers. Version 10.2.1. Franklin, Tn.: 2013. Downloaded computer software.

[61] Vine, W.E. "Vine's Complete Expository Dictionary of Old Testament Words." *E-Sword*. Rick Meyers. Version 10.2.1. Franklin, Tn.: 2013. Downloaded computer software.

[62] Steve Jones former Calvinist

[63] Ruckman, Peter S. *The Books of Galatians Ephesians Philippians Collossians.* Pensacola: Pensacola Bible Press, 1973. Print. 229.

[64] Jamieson, Faussett, and Brown.

[65] Ironside, 104-106

[66] Jamieson, Faussett, and Brown.

[67] *Pulpit Commentary. Ephesians. E-Sword.* Rick Meyers. Version 10.2.1. Franklin, Tn.: 2013. Downloaded computer software.

[68] Bliss, Philip P. *Free from the Law.* Sunshine for Sunday Schools. 1873. Cyberhymnal.org. Web. 25 August 2017.

[69] Strouse, Dr. Thomas M. *Ye are the Body of Christ.* Cromwell, Ct.: Baptist Bible Theological Seminary, 2010. Print 9-13.

[70] Strouse. 14.

[71] Webster

[72] Ironside. 150

[73] Strong's

[74] Ironside, 159-160

[75] "Gaither Vocal Band - The Love Of God Lyrics." MetroLyrics.com. April 25, 2016.

[76] Webster

[77] Webster

[78] Webster

[79] Zodhiates, Spiros and Baker, Warren and Carpenter, Eugene. "The Complete Word Study Dictionary, Old and New Testaments." 1992. *E-Sword*. Rick Meyers. Version 10.2.1. Franklin, Tn.: 2013. Downloaded computer software.

[80] Webster

[81] Zodhiates

[82] Thayer

[83] Webster

[84] Gill

[85] Gill

[86] Evans, William. *The Great Doctrines of the Bible*. Chicago: Moody Press, 1949. Print. 109-114.

[87] Evans, 115

[88] Evans, 116-118

[89] https://www.gotquestions.org/eternal-Sonship.html. Copyright 2002-2017 Got Questions Ministries. May 2017

[90] Webster

[91] Choi, Charles Q. "Planet Earth: Facts About Its Orbit, Atmosphere & Size." Space.com. March 7, 2017.

[92] "Core-Mantel boundary." Wikipedia. 2017. Wikipedia Foudation, Inc. March 7, 2017.

[93] Zodhiates

[94] Webster

[95] Barnes

[96] Webster

[97] Thayer

[98] Webster

[99] Webster

[100] Statement by Dean Meeker, a friend, in the 1970's, he was on the Navigator staff.

[101] Thesaurus.com. synonyms of lying. 5-11-16

[102] Brown, Francis and Driver, R. and Briggs, Charles. "Brown-Driver-Briggs Hebrew Definitions." 1906. *E-Sword*. Rick Meyers. Version 10.2.1. Franklin, Tn.: 2013. Downloaded computer software.

[103] Ruckman, pg. 288.

[104] Ironside, pg. 227

[105] Webster

[106] Webster

[107] Word Study

[108] Webster

[109] Wikipedia

[110] Webster

[111] Webster

[112] Webster

[113] Got Questions Ministries. *What does the Bible say about transsexualism / transgenderism? Is gender identity disorder / gender dysphoria the result of sin?* www.gotquestions.org/transsexualism-gender-identity-disorder.html. 2002-2014. Web. 10 Nov. 2017

[114] Webster

[115] Webster

[116] "OH Schools Study Federal Transgender Bathroom Directive." May 21, 2016. Gadgets and Technology News.com. 2015. Web. May 21, 2016.

[117] McNugh, Paul. 'Transgenderism: A Pathogenic Meme." The Witherspoon Institute Public Discourse. June 10, 2015. Web. May 21, 2016.

[118] "Chromosomes and Gender." Winthrop University. Web. May 21, 2016.

[119] Wikipedia, https://en.wikipedia.org/wiki/Cross-dressing. web. 10 Nov. 2017.

[120] Guzik, David. Enduring Word Commentary. Enduring Word Media. 2014. *E-Sword*. Rick Meyers. Version 10.2.1. Franklin, Tn.: 2013. Downloaded computer software.

[121] Webster

[122] Word Study

[123] Barnes

[124] Vine's NT

[125] Gill

[126] Walvoord, John F. The Holy Spirit: A Comprehensive Study of the Person and Work of the Holy Spirit. Zondervan.com/ Authortracker: 2010. Kindle E-pub. 2016

[127] Walvoord,

[128] Ryrie, Charles. Balancing the Christian Life. Moody Publishers: Chicago, 1994. Kindle e-book. 2016.

[129] Bridges, Jerry, The Pursuit of holiness. Navpress: Colorado Springs. 1978. Print. 2016.

[130] Bridges

[131] Bridges

[132] D. Martyn Lloyd-Jones. The Sons of God-Exposition of Romans 8:5-17 (Edinburgh: The Banner of Truth Trust, 1974). p. 124. Cited in Bridges. 1 Jan. 2018.

[133] Bounds, E. M. Purpose in Prayer. (a collection of statements from the book). Moody Press: Chicago. Print. 29 Dec. 2017.

[134] Mills, Eddie. Facebook post. 10/31/2016. Accessed 10/2016

[135] Word Study

[136] Perronet, Edward. "All Hail the Power of Jesus' Name." 1780. Hymnary.com. Web. May 16, 2016

[137] Word Study

[138] Thoughtco.com. Espie Estrella. "An Introduction to the Elements of Music." 5 Aug. 2017. Web. 12 Dec. 2017

[139] Runhart, Melissa. "7 Elements of Music." Pezi.com. 16 Sept. 2015. Web. 12 Dec. 2017.

[140] Merriam-Webster. https://www.merriam webster.com/dictionary/rhythm. 5 Jan. 2018.

[141] Dictionary.com. "Rhythm." Web. May 16, 2016.

[142] Dictionary.com

[143] Dictionary.com

[144] Goodreads. https://www.goodreads.com/quotes/tag/melody. 5 Jan. 2018.

[145] Saloman Jadassohn. cited in *Bible Guidelines for Christian Music*. Dial the Truth Ministries: http://www.av1611.org/cqguide.html. 5 Jan 2018.

[146] Joseph Haydn. cited in *Bible Guidelines for Christian Music*. Dial the Truth Ministries: http://www.av1611.org/cqguide.html. 5 Jan 2018.

[147] Leonard J. Seidel. (concert pianist and twenty-five year Christian music scholar). Face the Music – Contemporary Music On Trial, pp. 46-51 cited in *Bible Guidelines for Christian Music*. Dial the Truth Ministries: http://www.av1611.org/cqguide.html. 5 Jan 2018.

[148] Webster

[149] Giovanni Pierluigi da Palestrina (c. 1525-1594). Cited in *Bible Guidelines for Christian Music*. Dial the Truth Ministries: http://www.av1611.org/cqguide.html. 5 Jan 2018.

[150] Webster

[151] Thayer

[152] "Phobia." Wikipedia.com. Web. 8 May 2016.

[153] Webster

[154] Webster

[155] Webster

[156] Thayer

[157] Word Study

[158] Webster

[159] Turning Point radio broadcast, unknown time.

[160] Webster

[161] Webster

[162] Webster

[163] Wesley

[164] Webster

[165] Wright, Fred H. Manners and Customs of bible Lands. Chicago: Moody Bible Institute. 1953. Kindle. Amazon.com. Loc. 3873.

[166] "Slavery in Ancient Rome. Wikipedia. Web. May 24, 2016.

[167] ⁂ "Slavery." Wikipedia. Web. May 24, 2016.

[168] "Baldric-Roman Balteus." Wikipedia. Web. May 25, 2016.

[169] MacDonald and Farstad

[170] Ironside

[171] Clarke, Adam. "Adam Clarke;s Commentary on the Bible." 1810-1826. *E-Sword*. Rick Meyers. Version 10.2.1. Franklin, Tn.: 2013. Downloaded computer software.

[172] Henry, Matthew. "Matthew Henry's Commentary on the Whole Bible." 1708-1714. *E-Sword*. Rick Meyers. Version 10.2.1. Franklin, Tn.: 2013. Downloaded computer software.

[173] Barnes

[174] Henry

[175] Webster

[176] MacDonald and Farstad

[177] Ironside, 340.

www.ingramcontent.com/pod-product-compliance
Lightning Source LLC
Chambersburg PA
CBHW070719160426
43192CB00009B/1240